The Bride's Pearl

The Bride's Pearl

A Commentary on Ephesians

BY BRIAN KINSEY

The Bride's Pearl
A Commentary on Ephesians

by Brian Kinsey

©1993, Word Aflame Press
  Hazelwood, MO 63042

Cover Design by Tim Agnew

Printed in United States of America

Printed by

Library of Congress Cataloging-in-Publication Data

Kinsey, Brian, 1957-
    The bride's pearl : a commentary on Ephesians / by Brian Kinsey.
        p. cm.
    Includes bibliographical references.
    ISBN 1-56722-017-7 :
    1. Bible. N.T. Ephesians—Commentaries. I. Title.
BS2695.3.K567 1993
227'.5077--dc20   93-21382
                                                                 CIP

To Lanette, my wife and my friend,
whose encouragement and unwavering support
produced this book

Contents

Foreword

Ephesians—this great instructor as well as illuminator of the church has been called Paul's finest work. Brian Kinsey's rich analysis of the hidden pearls belonging to the bride of Christ sheds additional light on this most enlightening epistle.

You will be led into the bride's riches in Christ, the bride's walk in Christ, the bride's standing in Christ—as well as many tributaries that break off from the mainstream.

Some think that God created the world and then sat down. God is still creating. He has creative thoughts. When the mind of Christ is resident in you, you have a creative mind. God has endowed Brian Kinsey with a creative mind. One way to determine if someone has the mind of Christ is to see if he is a creative thinker. The author fits this criterion.

When the church on earth loses its direction, it creates enemies for the cause of God. The Book of Ephesians, along with this commentary by Brian Kinsey, can serve as a midcourse correction. It is stated that the Apollo moon mission was only on course no more than one percent of the time; yet the astronauts reached the moon. How? By constant correction. That's the story of life.

I commend to you the message of Ephesians—from the mind and heart of the apostle Paul freshly illuminated from the soul and spirit of Brian Kinsey. It is written to the glory of the bride's Groom, His Majesty, the Lord Jesus Christ.

T. F. Tenney

INTRODUCTION

I. The Song of Solomon of the New Testament

The Old Testament contains many spiritual types and shadows of truths that are developed more fully in the New Testament. Placed within the old covenant are events and character sketches for our example and admonition. "Now all these things happened unto them for ensamples: and they are written for our admonition, upon whom the ends of the world are come" (I Corinthians 10:11). Therefore, it is our right to compare Old Testament shadows with New Testament substance. The purpose of this study is to uncover the riches of every believer's inheritance in Christ Jesus by unlocking the treasure of the Epistle to the Ephesians.

Ephesians can be compared to the Old Testament book the Song of Solomon because of the parallels found in them. The Song of Solomon is the shadow; Ephesians is the substance. It reveals God's love for His bride, the church, as expressed through the loving sacrifice of the Bridegroom, Jesus Christ. The Song of Solomon expresses this truth like no other in the Old Testament, revealing a love that transcended the law, a love burning in the heart of God for Israel. It was a passion that would not cool in spite of her mistakes and shortcomings. "He hath not beheld iniquity in Jacob, neither hath he seen perverseness in Israel" (Numbers 23:21). This love God had for Israel, as shown in the Song of Solomon, is wonderfully typical of the love that Jesus Christ has for His church. No other epistle in the New Testament expresses this truth more eloquently than Paul's Epistle to the Ephesians.

The Song of Solomon speaks not only of the bridegroom's admiration of his bride's beauty, but also of her position alongside him. The relationship of a husband and wife is gloriously typical of the relationship of Jesus Christ and His church (Ephesians 5:32). Jesus Christ has made this relationship a reality in our lives through the cross of His redemption.

As saints, we have long rejoiced in the revelation of the Savior's love for us. We have given thanks for the truth that He has pledged His troth to us, yet perhaps something has been missing from our spiritual understanding. We have often failed to see the riches that our inheritance has purchased for us. The Savior has not only revealed His love for us but also has made known unto us "what is the exceeding greatness of his power to us-ward who believe" (Ephesians 1:19).

God esteems His church highly above all others, and Paul wrote in this most eloquent of letters a description of the riches of our inheritance, the responsibility of our walk, and the authority to take a stand against the enemy in spiritual warfare. "The exceeding riches of his grace" (Ephesians 2:7) are ours to enjoy and to share, if we are faithful to "walk worthy of the vocation wherewith [we have been] called" (Ephesians 4:1). This relationship of riches and walking with Him gives us power and authority "to stand" against the enemy (Ephesians 6:13-14). Therefore, not only do we rejoice over the beauty of our Redeemer's love for us, but we can also act on the privileges of the covenant by calling upon the resources of our inheritance to meet the needs of this generation. Because of these riches, Ephesians is the bride's pearl, her crowning diadem.

II. The Uniqueness of Ephesians

The Epistle to the Ephesians is called the crowning diadem of Pauline theology. It is said that because of the many uncommon revelations of the riches of God's grace and their matchless presentation, Ephesians captures the essence of the Christian religion, eloquently presented by the apostle who knew above all else just how wonderful the richness of God's grace can be. Paul, who was a persecutor of the church, became a prime example of the wonder of God's grace. He was transformed into a mighty warrior of the Cross. Only grace could have accomplished such a feat. An understanding of these revelations illustrates how the Epistle to the Ephesians stands out among the other epistles and causes us to rejoice in the glory of Christ's redemption.

Another reason Ephesians is unique is because of its absence of personal references. Outside Paul's reference to himself, his bonds, and Tychicus, the bearer of the letter, there are no personal references or greetings. He did not include any messages to or from any individuals he might have known, especially in Ephesus. This is quite unusual, considering his many acquaintances and his great love for the church in Ephesus. Acts 20:17-38 relates the story of Paul's departure from Ephesus and the reaction the elders had to his leaving. Verse 17 states, "And from Miletus he sent to Ephesus, and called the elders of the church." Verses 37 and 38 continue, "And they all wept sore, and fell on Paul's neck and kissed him, sorrowing most of all for the words which he spake, that they should see his face no more." Considering their love for the apostle and his love for them, it is strange indeed that there would not be some reference in the epistle to at least one of these elders.

The apostle obviously had another objective in mind. Rather than draw attention to any individual, it seems he desired the glory of redemption to take preeminence. Paul's message is simple. He wanted this epistle to express the faith he would have readily died to preserve. Paul wanted nothing to distract his or anyone else's attention from "the fellowship of the mystery" (Ephesians 3:9) or the "exceeding riches of his grace" (Ephesians 2:7). He wanted to draw the reader's attention directly to the beauty of Christ's redemption and to ponder the riches of his inheritance. His purpose was to totally captivate the reader with the wonder of it all, so that the reader would rejoice at what the Savior has purchased for him. He wanted the reader to be able to exclaim, "O what a Savior; O what amazing grace!"

A. An Advanced Development of Divine Revelation

An important characteristic of Ephesians is that Paul made no attempt to address any specific problems. He did not try to correct any faults in the lives of people, as he did in the other epistles. In Ephesians he made no attempt to correct the Judaizers of Galatians or the Gnostics of Colossians. He simply extolled the glory and the grace of Jesus Christ.

These facts demonstrate that Ephesians is an advanced development of divine revelation. It expresses the very soul of God's eternal purpose for His church. Each time Paul dipped his quill in the ink to write on the theme of redemption, it evolved into a more picturesque view of God's glory as seen in the unfolding drama of redemption. Therefore, Ephesians is the culmination of many arguments that had already been settled by earlier letters. Now Paul had no need to argue but to proclaim directly the glorious truths of redemption. This he did with an eloquence unmatched by the other writers of the New Testament.

Indeed, it is safe to say that Ephesians is a result of all the trials, arguments, and debates Paul had experienced in his ministry. The Book of Ephesians, the bride's pearl, was formed in the heart of the apostle as a result of all the irritants of past battles. His pearl had cost him a great price. Yet he knew that every verse written and every glorious truth expressed would make his efforts and battles all worthwhile, especially since he realized the tremendous benefits his revelation of redemption would provide for each succeeding generation. If they would receive this revelation into their spirit, it would empower them to go forth with the whole armor of God and thereby be propelled to victory.

B. The Crowning Glory of Paul's Revelation of Jesus Christ

Another possible reason for Paul's lack of doctrinal argument is that he may not have wanted anyone to think that his whole ministry was simply confined to arguing and debating false doctrines. There comes a time, even in the ministry of an apostle, when he must lay down his arguments and simply extol what he truly believes. It is evident that the convictions of the apostle were unwavering, for he praised the glory of Christ's work of redemption, unashamed and without fear. Paul was trying to purify his motive for ministry. He cleared his perspective in order to renew his faith and increase his fervency.

This spiritual cleansing produced for us the crowning glory of Paul's revelation of Jesus Christ. Paul knew that if he was successful in communicating this knowledge of Christ Jesus to all believers, it would revolutionize their walk with God and give them the power they needed to defeat the enemy. Ephesians 1:17-19 beautifully expresses this truth: "That the God of our Lord Jesus Christ, the Father of glory, may give unto you the spirit of wisdom and revelation in the knowledge of him . . . that ye may know . . . what is the exceeding greatness of his power to us-ward who believe, according to the working of his mighty power."

C. Ephesians—The Bride's Pearl

Paul's clear perspective produced a literary master-piece of divine revelation, a concise declaration of important gospel truths that had been revealed to all the gospel writers. However, Paul's eloquence in describing them gives him a special place among the writers. He gathered together in one all the important truths, as did the merchant of pearls who consolidated all his treasures and invested them in one pearl of great price. "Again, the kingdom of heaven is like unto a merchant man, seeking goodly pearls: who, when he had found one pearl of great price, went and sold all that he had, and bought it" (Matthew 13:45-46). The merchant consolidated all he had in order to purchase the supreme pearl. Paul took his treasures of spiritual understanding and his revelations, combined them in one letter, and with loving tenderness presented to the bride her pearl—born of anguish and trial, but gloriously triumphant in the end.

The reason for calling Ephesians the bride's pearl is quite simple when one understands how a pearl is made. *Collier's Encyclopedia* states, "The genuine pearl is the only gem that comes from the sea and the only one made by a living process." Its value is unique because it is born from the pain of a living organism. Collier's explains this process:

> Genuine pearls are the result of an accidental entry of foreign matter into a pearl oyster. This may be tiny grains of sand or possibly a parasite, which upon entry into the pearl oyster sets up an irritation. The pearl oyster, unable to rid itself of the unwelcome intruder, seeks to reduce the attendant irritation by coating the foreign substance with nacreous material. The final result is a calcareous concretion built layer upon layer. Many genuine pearls, when sectioned, reveal no evidence whatever of an irritant.[1]

Paul's Ephesians was produced as a result of the many irritating arguments and debates of past writings, yet he proved to be the conqueror. By his spiritual walk with God he covered the irritant of theological debate with the pearl of the gospel and thereby provided us with a statement of victory that surpassed anything else he had previously produced. So well conquered was this irritant or argument that even after one sections the epistle, no trace of the irritant can be found anywhere, just pure pearl.

III. Ephesians Compared to Colossians

Paul drew from various sources of Christian language to describe in the Epistle to the Ephesians the majesty of God's eternal purpose as manifested in the church. To demonstrate this point, let us discuss the similarities between Ephesians and Colossians, for they show that the bride's pearl is a combination of the riches of New Testament thought.

Scholars have been unable to agree on a precise number of parallels. Mitton stated, "More than one-third of the words in Colossians reappear in Ephesians."[2] Other scholars such as Wood[3] and Foulkes have estimated that either 73 or 75 of the 155 verses of Ephesians are found in Colossians.[4] The numerous parallels of expression do reveal a special connection between Ephesians and Colossians. No other epistles in the New Testament contain as many parallels as these two.

By studying the list of parallels Bible students will recognize that both epistles have similar patterns by which the apostle conveyed the riches of God's grace. (See Table 1.) Certain expressions are found that occur only in these two epistles. These expressions are not found in any other of the Pauline Epistles, further strengthening the special connection that exists between the two epistles. However, some of these expressions hold a different meaning and are used to express a different truth. Their usage is not always the same.

A. An Expansion of Colossians

These parallels are too numerous to be coincidental. Whether one considers the list of parallels given or the original expressions, it becomes obvious that the Epistle to the Ephesians is an expansion of truths and doctrines declared in Colossians. For example, Colossians reveals Jesus Christ as triumphant over all principalities and powers. His superiority over all His enemies is clearly seen in Paul's colorful description of victory: "And having spoiled principalities and powers, he made a shew of them openly, triumphing over them in it" (Colossians 2:15). In Colossians, Paul's emphasis is on Jesus Christ and how the eternal purpose of God is realized in His triumph. This emphasis is not new to Paul, for he expressed it in other epistles as well (I Corinthians 8:6). However, when we examine Ephesians, the role of Jesus Christ in God's eternal purpose is assumed, and the emphasis shifts from Christ to the church. The church is seen as the chosen vessel by which God will fulfill the work of Christ. In Colossians, Paul did not address the church's role in God's purpose, but in Ephesians he centered his entire theme on the church's role in God's eternal purpose.

Another treasure Ephesians uncovers, which is assumed in Colossians, is God's purpose of reconciliation (Colossians 1:20). Colossians expresses the importance of the role that Jesus Christ played in reconciling humanity to God. Ephesians expands this thought to include the reconciliation of people one to another, emphasizing that "the middle wall of partition" has been removed (Ephesians 2:14). In Colossians peace is made with God. In Ephesians peace is made with people.

Unveiled before us is a panoramic view of redemption. Paul first wrote Colossians and revealed to us the wonder of the eternal purpose of God as realized in Christ Jesus. He then began to write Ephesians, extending the marvel of God's purpose to include the church. This purpose is twofold: first, Christ would reconcile humanity to God, and then humans would become reconciled to one another in one body. Here we have a greater view of the purpose that He intended to bring to fruition. Colossians focuses on God in Christ; Ephesians on Christ in the church.

Unfortunately, much of the religious world overlooks

the importance of God's eternal purpose and cannot appreciate the view Paul presented to us in these two epistles. Many in Christianity consider the doctrine of justification by faith to be the only doctrine Paul taught that is of any significance. However, Paul's revelation of the redemptive work of Christ goes far beyond the initial legal grounds by which we have been given a right to claim salvation. He has given us some precious insights into the believer's position and purpose in Christ, opening to us a share in the bounty of the triumph He secured through the Cross.

Most of Christendom emphasizes Romans and Galatians, but Ephesians and Colossians are not to be underrated. Although Ephesians affirms justification by faith, it also proclaims God's plan to use the church as His means of consummating His eternal purpose and setting up His kingdom as ruler of the universe. No epistle of Paul reveals such treasure as does Ephesians. As F. F. Bruce declared, "True Paulinism has room for both, and our Christian thinking must similarly make room for both if it is not to become lop-sided and defective."[5]

Considering all the parallels that can be drawn from these two very special epistles, it becomes apparent that the writer of Ephesians was full of the language and theme of Colossians, setting forth a special expansion of thought, not in an "argumentative style with which we are so familiar from other letters of his, but in an inspired mood of meditative adoration and prayer."[6]

B. Question of Authorship

These similarities have often been used to dispute Pauline authorship. Most of the evidence presented to challenge Pauline authorship is internal evidence. Evanson and de Wette were among the first to challenge Pauline authorship, and their ideas were propagated by Mitton and Goodspeed. These scholars maintained that another writer, an impostor, whose mind was filled with the language of Colossians and the other writings of Paul, actually wrote Ephesians. "The argument has to be developed exclusively in terms of internal evidence, because the external attestation is unassailable."[7] Three basic reasons have been given why Pauline authorship is questioned. We will now turn to those reasons and consider their validity.

1. Tychicus, the Bearer of the Letter

Ephesians 6:21-22 and Colossians 4:7-8 identify Tychicus as the bearer of each letter, showing a definite connection. In many of the other parallel expressions, the wording is similar, but never exact. In this particular instance, however, most words are identical. Mitton pointed out that there are "as many as thirty-two consecutive words (apart from an omission of two words)" that are repeated exactly.[8] Mitton assumed that this repetition reveals a literary dependence that gave him sufficient ground to question authorship. However Mitton did make this concession, "Though Ephesians is often dealing with the same theme as Colossians and in similar words, never more than seven or eight identical words, at most, are repeated in the same sequence, and only rarely so many."[9]

2. Different Meaning of Words

Another reason scholars have questioned Pauline authorship is that the words used in one instance in Ephesians may have a different meaning in Colossians. But

Paul, on other occasions, used his words and expressions in a different light to capture a new splendor of thought. For example, Colossians 3:14 calls charity the "bond of perfectness," but Ephesians 4:3 implores us to "keep the unity of the Spirit in the bond of peace." Though the expressions are used in a different light, their use does not change any theology. Similarly, Paul used the phrase "in the name of the Lord Jesus" (Colossians 3:17) to refer to doing all things in Christ's name, but in Ephesians 5:20 "in the name of our Lord Jesus Christ" refers to a more specific act of giving thanks. Before any of this evidence can seriously dispute authorship, the basic theology of it would have to be proven contradictory, and that would be difficult when one considers it in light of other passages of Paul's writings.

IV. Ephesians Compared to Other New Testament Writings

The dispute about the authorship of Ephesians has also been fueled by the similarities found when it is compared to the rest of the New Testament. Much of the Epistle to the Ephesians has parallels in the other writings of Paul. Those who have opposed Pauline authorship have speculated that an imitator wrote Ephesians at a later date as a cover letter to introduce the rest of Paul's letters. They suppose that this imitator wrote Ephesians to help relate Paul's teachings to a later generation. However, this argument becomes invalid when we consider the unusual characteristics of the epistle. Foulkes and Wood observed that one could use this same argument against this theory by stating that Paul's intention in writing Ephesians was obviously to provide a comprehensive synopsis of his teachings. (See Table 2.)

Foulkes commented:

> We would expect Ephesians to resemble most closely those Epistles which have greater doctrinal sections than the others (e.g. Romans and Colossians), and this is the case. We would expect to find that Ephesians, if it were a letter of pure Pauline doctrine and ethics without local references, had a greater number of verses or expressions in common with other Pauline Epistles than would one of the letters which abound in local reference. This again is undeniably the case.[10]

Because of the importance of Ephesians and its purely doctrinal and practical nature, let us look at how Ephesians compares with other non-Pauline writings in the New Testament.

A. Acts and Luke

In comparing Acts and Luke to Ephesians, many similarities begin to surface. Some scholars such as Mitton and Goodspeed, have indicated that Acts reflects Pauline theology very poorly, and Mitton argued against the Pauline authorship of Ephesians on the ground that it is a poor reflection of Paul's true theology. This view results from a limited interpretation of Paul's theology that has hindered a full understanding of gospel truth.

Many scholars give Acts historical validity but little theological value, rejecting it as a divine blueprint for the church's doctrine and ministry. Actually, however, Acts plays an important role in revealing the kind of church

Jesus came to establish. It demonstrates how the apostles interpreted the teachings of Jesus and how they put His principles into action.

Ephesians likewise deals with the church and her place in Jesus Christ, showing the privileges connected with this position. It further discusses the function of the church in her place in Christ, the effect of the ministry upon the church, and the church's warfare against the enemy. By addressing these practical principles, Ephesians provides an explanation of the methods used by the apostles in the Book of Acts. Ephesians deals with the privileges of the believer, and Acts reveals these privileges in practical application. Acts shows us what the church is capable of accomplishing, while Ephesians explains why we are able to accomplish these things.

Paul never intended to change the message of Acts by any of his theology but simply set forth sound doctrinal explanations of how and why the church is given such power. Paul's gospel was not just a gospel of intellectualism, but also a gospel of power. The gospel does not remove the intellect, but it can and does operate in spite of the limitations of the intellect. Paul never intended for the gospel of power to wane into a haze of intellectual foolishness.

To scholars such as Mitton and Goodspeed, the redemption glories revealed by Paul through his epistles are privileges obtained by a simple acceptance of the historical fact of Christ's existence and crucifixion. This gives birth to a doctrine of "easy believism" that possesses only a remote resemblance to what Christ Himself taught and the apostles in Acts exemplified. Faith is much more than simply making an intellectual decision for Christ. The

Book of Acts reveals the total involvement of faith, which causes the individual to repent, acknowledging his sinfulness and His need of a Savior. Christ clearly stated, and the apostles, including Paul, proclaimed that repentance is incomplete without water baptism by immersion in the name of Jesus Christ. Acts and Ephesians further recognize that the witness from God of the genuineness of faith is the gift of the Holy Ghost as the promise of the Father, the seal of the Spirit.

Acts plays a more distinct role in giving sound interpretation to the epistles of Paul than most scholars have given it. We must give Acts this place of prominence because it is in the canon of Scripture, which means it is inspired of the Holy Ghost. If we do not interpret the epistles of Paul by the light of the apostles' actions in Acts, then we do not have a clear and concise guide for the practical application of principles given in the epistles. The alternative is various methods of interpretation that are not sanctified by the Holy Ghost. We must allow Scripture to interpret Scripture, or interpretation erodes into an intellectual free-for-all that leads to confusion and false doctrine.

In Acts, we do not see the infilling of the Spirit discussed as a religious platitude, but we see an actual demonstration of it taking place. Acts exists to show a literal example of someone being filled with the Spirit, while Ephesians explains how and why we can remain filled with the Spirit.

Ephesians also bears some striking similarities to Luke. Luke was the writer of both Acts and Luke, and was present with Paul on several missionary journeys; this should be sufficient explanation as to why these similarities exist. If the inspiration of Paul seeded the heart of Luke and then Luke produced fruit from Paul's ministry in writing his Gospel and the historical account of the early church, then we would expect his writing to show evidence of that fruit. Considering the amount of time Luke spent with Paul and considering these similarities, we can see the true emphasis Paul made in his ministry being mirrored in Luke. Too many scholars do not interpret Paul's theology in light of the way he lived, especially the way he lived as described by Luke in the Book of Acts. (See Table 3.)

Paul and Luke knew that the church would continue into the future and did not want her to lose the spiritual function she had enjoyed in the beginning. The church today cannot afford to lose her connection with the apostles' doctrine as described in Acts. She must remember that she was born of a Jewish background, and though Jesus has waited for two millenniums to return, He desires to return to an apostolic church founded on the truths revealed in Acts and Ephesians.

B. Hebrews

The doctrines of the early church were definitely in view when Ephesians was written, and the same is true with Hebrews. The latter book, first written to a specific audience, sets forth the inimitable doctrines of Christ as a superior revelation to the old covenant. Naturally we would find these similarities, none of which could be used to dispute Pauline authorship. (See Table 4.)

C. I Peter

Significant parallels exist between Ephesians and I

Peter. The opening doxologies hold to a basic form of greeting not unlike that of I Corinthians 1:3. Emphasis is placed on the spiritual aspect of Christ's ministry and the Christian's ministry in warfare. (See Table 5.)

One word that has added fuel to the controversy of authorship is the word *eusplanchnoi,* which is translated "tenderhearted" in Ephesians, while it is translated "pitiful" in I Peter. It is used only in Ephesians 4:32 and I Peter 3:8. This similarity is easily explained when we consider that Paul and Peter were concerned about seeing Jesus Christ formed in the lives of believers, not just doctrinally, but also on a practical level. It is obvious they would call attention to the need for believers to be tenderhearted toward one another.

Similarities among the New Testament books should not seem suspect when we consider that the apostolic doctrines had, by this date, solidified into a strong unity of belief. Therefore, it is to be expected that the language would be similar among the different writers of the New Testament. Ephesians is obviously one of Paul's most mature works, and he drew from all the language of the early church in writing this letter.

D. John's Writings

The language of Ephesians bears certain similarities to John's writings that are expected when we consider that both writers dealt with the theme of redemption. Key words used by both authors demonstrate that the doctrine of the apostles had developed a unity of faith. (See Table 6.)

We can best explain the similarities between Ephesians and John's writings by realizing that a revelation of redemption demands the use of common terms to express that redemption. The terms common to these writings actually reveal their authenticity. Once again, Ephesians expresses God's purpose in language that is compatible with every writer of the New Testament. Therefore, a comparison with the expressions of John's writings cannot be used to argue the question of authorship.

Parallels also exist between Ephesians and Revelation, particularly that the church at Ephesus is mentioned in the second chapter (Revelation 2:1). (See Table 7.) However, considering that the Book of Revelation was the last New Testament book to be written, it would be normal for John to have used symbolism and language common to the early church writers to describe the awesome revelation of Jesus he had received.

Undoubtedly there are many parallels between Ephesians and the non-Pauline writings. But the same can be said about the other Pauline writings when compared to the rest of the New Testament. The fact that Ephesians is not a controversial writing and no particular problems are being dealt with, explains why these parallels exist.

> We may well ask whether the similarities between Ephesians and these various writings are not simply eloquent testimony to the great and increasing measure of unanimity in the early Christian preaching and teaching, whether in Asia, Rome, Ephesus or Antioch, whether from the lips of Peter, Paul, John or any other.[11]

V. The Vindication of Pauline Authorship
A. *External Evidence*

The scholars who dispute the Pauline authorship of

Ephesians appeal to the internal text of the epistle and create an imaginary scenario in which a disciple of Paul, later in the first century, compiled a collection of Paul's letters and wrote a cover letter to introduce that collection, writing it in Paul's name. If indeed a disciple of Paul wrote Ephesians, he was a literary genius equal to Paul, but there is no record in the early church history of such a genius. The historical assumption by every writer and scholar of the early centuries that Paul wrote Ephesians provides an unbeatable argument. Because of the confirmation given by early writers, such as Ignatius, Tertullian, and Origen, of the validity of Ephesians, an opponent would have to explain why their view was unquestioned for seventeen centuries. That explanation has not been given.

If there had been any question among the ancient Christian writers as to the authenticity of the epistle, it is possible that the authorship of Ephesians could be called into question. Since no such question was raised among these early writers, the epistle still stands as Paul's.

B. Internal Evidence

Some have disputed the authorship of Ephesians by claiming that its doctrine is not compatible with the other Pauline epistles. However, they do admit that the doctrine of Ephesians is consistent with the rest of the New Testament writings. Unfortunately, this type of theorizing hints that most scholars view Paul's epistles as a higher revelation than the rest of the New Testament writings. It seems they believe Paul changed the doctrine of the early church to better accommodate the Gentiles. This view is erroneous.

Paul's revelation of Christ and the church was progressive in that it offered a greater understanding and explanation of Christ's redemptive work. But by no means did it change the teachings of Jesus or of the other disciples. Certainly, it did nothing more than enhance the beauty of the Acts of the Apostles by showing us the glory of Christ and His purpose being worked out through the church. An examination of these disputed doctrines will show that they are completely compatible with Paul's other epistles.

Much of Christendom has divided the Godhead into three distinct persons. This view is unscriptural. The Godhead consists of only one undivided being (Deuteronomy 6:4), and Jesus Christ is the "express image of his person" (Hebrews 1:3). Even trinitarian scholars admit that "to the apostle, what is the work of the Father is the work of the Son."[12] Christ's work of redemption included forgiveness of sins, and God manifested Himself in Christ, thus reconciling the world unto Himself. As a result, we can attribute both forgiveness and reconciliation to God and to Christ. When we understand the biblical teaching of one God who became our Savior, we see that Ephesians harmonizes with the rest of the Pauline epistles.

Some critics have stated that unlike some other Pauline epistles, Ephesians and Colossians seem to anticipate a long time before the second coming of Jesus Christ. The emphasis in Ephesians is indeed different. Paul realized that the coming of the Lord would come later and prepared the church by writing Ephesians and other epistles as well (II Thessalonians and Philippians).

Mitton stated that the hope of the *parousia* (Second Coming) was lost in Ephesians, which to him spoke against Pauline authorship. A careful study of the text refutes this idea, however. The Second Coming is definitely in view when Paul referred to the "redemption of the purchased possession" and spoke of the seal of the Holy Spirit given to believers "unto the day of redemption" (Ephesians 1:13-14; 4:30). Moreover, Ephesians 5:27 states that Christ intends to present the church without spot or wrinkle unto Himself.

Ephesians also warns the children of disobedience of the day of God's wrath (Ephesians 5:6) and promises a time of reward for those who do good (Ephesians 6:8). Ephesians prepares the church for a waiting period before Christ's return but by no means changes the expectation of Christ's second coming.

The doctrine of Ephesians is unquestionably Paul's and is compatible with every epistle in the New Testament. At most Ephesians should only be considered an expanded revelation or explanation of previously revealed truths.

VI. Destination

To whom the letter is addressed is uncertain. By the second century the title, "To the Ephesians," was almost universally accepted. It appears in all the extant Greek manuscripts. However, the oldest manuscript of Ephesians, the Chester Beatty Papyrus P46 dating from about A.D. 200, along with the fourth-century codices Sinaiticus and Vaticanus do not contain the words "at Ephesus" as we have them in Ephesians 1:1. Origen, Basil, and Jerome all stated that the manuscripts they possessed did not contain the words either.

Other questions arise when the letter is examined internally. It appears that Paul was not well acquainted with the readers of this letter because it states that he has only heard of their faith and love (Ephesians 1:15). They, in turn, have only heard about the stewardship of God's grace entrusted to him to preach the gospel to the Gentiles (Ephesians 3:2). This wording is puzzling, considering that Paul stayed in Ephesus for over two years and the mutual affection of Paul and the Ephesians is clearly seen in his farewell to the elders (Acts 19:8-10; 20:36-38). The fact that Paul was so well acquainted with the Ephesian church and yet the letter contains no personal greetings or references adds a further question.

It seems clear that Paul wrote Ephesians to a larger audience than just his personal acquaintances. He did not address merely his friends and did not intend for this letter to be read exclusively by those he met on his second missionary journey. One explanation is that Paul indeed wrote this letter to the Ephesians, but the church in Ephesus sustained an incredible amount of growth from the time of Paul's departure and the time he wrote the epistle from Rome. Recognizing this fact, Paul referred to the believers in this more impersonal manner. This could also explain why he could only assume they had been taught the truth about Jesus (Ephesians 4:21).

Many scholars conclude that Paul did not address the letter specifically to the Ephesians. In this case two questions need to be answered. To whom was the letter written, and how did it become known as the Epistle to the Ephesians? Two theories have found favor with scholars over the years.

1. *The letter to the Ephesians is actually the lost*

letter to Laodicea. Marcion, in the second century, claimed to have a copy of Ephesians with the words "at Laodicea" inserted. "This may have been because . . . it was a deduction from the reference to the letter 'from Laodicea' in Colossians 4:16."[13] Marcion's claim that Ephesians was written to the Laodiceans does not have much support because Marcion notoriously changed the actual text of the Scripture to suit his own views. However, Marcion would gain no theological advantage for changing the title, so it is unlikely that he did so. Even at that, Marcion's claim still does not receive much support because the Muratorian Fragment mentions two epistles, one to the Ephesians and another to the Laodiceans. Some have supposed that the name Laodicea was removed and Ephesians inserted into the letter because the church at Laodicea was judged by God and its candlestick removed.[14]

Ephesians does seem to answer the need of the Laodiceans to awaken from their spiritual blindness by anointing their eyes with eye salve and allowing the eyes of their understanding to become enlightened (Ephesians 1:18; Revelation 3:17-18). Ephesians makes the believer aware of his riches in Christ, and Jesus requested the Laodiceans to "buy of me gold tried in the fire that thou mayest be rich" (Ephesians 1:7, 18; 2:7; 3:8, 16; Revelation 3:18). Ephesians calls every believer to "put on the whole armour of God," and Jesus tells the Laodiceans to buy raiment that they may be clothed (Ephesians 6:11; Revelation 3:18).

This theory has many problems, however, and has not met with a great deal of support. In particular Colossians 4:16 speaks of a letter "from Laodicea," not "to Laodicea." Moreover, it would seem strange for Paul to greet the Laodiceans in Colossians 4:15 while at the same time writing them another letter.

2. *The letter was written to several churches in the Roman province of Asia.* Since Ephesus was the capital, it would be the most strategic place for distribution. This theory has been the most widely accepted because it is strongly supported by both the internal and external evidence. Some have proposed that the letter was sent from church to church and the bearer of the letter would fill in the blank space to personalize the letter as he reached his destination. As a result, in the process of time, since Ephesus was the capital and contained the most important church of that area, the letter became accepted as "the Epistle of Paul to the Ephesians." F. F. Bruce adopts this explanation:

> The most acceptable view, having regard to the general character of the letter, is that it was intended for all the churches of the province of Asia, some of which were personally known to Paul, while others were not (cf. Col. 2:1). . . . We may quite justifiably call it "The Epistle to the Ephesians," provided that we remember that it was sent also to other churches in the province of which Ephesus was the capital city.[15]

VII. Date

Three times Paul referred to his imprisonment in Ephesians. He referred to himself as "I Paul, the prisoner of Jesus Christ," as "the prisoner of the Lord," and as "an ambassador in bonds" (Ephesians 3:1; 4:1; 6:20). This leaves no doubt that Ephesians was written during one of Paul's imprisonments. We know from the account given to us in the Book of Acts that Paul was imprisoned at least twice, once in Caesarea and again in Rome. Both of these imprisonments lasted at least two years (Acts 24:27; 28:30). Obviously, the one night of imprisonment in Philippi would not be considered (Acts 16:23). However, Paul was imprisoned on other occasions beside these (II Corinthians 11:23). It is very likely, considering the opposition he met in Ephesus, that he was imprisoned during his ministry there (I Corinthians 15:32). Because of this, some have proposed that he wrote Ephesians while imprisoned in Ephesus. This does not seem likely in light of the absence of personal references or greetings. Moreover if Ephesians were written from Ephesus, the date would have to be about A.D. 54 or 55, which is unlikely since it seems to represent a later stage of development in Paul's writing.

The traditional view is that Paul wrote Ephesians, Colossians, and Philemon while imprisoned in Rome, and that these three epistles were sent with Tychicus and Onesimus (Ephesians 6:21; Colossians 4:7-9; Philemon 12). Considering this evidence, it is highly possible that the three epistles were written together and sent out at the same time. The evidence also indicates that Philippians was written from Rome at about the same time. Support for this view becomes substantial when one considers that Timothy was with Paul during the writing of Philippians, as well as Colossians and Philemon (Philippians 1:1; Colossians 1:1; Philemon 1). When Paul wrote to the Philippians, he said that he enjoyed liberty in preaching the gospel. He stated the same in Ephesians (Philippians 1:13;

Ephesians 6:20). Paul also expressed to the Philippians and to Philemon his confidence that he would soon be released from his imprisonment (Philippians 2:24; Philemon 22). It becomes obvious that if any of these epistles were written from Rome, they all were.

In conclusion, it can be surmised that Ephesians was written from Rome during Paul's imprisonment there, sometime between A.D. 60 and 61. Paul wrote Colossians first and then Ephesians and sent them along with Philemon and perhaps Philippians as well by the hand of Tychicus. Tychicus, being instructed that the epistle needed to be read by the churches throughout the province of Asia, bore the letter with a blank space that he would fill in as he arrived in each city. (This explains Marcion's copy of this letter with the words "at Laodicea" inserted.) Since Ephesus was the capital and most important church in the province, the only place identified in the epistle was Ephesus, and thereby the letter became known as the Epistle to the Ephesians.

VIII. Occasion and Purpose

Paul's first trip to Ephesus came at the end of his second missionary journey. He had completed his work at Corinth and proceeded to Ephesus, accompanied by Aquila and Priscilla. While he intended to leave Aquila and Priscilla in Ephesus to continue the work of the Lord, Paul entered into the synagogue and immediately began reasoning with the Jews. They desired that he would remain with them, but he revealed his plans to return to Jerusalem and keep the feast (Acts 18:18-21).

In Paul's absence, Aquila and Priscilla converted Apollos, an eloquent man who was well versed in the

Scripture. They "expounded unto him the way of God more perfectly." He then began to preach Christ and many Jews were converted (Acts 18:24-28). Apollos left Ephesus, and a letter was sent with him that the brethren might receive him. His travels took him as far as Corinth.

While Apollos was in Corinth, Paul began his third missionary journey. He returned to Ephesus and found certain disciples of John the Baptist, who had only received the baptism of John. Paul proceeded to explain to them the "way of God more perfectly" by asking them, "Have ye received the Holy Ghost since ye believed?" (Acts 19:2). They had not heard that the Holy Ghost was available but knew by John's preaching that it would soon be given. Paul laid hands on them, and they received the Holy Ghost and began to speak with tongues and prophesied (Acts 19:3-6). The church at Ephesus, under Aquila, Priscilla, Epaphras, and Paul, began to flourish. The gospel began to spread throughout the entire region, Ephesus being the headquarters for this evangelistic thrust.

For three years, probably from the summer of A.D. 52 to the spring of A.D. 55, Paul ministered in Ephesus and in the surrounding area. Miracles and mighty wonders were wrought through Paul to help establish the gospel of Jesus Christ. Sorcery and necromancy were prevalent in that society, but the Word of God prevailed so that "many of them also which used curious arts brought their books together, and burned them before all men: and they counted the price of them, and found it fifty thousand pieces of silver. So mightily grew the word of God and prevailed" (Acts 19:19-20). The faith of the people grew to such an extent that aprons and handkerchiefs were anointed and sent out and by this means the sick were healed (Acts 19:12). The church at Ephesus was founded on the preaching of the gospel of Jesus Christ, which was confirmed by signs and wonders.

Epaphras was instrumental in helping Paul establish churches in the entire Lycus Valley, over which Ephesus was the capital. The churches he helped to establish by Paul's instruction were Colossae, Hierapolis, and Laodicea (Colossians 1:6-7; 4:12-13; Philemon 23).

Paul departed from Ephesus into Macedonia and Greece, then returned to Jerusalem via Miletus. At Miletus, before departing for Jerusalem, he called for the Ephesian elders and gave them one final charge, knowing that he most likely would never see them again (Acts 20:17-38). Upon arriving at Jerusalem, Paul was falsely accused by the Jews and imprisoned, and he barely escaped with his life (Acts 21:27-36). He was then sent to Caesarea, along with two centurions, two hundred soldiers, seventy horsemen, and two hundred spearmen to provide protection from the Jews. They even had to leave at night because of the stir Paul had caused (Acts 23:23). For two years he was held by Felix and Festus as a prisoner in Caesarea, and by virtue of his appeal to Caesar, was sent to Rome (Acts 24:27; 25:11-12).

Thus began Paul's two-year imprisonment at Rome, where it is believed he wrote the Epistle to the Ephesians. It was in Rome that he met and converted the runaway slave Onesimus. Onesimus had run away from his master, Philemon, who lived in Colossae (Philemon 10). Tychicus, a native of Ephesus, was also with Paul in Rome at this time. Paul prepared a letter to be sent back with Tychicus and Onesimus to Philemon with the hope that Philemon would receive Onesimus again as a brother and not just a servant.

Before their departure, Epaphras, Paul's fellow minister, came to visit him in Rome to tell him of the condition of the churches in the Lycus Valley. Paul was concerned about the heresy that was spreading in Colossae and wrote Colossians as an answer to that heresy.

Epaphras brought Paul the news that the Colossian church was being infiltrated by a mixture of "Jewish and pagan elements which made much of the hierarchies of principalities and powers in the universe. It was hospitable enough to make room for Christ in its scheme of things, but its whole tendency was to deny His supremacy and the completeness of His redemptive work."[16]

False teachers (or possibly a single false teacher) were trying to make too much of the worship of angels, principalities, and powers. In answer to this, Paul set forth a doctrinal statement of Jesus Christ, explaining that Jesus had conquered all principalities and powers and made a show of them openly. He declared that Christ's redemption put this defeat on display before the whole universe, and by virtue of His victory, Christ deserved total worship and admiration of the believer. Hence we have Colossians, an epistle that "contains one of the most powerful presentations of the doctrine of Jesus Christ in the Scriptures."[17]

It is probable that Paul, after considering his reply to the Colossian heresy, began to ponder not only the work of Jesus Christ in God's eternal purpose, but also the work of the church and how it affects God's eternal purpose. He then picked up his pen and began to write Ephesians. The theme of Ephesians was definitely relevant to what was happening in the area at this time. The truths revealed not only counteracted the false doctrine being propagated but also provided practical application necessary for the church to carry out her mission. Thus we have Ephesians as a fuller proclamation of Paul's grandest theme: Christ accomplishing His purpose through His church. "Unto him be glory in the church by Christ Jesus throughout all ages, world without end. Amen" (Ephesians 3:21).

IX. Conclusion

Without question, the style of Ephesians is quite different from Paul's other epistles. Ephesian's purpose is more objective than that of Colossians because Paul was attempting "to rise above the smoke of battle and capture a vision of God's sovereign plan that transcends the bitterness of controversy."[18] With his mind free of debate, Paul was able to write Ephesians and incorporate the church into God's eternal purpose. He wrote, unshackled by chains of argument, of the riches of Christ's redemption and its effect on the daily lives and relationships of believers. Because Ephesians contains no pattern of argument and no hard-hitting answers to theological questions, Paul had the liberty to set forth the beauty of Christ's redemption in poetic expressions that still amaze even the greatest of scholars.

Considering Ephesians and its relationship to Colossians, we come to the following conclusion. Paul, after writing Colossians and being filled with the language and thought of Christ's eternal purpose, began to write Ephesians to present to the church a pearl formed in his heart as a result of his personal triumph over all the controversies he had faced. Then after writing both epistles, Paul sent them at the same time by the hand of Tychicus. Charles Hodge explained, "All these characteristics of similarity, dissimilarity and mutual independence, are naturally accounted for on the assumption that the two epistles were written at the same time, the one for a particular congregation, the other for a particular class of readers."[19] The evidence clearly indicates that Ephesians belongs to the genius of Paul, and the title as written in the King James Version still stands: "The Epistle of Paul the Apostle to the Ephesians."

X. Definition of Key Terms

Accepted: Past tense, referring to our redemption accomplished by the Cross. It has already been accomplished, and we are accepted because the blood of Jesus has atoned for our sins. We are "accepted in the beloved" (1:6). We do not earn this acceptance but receive it through a living relationship with the beloved Son of God.

Access: The privilege of making requests and having prayers answered, given to every believer through the Spirit. According to 2:18, the Spirit gives us access to the Father. In 3:12, we have "boldness and access with confidence" by faith in Christ.

Adoption (1:5): The process of becoming a part of a family with all its rights and privileges, even when one is not a natural-born member of the family.

Armor of God (6:11): (1) Protection provided for the believer who prays. (2) It can mean God Himself is our armor. The various pieces of the armor simply describe what God is to us.

Children of disobedience: Ephesians provides lists of

sins that the children of disobedience commit (2:1-3; 4:17-31; 5:3-6). They walk in their own lusts, offend with evil communication, and are called the children of wrath (2:2-3; 4:29; 5:6). Disobedience incurs the wrath of God.

Children of the light (5:8-21): Those who choose the best course of action when confronted with evil. That course of action will always be what pleases God the most.

Dispensation: Oikonomia is translated as "dispensation" in Colossians 1:25; Ephesians 1:10; 3:2. In Colossians the word refers to a stewardship that God had given to Paul. In Ephesians 1:10 and 3:2 the word refers to a plan that God Himself has made, which is more general than specific. In Colossians, the specific purpose is being expounded, revealing God's plan for the Incarnation. Ephesians was written with the intention of revealing to the church as a whole the broad spectrum of God's eternal purpose.

Exceeding: God's ability to do great things, above and beyond the comprehension of the human mind (1:19; 3:20). This power is seen in the Resurrection, which is the power of salvation. God's power is not limited to our finite comprehension or ability to pray. He exceeds all that. That is why the Spirit must intercede for us (Romans 8:26).

Fellow citizens (2:19): The Gentiles, who were totally alienated from all God's promises, can now belong to the commonwealth and become citizens along with the Jews in Christ's economy.

Fitly framed together (2:21): The Jews and Gentiles are built together in the superstructure of the church. The church is a building firmly fitted on the foundation of the apostles and prophets, Jesus Christ Himself being the chief cornerstone (2:20).

Fitly joined together (4:16): The church is described as a body with Christ as the head. Each member is joined together as the members of a physical body, with each one supplying nourishment to the other members.

Fullness: Pleroma is translated "fullness" in Colossians 1:19; 2:9; Ephesians 3:19; 4:13. Colossians describes Christ as embodying all the fullness of the Father and of the Godhead. In Ephesians, the word "fullness" has two different uses: (1) The fullness of God as possessed by the individual believer through Christ (3:19). (2) The fullness of Christ as obtained by the church collectively (4:13). Colossians reveals that the fullness dwells in Christ, and Ephesians reveals that the fullness is possessed by the church through Christ.

Heavenly places: The literal rendering is "in the heavenlies," referring to where Jesus dwells. He is seated in heaven in power and authority. The believer is also seated with Him in the same power and authority. Ephesians mentions this heavenly realm four times, and each time it refers to a different aspect. The heavenly places are: (1) the *location* of the believer's blessings (1:3), (2) the *dwelling* of Jesus Christ (1:20), (3) the *dwelling* of the believer (2:6), and (4) the *battlefield* for the church's warfare (3:10; 6:12). The heavenly places contain the blessings, the Savior, the dwelling, and the warfare of the church, and they are obtained through obedience to the will and power of the Lord Jesus Christ.

Hymns, psalms and spiritual songs (5:19): Gives insight into the type of church services the early church experienced, which included singing and music. (1) They sang hymns. These could have been songs written by the members of the early church or even old hymns sung by the Jewish people that were adapted to the Christian viewpoint. (2) They sang psalms. Most likely these were the Psalms of the Old Testament. However, we cannot rule out the possibility that the early church wrote and sang new psalms. (3) They sang other songs as they were moved upon by the Spirit.

Middle wall of partition (2:14): A unique phrase used to describe the division between Jews and Gentiles, referring to the wall in the Temple that divided the Court of the Gentiles from the rest of the Temple. Access to the inner sanctuary was denied the Gentile proselyte. Jesus Christ ended this enmity and tore down the wall. This occurred for two reasons: (1) To give Gentiles access to the promises of Christ's redemption; (2) To make one new church out of the formerly separated peoples.

Mystery: Musterion in Colossians 1:27 and Ephesians 3:3, 9. Something that has been hidden in ages past but is now revealed. In Colossians, Paul expounded the "mystery" of "Christ in you the hope of glory," while in Ephesians he used the word "mystery" to show that the Gentiles are fellow heirs with the Jews. Reconciliation in Colossians is between God and man, whereas Ephesians reveals the harmony God has created between Jews and Gentiles. The revealed mystery is twofold: (1) the relationship between God and man restored by Christ's atonement, and (2) the resulting new relationship between man and man, specifically, between Jew and Gentile (1:9; 3:3-9; 5:32; 6:19).

Perfect man: This expression sums up the ultimate purpose of the ministry, namely, the perfecting, edifying, and equipping of the saints (4:12-13).

Predestinated: In every reference the plural form is

45

used. It refers to the collective purpose of God rather than the individual's destiny (1:5).

Prince of the power of the air: Satan, or Lucifer. His sphere of influence is this planet, and his kingdom encompasses the governments of this world. He is the spirit that works the disobedience in the lives of those who do not belong to Jesus Christ (2:2).

Principalities (6:12). Satan rules not only over the children of disobedience, but also demon powers who help him with his diabolical schemes. Some demons are called "rulers of the darkness of this world," and they have "principalities," or positions of rule in Satan's kingdom. In Daniel 10:13, 20 some demonic princes are associated with geographical areas.

Riches: Redemption has made all believers, including Gentiles, rich in grace (1:7; 2:7), glory (1:18; 3:16), and Christ (3:8). All the riches of Christianity flow through Christ.

Sealed: The seal in Ephesians is a symbol of the Holy Ghost and refers to ownership. Through the Holy Ghost God claims possession of His people (1:13; 4:30).

Spiritual blessings(1:3): All the possessions of believers that we obtain through Christ. This expression sums up all the riches of God's treasure of redemption. These blessings are not material, but spiritual, and they come from God the Father to the church, His children.

Unity: One of the greatest duties of believers is to keep the unity of the church (4:3). They must endeavor to do so by developing the proper spiritual virtues as described in 4:1-2. The bond of peace is the only force strong enough to keep this unity. All the actions of believers must be weighed in the balance of peace. They must determine whether their actions and attitudes are divisive or unifying. Ephesians 4:13 speaks of the unity of the faith, which is accomplished by a steady diet of the Word from the ministry (4:11-12).

TABLE 1

A Comparison of Ephesians and Colossians

Ephesians	Similarity	Colossians
1:2	Grace and peace from God and Christ	1:2
1:7	Redemption through Christ's blood	1:14
1:7, 18; 2:7; 3:8, 16	Redemption's riches	1:27; 2:2
1:9; 3:3-9; 6:19	Mystery revealed	1:26-27; 2:2; 4:3
1:10; 3:2	Dispensation (stewardship or plan)	1:25
1:13	Word of truth	1:5
1:16	Thanksgiving and prayer	1:3
1:22-23; 4:12; 5:23, 30	The church as Christ's body	1:18, 24
1:23; 3:19; 4:13	Fullness of God	1:19; 2:9
2:1, 5	Christians once dead in sin	2:13
2:2; 4:17	Used to walk in sin	3:7
2:5	Made alive in Christ	3:3-4
2:6	Risen with Christ	2:12; 3:1
2:10; 4:1; 5:2, 8, 15	Walk of holiness	1:10; 2:6; 4:5
2:12; 4:18	Once alienated from God and grace	1:21
2:13-16	Reconciled through death of Christ	1:20-21
2:16; 4:4	One body	3:15
2:20; 3:17	Built as a structure on a foundation	1:23; 2:7
3:1-7	Divine commission to make known the mystery of the gospel	1:23-29
3:17	Rooted in Christ	2:7
3:21	Ages	1:26
4:2-3, 25; 5:5	Sins reproved; virtues enjoined	3:5, 8, 12-14
4:2	Forbearing one another in love	3:13
4:3	Bond of peace and perfectness	3:14
4:16	Nourishment to the body	2:19
4:15-16	Growth of the body	2:19
4:18; 5:8	Once in darkness	1:13

continued on next page

TABLE 1 (continued)

A Comparison Of Ephesians And Colossians

Ephesians	Similarity	Colossians
4:22-24	Old man and new man	3:9-10
4:32	Forgiving one another as Christ has forgiven us	3:13
5:5	Covetousness defined as idolatry	3:5
5:6	Wrath of God coming	3:6
5:8-9	Walking in the light	1:12
5:16	Redeeming the time	4:5
5:19-20	Thanksgiving in psalms, hymns, spiritual songs	3:16
5:22-6:9	Duties and relationships in the home	3:18-4:1
6:18	Prayer and intercession	4:2-3
6:18-20	Mystery of the gospel and Paul's bonds	4:3
6:21	Character and commission of Tychicus	4:7

TABLE 2

A Comparison of Ephesians with Other Pauline Epistles

Ephesians	Similarity	Other Pauline Epistles
1:21	Christ is above all principality and power	I Corinthians 5:24; Philippians 2:9
2:8-9	Salvation by grace through faith	Romans 3:24-25; Galatians 2:16, 20
4:4	One body and one Spirit	Romans 12:5; I Corinthians 10:17; 12:4, 13
4:4	Called in one hope of our calling	I Corinthians 7:20; 13:13
4:5	One Lord, one faith, one baptism	I Corinthians 8:6; 12:5; 12:13; 13:13
4:6	One God and Father of all	Romans 9:5; I Corinthians 8:6; 12:6
4:6	God is above all, through all, and in us all	Romans 9:5; 11:36; I Corinthians 12:6

TABLE 3

A Comparison of Ephesians with Luke and Acts

Ephesians	Similarity	Luke and Acts
1:5	The good pleasure of God	Luke 2:14; 12:32
1:20; 4:8-10	Importance of the ascension and exaltation of Christ	Luke 24:51; Acts 1:9; 2:32-36; 7:55
4:24	Purpose of Christ's ministry to produce holiness and righteousness in the saints	Luke 1:75
5:8-13	Contrast between light and darkness	Luke 11:33-36; Acts 26:18
6:13	Ability of the church to withstand the devil	Luke 10:17-20; 21:15

TABLE 4

A Comparison of Ephesians and Hebrews

Ephesians	Similarity	Hebrews
1:4	Purpose of God settled before the foundation of the world	1:1-2
1:7, 14	Redemption through Christ	9:12
1:20	Exaltation of Christ	8:1
2:18; 3:12	Access to God through Jesus Christ	10:19
5:26	Cleansing and purification of the church	9:13-14

TABLE 5

A Comparison of Ephesians and I Peter

Ephesians	Similarity	I Peter
1:4	Purpose of God settled before the foundation of the world	1:19-20
1:4	The church as God's own possession	2:9
1:20-21	Christ's exaltation bringing triumph over all principalities and powers	3:22
2:2-3	Putting away the lusts of the flesh	1:14; 2:11
3:5-10	Gospel once hidden but now made manifest	1:10-12
4:25, 31	Putting away guile and evil speaking	2:1
5:22-33; 6:5-9	Relationships	2:18-3:7
6:10-11	Christian warfare	5:8

TABLE 6

A Comparison of Ephesians and John

Ephesians	Similarity	John
1:6	Jesus called the beloved	3:35; 10:17; 15:9; 17:23-26
2:5	A Christian's life found in Christ	10:10
3:17; 5:26	Life sustained by Christ dwelling within, producing sanctification and cleansing	14:20; 15:3-7; 17:17-19
4:3, 11-13	Unity in the church	17:22
4:8-10	The condescension and ascension of Jesus Christ for our redemption	3:13, 31; 7:39

TABLE 7

A Comparison of Ephesians and Revelation

Ephesians	Similarity	Revelation
1:1	The church at Ephesus mentioned	2:1
1:4-12	First love of the church (Christ Himself)	2:1-7
1:13; 4:30	Symbol of the seal (In Ephesians the seal is a symbol of the Holy Spirit, whereas in Revelation it is a symbol of pending judgment.)	7:2
2:6	Saints sitting in heavenly places	3:21
2:20; 3:5	Apostles and prophets the foundation of the church	10:7; 18:20; 21:14
5:11	Saints urged not to partake of evil or have any fellowship with darkness	18:4
5:25, 32	Church referred to as the bride of Christ	19:7

Notes

[1]*Collier's Encyclopedia,* (New York: Macmillan, 1984), 18:517.

[2]C. L. Mitton, *Ephesians,* vol. 19 of *The New Century Bible Commentary* (Grand Rapids: Eerdmans, 1973), 11.

[3]A. Skevington Wood, *Ephesians,* vol. 11 of *The Expositor's Bible Commentary* (Grand Rapids: Zondervan, 1978), 6.

[4]Francis Foulkes, *The Epistle of Paul to the Ephesians,* vol. 10 of *The Tyndale New Testament Commentaries* (Grand Rapids: Eerdmans, 1956), 20.

[5]F. F. Bruce, *The Epistle to the Ephesians* (Old Tappan, NJ: Fleming H. Revell, 1961), 15.

[6]Ibid.

[7]Wood, 5.

[8]Mitton, 11.

[9]Ibid.

[10]Foulkes, 26.

[11]Ibid., 30.

[12]Ibid., 36.

[13]Ibid., 17.

[14]Wood, 10.

[15]Bruce, 13.

[16]Ibid., 14.

[17]David Bernard, *The Message of Colossians and Philemon* (Hazelwood, MO: Word Aflame Press, 1990), 11.

[18]Wood, 17.

[19]Charles Hodge, *An Exposition of Ephesians* (Wilmington, DE: Associated Publishers and Authors, 1972), 5.

I.

PAUL'S SALUTATION

(1:1-2)

(1) Paul, an apostle of Jesus Christ by the will of God, to the saints which are at Ephesus, and to the faithful in Christ Jesus: (2) Grace be to you, and peace, from God our Father, and from the Lord Jesus Christ.

The salutation Paul used in Ephesians was patterned after the normal letter writing of his time. The salutation has three parts: the identification of the writer, the naming of the recipients, and a greeting. Paul expanded the greeting of Ephesians to include a blessing for the reader. This blessing resembled the blessing God commanded the high priest to bestow upon Israel (Numbers 6:23-27).

The salutation of Ephesians omits the names of Paul's companions at the time, which is in keeping with the nonpersonal nature of the entire epistle. (Note the contrast to I Corinthians 1:1; Philippians 1:1; Colossians 1:1; I Thessalonians 1:1; II Thessalonians 1:1; Philemon 1:1.) Paul made no personal references throughout Ephesians because he did not direct the letter toward acquaintances he had made on his journeys, but rather it is a simple declaration of the gospel. This declaration highlights the will of God for the church and outlines the ministries needed to bring life to Christ's body, the church.

Verse 1. Paul described himself as an apostle, identifying his calling and ministry. By the will of God, his ministry was a specific calling that applied directly to the Gentiles. Knowing that, he was able to focus his energy in a definite manner, increasing the effectiveness of his ministry.

Paul identified his calling as "an apostle of Jesus Christ" (Greek: *apostolos*). Paul knew that his apostleship was not granted because of any personal merit or ability, but simply "by the will of God." This attitude is seen clearly throughout Paul's writings (I Corinthians 15:9; Galatians 1:13-15; I Timothy 1:12-16). His apostleship demanded total commitment to Jesus Christ Himself, not just Christ's work or will, but to His person. As R. W. Dale explained, Paul's assurance of his calling was vital to the success of his labor:

> The vigour and hopefulness of our work for others are lessened by the uneasy consciousness that we are wanting in spiritual fervour and force; by the fear that our motives are not perfectly unselfish, that our consecration is not complete, that our intellectual qualifications are inadequate. Thoughts like these are sufficient to paralyse the strength of the strongest and to quench the fire of the most zealous.[1]

A study of the salutation shows that all salvation and ministry depend on the will of God. "And all things are of God" (II Corinthians 5:18). Without God's commission and decisive call, a person, especially the minister, will never find true, godly success.

Paul identified the people he wrote to as "the saints which are at Ephesus" (1:1). His audience dictated his approach and style of writing. Paul's attitude towards his readers set the tone for his letter. He considered them to be "the faithful in Christ Jesus" (1:1).

The word "saints" (Greek: *hagioi*), means "the set apart ones." Paul called them "the faithful" (Greek: *pistoi*), meaning that they had obtained a state of trustworthiness; they could be trusted in a storm or trial. The purpose of ministry is not just to comfort the weak and tend to the hurts of people, but also to set people apart for a specific work and to generate in them a character that is trustworthy, so that even when persecution comes their faith in Christ is not diminished.

Paul immediately connected sainthood with a relationship and fellowship with God. The word "saints" does not refer to special people who perform various miracles and are then canonized after their deaths. It refers to a spiritual relationship with God enjoyed by all those who are faithful in Christ Jesus.

The words "in Christ" are used twenty-seven times in Ephesians. Condemnation no longer exists for a saint who abides in Christ Jesus (Romans 8:1), and the hope of the resurrection awaits if the saint abides in Christ (I Corinthians 15:17-23). Every saint can only claim the privilege of being a new creation by abiding in Christ (II Corinthians 5:17). Being "in Christ" means developing a personal relationship with Him, which is the ultimate purpose of ministry.

Verse 2. Paul pronounced a blessing of grace and peace specifically to the people of Ephesus and also upon believers in general. From the start, Paul defined the blessing he wished to impart to the readers of this epistle. The rest of the epistle should be viewed in light of the ultimate blessing he desired to confer.

"Grace" is translated from the Greek word *charis,* meaning "charm" or, in the biblical context, a godly life influenced by God's Spirit. The ministry must desire to create an atmosphere where saints can be influenced by God's Spirit and through His Spirit become more like the image of Jesus Christ.

Paul used "peace," from the Greek *eirene,* as the counterpart of the Hebrew word *shalom,* meaning "the highest good." The peace that a Christian enjoys is not an absence of troubles or trials, but rather the confidence that all things are working for their highest good and for the fulfillment of God's eternal purpose (Romans 8:28).

We cannot enjoy true grace and peace unless we know God as Father, the one who has taken the responsibility to supply every need that His child possesses. The Father-child relationship offers to every believer the peace that passes all understanding (Philippians 4:7). We cannot claim the wealth of this blessing of peace except by grace, the unmerited favor of God toward us.

The only means of truly knowing God as Father is to become acquainted with the Lord Jesus Christ. When Christ establishes His kingdom and lordship in our lives, then we can look up to God and call Him Father.

The phrases "God the Father" and "the Lord Jesus Christ" do not refer to two separate persons in the Godhead, but rather identify the means by which we may know the one Spirit of God—as Father through the person of Jesus Christ. Christ is the "express image of his person" (Hebrews 1:3). The word "person" is singular;

revealing that the only visible expression of the Father is Jesus Christ. "Person" is translated from the Greek *hupostatis,* meaning "a person or substance under or standing in a position." Only through the person of Jesus Christ can we truly know the Father (John 14:6, 9-11). The Incarnation and Atonement secured for all humanity the opportunity to know God as Father for all humanity (John 10:30; I Timothy 2:5; 3:16; Hebrews 9:14).

David Bernard explained that Paul's salutations do not divide God into two persons but actually identify Jesus with God:

> When we compare Romans 1:7 with similar phrases elsewhere in Paul's epistles, we find a strong indication that Paul meant to identify God the Father and the Lord Jesus Christ as the same being. For example, II Thessalonians 1:12, I Timothy 5:21, II Timothy 4:1, and Titus 2:13 all identify God and Jesus Christ as one and the same being.[2]

Paul's ministry was effective because he knew his calling was from God, he knew what his calling required, he identified his audience, and he met their need by bestowing upon them the proper blessing.

Notes

[1]R. W. Dale, *The Epistle to the Ephesians, Its Doctrine and Ethics* (London: Hodder and Stoughton, 1897), 14.

[2]David Bernard, *The Message of Romans* (Hazelwood, MO: Word Aflame Press, 1987), 37.

II.

THE BRIDE'S RICHES IN CHRIST

(1:3—3:21)

A. Praise for the Bride's Possessions (1:3-14)
　1. All Spiritual Blessings (1:3-6)
　　a. The Privilege of our Relationship
　　b. The Possession of the Riches
　　c. The Position Gained by the Riches
　　d. Election
　　e. Adoption
　　f. Acceptance in the Beloved
　2. Redemption through the Blood (1:7-8)
　3. The Mystery of His Will (1:9-12)
　　a. Dispensation
　　b. Times
　　c. Gathering Together
　　d. The Restoration of Unity
　　e. An Inheritance
　　f. Predestination
　4. Sealed by His Spirit (1:13-14)
B. Prayer for the Bride's Enlightenment (1:15-23)
　1. The Revelation and Knowledge of Christ (1:15-19)
　　a. The Hope of His Calling
　　b. His Inheritance in Us
　　c. His Exceeding Great Power
　2. The True Power of the Resurrection (1:20-23)

C. The Bride's New Condition (2:1-10)
  1. Our Miserable Condition before Conversion (2:1-3)
  2. Our New Condition after Conversion (2:4-10)
D. The Bride's New Privileges (2:11-22)
  1. The Gentiles' Old Position (2:11-12)
  2. The Gentiles' New Privileges (2:13-22)
     a. The Blood Makes Peace
     b. Reconciliation by the Cross
     c. Access to God
     d. Fellow Citizens of the Same House
E. The Bride's Revelation of the Mystery (3:1-13)
  1. Paul, a Prisoner (3:1)
  2. The Mystery Made Known to Paul (3:2-5)
  3. The Fellowship of the Mystery (3:6-13)
     a. The Gentiles As Fellow Heirs and Partakers
     b. The Manifold Wisdom of God
     c. Boldness in Christ
F. Prayer for the Bride to Receive Fullness (3:14-21)
  1. The Riches of His Glory (3:14-18)
     a. Strengthened with Might
     b. Rooted and Grounded in Love
     c. Comprehending the Love of God
  2. Filled with All the Fullness of God (3:19)
  3. Paul's Prayer Directly to God (3:20-21)

A.

Praise for the Bride's Possessions

(1:3-14)

In the Greek, verses 3 through 14 comprise one long sentence that defines in progression the specific possessions granted to every believer through Christ. This long sentence was best described by R. W. Dale when he said, "One proposition melts into another. Thought flows into thought. No one sentence is complete, apart from the sentence which precedes it and the sentence that follows it."[1]

The opening verse sets the tone for what follows. Everything between the beginning of verse 3—"Blessed be . . . God"—and the ending of verse 14—"to the praise of his glory"—creates an atmosphere of praise in the heart of the recipient for the blessing of the riches bestowed through God's grace. These blessings lead us to "the praise of his glory." They are unsearchable, yet capable of being possessed.

1. All Spiritual Blessings (1:3-6)

(3) Blessed be the God and Father of our Lord Jesus Christ, who hath blessed us with all spiritual blessings in heavenly places in Christ: (4) according as he hath chosen us in him before the foundation of the world, that we should

be holy and without blame before him in love: (5) having predestinated us unto the adoption of children by Jesus Christ to himself, according to the good pleasure of his will, (6) to the praise of the glory of his grace, wherein he hath made us accepted in the beloved.

Verse 3. Paul explained from the beginning that the person responsible for opening the storehouse is God almighty. No one has taken this honor upon himself. God has made a sovereign choice, according to the good pleasure of His will.

When the word "blessed" is used in the Old Testament in reference to God, it refers to His covenant relationship with His people (Genesis 9:26; 24:27; Psalm 41:13; Isaiah 61:9). The same word is used eight times in reference to God in the New Testament (Mark 14:61; Luke 1:68; Romans 1:25; 9:5; II Corinthians 1:3; 11:31; Ephesians 1:3; I Peter 1:3). Each time it means that God is to be praised for His faithfulness in keeping the covenant.

Under the inspiration of the Holy Ghost, Paul altered the former pattern, identifying God by a new covenant title: "the God and Father of our Lord Jesus Christ" rather than "the God of Israel," signifying the new covenant that completed the old in the person of Jesus Christ. (See also II Corinthians 1:3; I Peter 1:3.) An access route to a new covenant relationship with the Father was established through the work and person of Jesus Christ, whose physical body bridged the gulf of sin between humanity and God at Calvary. The new covenant title and the person of Jesus Christ do not establish a separation of persons in the Godhead, for in Jesus "dwelleth all the fulness of the Godhead bodily" (Colossians 2:9), but do reveal the means that God used to bring about His new covenant relationship with the Jews and with the Gentiles.

Not only is God the Father of "the man Christ Jesus" (I Timothy 2:5), but He is also our Father. Through joint heirship with Jesus Christ, the fatherhood of God and its attached blessings now belong to His bride, the church. "God's love is very fatherly and His care of us is very practical."[2] God's concern for our well-being as a new community of believers is demonstrated by His making these spiritual blessings available. Without them the church could not properly function in this world and would be destitute of ministry and purpose.

For this reason Paul made known the privileges that govern our relationship with God: our election, adoption, acceptance, and forgiveness. Our relationship with God is not based on our righteousness, but by the counsel of His own will He allows us the privilege of forgiveness. A second set of four privileges (wisdom and prudence, the knowledge of His will, the inheritance, and the seal of the Holy Spirit) governs His purpose for our relationship.

a. The Privilege of our Relationship

Paul's praise led him to reveal the privileges, possessions, and position of the believer in verse 3, which serves as a summary for the subsequent verses. The greatest privilege the church can have is knowing that God "hath blessed us." The word "us" refers to the joining of believers in the body as one. Whether they be bond or free, Jew or Gentile, they have become one in Christ Jesus. The term "us" is all inclusive. No one can be excluded. What a privilege!

b. The Possession of the Riches

He "hath blessed us with all spiritual blessings." "All" means everything that Christ possessed in His inheritance has been bequeathed to the child of God. The verb "hath" reveals that the purpose has been fixed from the foundation of the world. The blessings themselves are fixed and cannot be removed. God counseled "with his own will" to bring this to pass before time ever began (Ephesians 1:11). His desire to equip the church and endow her with power is a part of the eternal scheme of God's redemption. The word "hath" speaks of what has already happened. It does not exclude the fact that it shall continue to happen. If a person is positioned properly, then every blessing promised belongs to him.

The spiritual blessings mentioned in verse 3 affect the inner man and allow him to identify with a great God through the operation of the Holy Ghost. The Holy Ghost provides the believer with the gifts and equipment needed to fulfill God's purpose—to create a family of sons through which He will rule His kingdom. First, God uses the church to help rescue lost souls. After being rescued from sin, they are equipped with power to rule. Rescue, restoration, and rulership are three elements of God's purpose.

c. The Position Gained by the Riches

Paul gave the location of these possessions by saying they are found "in heavenly places in Christ." The literal rendering is "in the heavenlies," referring to a specific place. Jesus dwells in this place, and He is seated there in power and authority. The believer is also seated with Him in the same power and authority. If we are positioned in the dwelling place of the Lord Jesus and if we are located in the heavenly sphere where the perfect will of God rules, then all the possessions of grace are ours. Without location there is no possession.

This heavenly sphere is mentioned four different times in Ephesians, and each time it refers to a different aspect. The "heavenly places" are (1) the location of the believer's blessings (1:3), (2) the dwelling of Jesus Christ (1:20), (3) the dwelling of the believer (2:6), and (4) the battlefield for the church's warfare (3:10, 6:12). The heavenly places contain the blessings, the Savior, the dwelling, and the warfare of the church, and they are obtained through obedience to the will and power of the Lord Jesus Christ.

God will use three phases of sonship to create a family of sons: obedience to His commands (knowing His voice), alignment with His perfect will (knowing His purpose), and personal acceptance of His rule through Christ (knowing Him).

Verse 4. "According" connects the spiritual blessings of the Father in heavenly places in Christ to the redemption plan that was in existence before the foundation of the world. Paul then began to identify the blessings that the Father has given to us through Jesus Christ.

d. Election

The first blessing described is election. The pronoun "us" refers to the one body made up of Jews and Gentiles under one head, Jesus Christ. That body is the church planned by God from the beginning, which is to be a universal people who claim Christ as Lord.

The phrase "before the foundation of the world"

reveals an unconditional, eternal plan of God to preserve and redeem humanity. The phrase is found three times in the New Testament, revealing three dimensions of God's eternal purpose:

1. In John 17:24 Jesus used it in reference to the love that the Father had for Him.

2. Ephesians 1:4 uses it in reference to the church being chosen in Christ.

3. In I Peter 1:20 the phrase refers to the redemption purchased by the precious blood of the Lamb.

The coming of Christ, the birth of the church, and redemption were all predetermined events in God's master plan to create in the believer the divine nature of God and holiness unto the Lord.

The purpose of redemption, which is purchased by the blood of the Lamb, is "that we should be holy and without blame before him in love." The word "holy" (Greek: *hagois*) means "separated unto God" to be a "peculiar" (unique, special) people (Titus 2:14; I Peter 2:9). Redemption carries with it the responsibility to live a life separated unto God and separated from the world (II Corinthians 6:17).

The church is to be "without blame" or "blameless" (Greek: *amomos*). This word alludes to the Old Testament sacrifices that had to pass inspection before they could be offered unto the Lord. Every offering had to be without blemish in order to pass inspection. God's redemptive plan includes not only a recovery process that brings humanity out of sin, but also a highway of holiness for us to walk in this life. (See Philippians 2:15; I Peter 1:19; Leviticus 1:3, 10; Isaiah 35:8.)

Holiness can only be acquired "before him in love."

The true basis for holiness is not the law of force, but the law of love. The law of love is a higher law than that of legalism. It actually demands more (James 2:8-9; I Peter 1:16). It is not legalism to expect results from the work of sanctification that will purify the carnal man. "Paul balances *doctrine* with *duty*. We *inherit* the wealth by faith and *invest* the wealth by works."[3]

e. Adoption

Verse 5. The doctrine of predestination is a topic of dispute in Christian teachings because some have defined it to mean that God chooses certain individuals for salvation apart from their personal decision. Paul's reference to predestination is not to the individual believer, however, but to the body of believers that resulted from the joining of Jews and Gentiles together in Christ. Paul never used a singular form when discussing the predestined but always used the plural forms of "we," "us," or "whom" (Ephesians 1:5, 11; Romans 8:29-30). Predestination, as described by Paul, refers to God's eternal plan to build a church comprised of one body of baptized believers from all the peoples of the earth.

The word "predestinated" comes from a Greek word *proorizo,* which means "to mark out beforehand the boundary or horizon." God marked the boundary of the church and its peoples before the world began by making provision for the adoption of the Gentiles as sons of God through Jesus Christ. The adoption extends the blessings of Abraham to those who are not entitled to His privileges by the natural birth (Romans 8:15; Galatians 4:6). The infilling of the Holy Ghost allows a person access to sonship through an adoption process.

The concept of adoption originated with the Romans and was a means whereby one was accorded all of the rights of a natural son under the Roman law. William Barclay described this procedure:

> It was, however, not uncommon, for children were often adopted to ensure that some family should not become extinct. The ritual of adoption must have been very impressive. It was carried out by a symbolic sale in which copper and scales were used. Twice the real father sold his son, and twice he symbolically bought him back; finally he sold him a third time, and at the third sale he did not buy him back. After this the adopting father had to go to the *praetor,* one of the principal Roman magistrates, and plead the case for the adoption. Only after all this had been gone through was the adoption complete.[4]

The process provided a complete change of identity and canceled the old name, the old rights, and the old debts of the person adopted. A new person emerged, hence Paul's use of the idea in relationship to adoption of sons by God. "Therefore if any man be in Christ, he is a new creature: old things are passed away; behold, all things are become new" (II Corinthians 5:17). The concept implies a giving up of the old life in order to receive a new life through regeneration and a supernatural birth.

The word "adoption" in the Greek is *huiothesia* which means "the placing of a son." The adoption process was secured "by Jesus Christ" through Calvary, and the Gentiles were allowed entry through the outpouring of the Holy Ghost on Cornelius's household in Acts 10. Calvary purchased this privilege; the believer has no right to claim it based on his own merit or ability. Jesus chose to bring the Gentiles into the church and confirmed this desire by pouring out the Holy Ghost on Cornelius's household. God's sovereign choice decided the matter, and based on that decision, adoption is now available.

Accepting the privileges that accompany sonship also requires sanctification by the Spirit in order to conform to the holy and blameless image of Jesus Christ. When Christ returns and perfects the church (Romans 8:29-30; Ephesians 1:14), then God's redemption will be complete, and God will have obtained perfect fellowship with the church through Jesus Christ.

In Ephesians, Paul referred to the justification of the believer by faith, which includes his initial step of faith in Christ, and also to the sanctification of the believer, which is the gradual perfecting process that God uses to purify the believer. Then he dealt with the future glorification of the believer. Without all three aspects our relationship with God would be incomplete.

God provided the adoption process "according to the good pleasure of his will." "Good pleasure" in the Greek is *eudokia* meaning that it seemed good or "satisfaction." In the Greek the word "will" is *thelema,* meaning "someone's choice." God chose to adopt a family from Jew and Gentile because it satisfied every aspect of His nature, His principles, and His purpose. W. Leon Tucker observed, "Back of the will of God there is not a word. His will is the secret and the sequence of it all. For, says the apostle, of Him (origin), and through Him (organ), and unto Him (object), are all things (Romans 11:36)."[5]

Tucker described God's will as the standard and measurement of God's mercy that has been extended to all who will accept it unto salvation. Because it seemed good to God, we now possess the "adoption of children." This is the basis for all salvation.

f. Acceptance in the Beloved

Verse 6. Paul used "to the praise of the glory" three times between verses 3–14 as though it was "a refrain at the end of successive stanzas of a poem."[6] Perhaps his intention was to ensure that no one person received the credit for salvation through grace by any means but God's redemptive power. He revealed the fullness of Christ's redemption while protecting God's glory, "which is the harmony of His attributes, His character."[7] The privilege of being called God's son through the grace of Jesus Christ will be the greatest song of praise in eternity.

The election of the bride and the adoption of children were planned "according to the good pleasure of his will" (verse 5), that it might lead "to the praise of the glory of his grace" (verse 6). The power of his grace "hath made us accepted in the beloved." The literal translation is "he has be-graced us." The word "made" refers to God's creative ability. Sin has infected the entire human race and made man unacceptable, even repulsive, to God; but now by God's own act of grace man has been made a new and acceptable creation (II Corinthians 5:17). God, through grace, has made a whole new creation, a new people who live solely for the purpose of praising Him. The word "accepted" is past tense, referring to a historical event that has already taken place. We do not gain acceptance by qualifying through a series of trials and tests, but by accepting the finished work at Calvary.

72

The term "beloved" is a messianic term that reveals Jesus Christ as the "beloved Son" who obtained favor because of His sinless life. God used the term at Christ's baptism and transfiguration (Matthew 3:17; 17:5). Jesus set a mark of excellence that was confirmed by the Father's declaration of Him as the "beloved Son." Any who choose to join themselves to Christ by faith and Spirit baptism will experience the same acceptance that Jesus did from His Father (Romans 8:15; Galatians 4:6). Acceptance comes through the redemptive power of Jesus Christ and has been freely given to the believer "in the beloved."

2. Redemption through the Blood (1:7-8)

(7) In whom we have redemption through his blood, the forgiveness of sins, according to the riches of his grace; (8) wherein he hath abounded toward us in all wisdom and prudence.

Verse 7. Jesus Christ lived a life of such perfection that He was accepted as worthy to purchase redemption for humanity. He has chosen, predestinated, accepted, and redeemed the church through His blood, thus becoming the Savior "in whom we have redemption." Redemption provides forgiveness of sin and allows the nature of "the old man" to be changed into the nature of "the new man" (Ephesians 4:22–24), through a partaking of the divine nature (II Peter 1:4).

"Redemption" (Greek: *apolutrosis*) means "ransom in full" or "something to loosen with." It conveys the idea of a slave who is powerless to free himself and needs someone to pay the price to purchase his freedom. Although the legal transaction was made at Calvary, the experience of being loosed occurs when the believer is sealed with the Holy Spirit of promise (Ephesians 1:13).

Jesus ransomed us "through his blood." Redemption refers back to the Old Testament concept of redeeming the land and person of a debtor (Leviticus 25:25-27, 47-49). Israel's redemption from Egypt is a foreshadowing of the blood redemption of humanity (Exodus 15:13), through Christ in the eternal plan of God.

Colossians 1:13-14 parallels Ephesians 1:7 and connects deliverance and spiritual translation to redemption. There Paul identified redemption specifically with forgiveness, thus attributing to redemption the power of forgiveness, cleansing, deliverance, and transformation under a new, governing Spirit. The consequences of sin may linger after the initial time of conversion, but forgiveness and liberty are provided through redemption.

"Forgiveness" (Greek: *aphesis*) means "to carry away" or "to remove." The word has the same meaning as the scapegoat that was sent into the wilderness with the sins of Israel imputed to it by the laying on of the hands of the high priest, removing the sins of Israel from the camp (Leviticus 16). "As far as the east is from the west, so far hath he removed our transgressions from us" (Psalm 103:12). "The forgiveness of sins" has provided deliverance for the soul and redemption for the body (Titus 2:14; Romans 8:23).

Redemption is actually portrayed in the New Testament as a process of being loosed or released from a type of prison or bondage (Luke 21:28; Romans 8:23), reminiscent of the time Lazarus was raised from the dead. Even though resurrection power was at work, his freedom was not complete until Jesus commanded the people, "Loose him, and let him go" (John 11:44).

Jesus submitted to the just punishment for sin to provide deliverance, which has a three-dimensional effect: God no longer retains His anger toward our sins, man's conscience is purged from guilt (Hebrews 9:14), and death no longer rules, having been conquered by the blood of Jesus Christ (I Corinthians 15:55-56).

God bequeathed this treasury of redemption to us "according to the riches of his grace." "For ye know the grace of our Lord Jesus Christ, that, though he was rich, yet for your sakes he became poor, that ye through his poverty might be rich" (II Corinthians 8:9). Paul mentioned the riches of the believers six times in Ephesians (Ephesians 1:7, 18; 2:4, 7; 3:8, 16). He identified these riches in four different ways:

1. the "riches of his grace"
2. the "riches of his glory"
3. "rich in mercy"
4. the "riches of Christ"

Jesus is the grace, the glory, and the mercy of God manifested in the flesh. (See I Timothy 3:16.) "Worthy is the Lamb that was slain to receive power, and riches, and wisdom, and strength, and honour, and glory, and blessing" (Revelation 5:12).

Verse 8. Out of the superabundance of God's riches He has made available every gift and spiritual blessing, "wherein he hath abounded toward us." This bounty of wealth was secured by the sufferings of the Savior. Because of the shed blood of Jesus, Paul could now show each benefit as the Holy Spirit led him.

Paul used the word "abound" quite often throughout his writings. In Romans 15:13 Paul stated his desire that Christians would "abound in hope, through the power of the Holy Ghost." Without the Holy Ghost the abundance of possessions that belongs to the bride of Christ can never be bequeathed to the believer. Faith in Jesus Christ must lead to the receiving of the Holy Ghost in order for there to be an abounding of hope, grace, and love (Romans 5:5; 15:13; II Corinthians 8:7; I Thessalonians 3:12).

The superabundance of God's grace has secured for the church election, adoption, acceptance, redemption, and forgiveness, but here Paul increased the possessions to include "wisdom and prudence." What good is it to be saved and not know why? God has allowed us the privilege of joining His inner circle of friends and to be included in His plans for the ages. "Surely the Lord GOD will do nothing, but he revealeth his secret unto his servants the prophets" (Amos 3:7).

The word "wisdom" (Greek: *sophia*) refers to God's eternal purpose and how people can fulfill that purpose in their own lives. This wisdom is given to the believer for the purpose of revealing God's plan and the believer's place in that plan.

To know God's will is not enough. We must also know God's *way* of bringing His will to pass. Before Moses asked to see the glory of God he first asked that God would "shew me now thy way" (Exodus 33:13). God has a will, but He also has a way of bringing His will to pass. His way ensures us that all the glory and the praise will be given unto Him, for He alone is worthy. Too many people do not wait on God to discover His way. They go about trying to fulfill the will of God, but they do it in their own way and for their own glory.

The New Testament also speaks of the wisdom of God as the "things" of God (Mark 8:33; Romans 8:5; Colossians 3:2). What belongs to God and His purpose is what grace has "abounded toward us." If God is going to give us a place in His purpose, then we must "set [our] affection on things above, not on things on the earth" (Colossians 3:2). What God wants should be more important than what we want. God's plan can only be fulfilled when this condition is met.

Paul prayed that the Colossians would "be filled with the knowledge of his will in all wisdom" (Colossians 1:9). Knowing God's will is one of the greatest privileges that He could ever bestow upon the bride of Christ. Not only has He made us to know His will, He has also revealed our place in that will. This place demands that we testify of God's grace to the whole world.

Paul told the Corinthians that the wisdom he preached was not the wisdom of the world but rather the wisdom of God that He ordained before the world for our glory (I Corinthians 2:6-7). He explained that the wisdom of which he spoke was the crucifixion of Jesus Christ, because God used Calvary to thwart the devil's plans and implement His plan of redemption (I Corinthians 1:30; 2:8). This glorious wisdom can only be revealed by the Spirit of God (I Corinthians 2:10). The church is in desperate need of a spiritual revelation, for this wisdom can only be discerned spiritually (I Corinthians 2:14).

God's will, revealed to us in wisdom, is something more than we know by intellectual understanding. It is something that we declare to the whole world. God's plan of redeeming the world by the cross of Jesus Christ is the eternal truth that we need to herald to the four corners of the earth. Our place in that plan is to go and preach this gospel to every creature (Mark 16:15).

The word "prudence" (Greek: *phronesis*) has a slightly different meaning than the word "wisdom." "Prudence" refers to the practical application of knowledge, or the "proper management of affairs." Wisdom reveals God's eternal plan and our place in that plan. Prudence gives us the ability to properly manage our affairs on a day-to-day basis, to allow for the fulfillment of God's plan in our life. Without a proper reaction to crisis on a daily basis, the eternal purpose will not succeed for us. Even though we may possess a knowledge of the eternal purpose and our place in that purpose, without the proper management of our daily life we will never be able to realize the true destiny that grace has purchased for us.

3. The Mystery of His Will (1:9-12)

(9) Having made known unto us the mystery of his will, according to his good pleasure which he hath purposed in himself: (10) that in the dispensation of the fulness of times he might gather together in one all things in Christ, both which are in heaven, and which are on earth; even in him: (11) in whom also we have obtained an inheritance, being predestinated according to the purpose of him who worketh all things after the counsel of his own will: (12) that we should be to the praise of his glory, who first trusted in Christ.

Verse 9. Paul's purpose in writing Ephesians was to reveal the place that the church holds in God's eternal plan, not only to give her the understanding of what the plan is, but also to equip her to carry out her purpose in that plan. For this reason Paul took the opportunity to praise God for all the bride's possessions. Included in this redemptive package is the prize of "having made known unto us the mystery of his will."

It is a mystery (Greek: *musterion*) to the world, but not to the church. Now it is made known. The word "mystery" suggests a secret that has been kept for an appointed time. When its time comes, it is revealed to those who will help bring the secret plan to pass.

Though this mystery can be known, it cannot be logically analyzed or humanly reasoned out. The revelation of this mystery must definitely come from God Himself. How can the church accomplish God's perfect will if it does not know what that will is? Paul understood the extreme importance of revealing God's will to the church, as he made clear in Colossians 1:9: "For this cause we also, since the day we heard it, do not cease to pray for you, and to desire that ye might be filled with the knowledge of his will in all wisdom and spiritual understanding."

Paul used the word "mystery" quite often throughout his writings in connection with the preaching of the gospel. This mystery was revealed to the nations "for the obedience of faith," and the mystery was defined specifically as the "preaching of Jesus Christ" (Romans 16:25–26). I Corinthians 2:10 shows that the mystery can only be understood by a spiritual revelation. Ephesians 3:9 defines the mystery as the formation of the church and the church fulfilling the purpose of God. But in Colossians 1:26–27 the mystery takes on a fuller meaning as the indwelling Christ, the only hope of obtaining the glory of God's inheritance. Understanding the full meaning of this mystery can better equip the church to carry out her mission. Paul basically defined the mystery in four ways: the church receiving Christ (Colossians 1:26–27), the church preaching Christ (Romans 16:25), the church living in Christ (Ephesians 3:9), and the church becoming like Christ (I Corinthians 15:51-57).

Though the details of the mystery have not yet been revealed, this does not mean it cannot be experienced and acted upon. I Corinthians 15:51 tells us about the mystery of the resurrection of every believer, that each member of the body of Christ is going to be changed into a new body. Even though we do not know all the details of this mystical change, we can accept it by faith and know that someday it will come to pass.

The privilege of knowing the mystery of God's will is a precious possession. God always reveals His plans to those He considered His friends. He revealed His plan to destroy Sodom and Gomorrah to His friend Abraham in Genesis 18. He never did anything without revealing to His prophets what He was going to do, whether it was the outpouring of His judgment or His redemptive provision of mercy. In either case, He told His people beforehand, and He will do the same today. He has given a marvelous pearl to the bride. If she will accept her rightful place in His purpose, God will reveal His will to her.

The revelation of the mystery of God's will has been done "according to his good pleasure which he hath purposed in himself." The mystery is God's will, God's good pleasure, and God's purpose "which he hath purposed in himself." This description lets us know that all of God's predetermined purposes are for the ultimate good of the church. His "good pleasure" actually means that He has never intended anything but the bride's ultimate good (Romans 8:28). From the beginning, God's intentions have never been anything but kind and good toward humanity. Moreover, God has never purposed anything that would be inconsistent with "himself"—His nature or character. All has been done to bring about the ultimate good of the universe, and it has all been done in congruence with His perfect holiness and nature.

Verse 10. Next Paul began to describe the mystery of God's will. He had already done so in other passages of Scripture, accentuating or highlighting certain aspects that reveal the place of the church in God's will. But in this verse Paul presented a new dimension that the church needs to understand if she is going to carry out her mission effectively: "That in the dispensation of the fulness of times he might gather together in one all things in Christ." This phrase sums up the mystery of God's will, and as we analyze each key word that fact becomes clearer. Jesus is placed in a position of such importance and power that everything else pales in comparison.

a. "Dispensation"

"Dispensation" (Greek: *oikonomia*) means "stewardship" or the "administration of the house." The word is translated as "steward" in I Corinthians 4:1-2; Titus 1:7; I Peter 4:10. In other cases where Paul used the word "dispensation" it was in connection with the time and commission God had given him to proclaim the gospel to the Gentiles (I Corinthians 9:17; Ephesians 3:2; Colossians 1:25). God's purpose from the beginning was to make Jesus Christ the "firstborn among many brethren," the Head of a family of believers (Romans 8:29). As the firstborn He had the responsibility for the entire "household of faith" (Galatians 6:10).

The ultimate goal of God's plan is to create a new body of people who have been redeemed from sin, with Jesus Christ as the head of this new household. The Old Testament also reveals that the government of this family would rest upon the shoulders of the Messiah (Isaiah 9:6). He, being the perfect example of holiness as seen in humanity, would become the perfect steward over all the new creation of God.

The church is not just an earthly institution that is organized for religious ritual. It is a living, breathing organism that is growing into a new creation of sons that will not only live forever with Jesus but will also rule with Him forever (II Timothy 2:12; Revelation 20:6). James 1:18 says, "Of his own will begat he us with the word of truth, that we should be a kind of firstfruits of his creatures." Jesus Christ is the beginning of a new people who will reign with Him throughout the endless ages of eternity.

b. Times

"Times" (Greek: *kairos*) means "particular events that conclude a matter." The dispensation of the fullness of times will come when all things are in their proper places and are arranged for the glorious return of Jesus Christ to the earth.

Paul and all the New Testament writers revealed that the cross of Christ made our redemption possible. But they also showed that the next thing on God's agenda is to equip the church to go forth into all the world and make disciples of everyone who will believe the report of Jesus Christ, thereby using the church to help create this family of sons. Then Christ will return a second time to catch them away. At this time, or at this *kairos,* He will "gather together in one all things in Christ."

c. Gathering Together

"Gather together" (Greek: *anakephalaiomai*) means

to "gather all that is in disorder or disarray and create a harmony." The word was used of gathering things together and presenting them as a whole. The Greek practice was to add up a column of figures and put the sum at the top, and this name was given to the process.[8]

This gathering together speaks of a restoration that has not yet happened but will come at the appointed time —at the return of Jesus Christ, "whom the heaven must receive until the times of restitution of all things, which God hath spoken by the mouth of all his holy prophets since the world began" (Acts 3:21).

Sin brought disorder to the world and disrupted the harmony of the universe itself, but because of Jesus Christ and Calvary, all things are going to be brought together in absolute harmony again. In Christ, all things will find true identity (Acts 17:28).

The disorder that sin has caused will be replaced by unity. Creation itself will rejoice at this time, as will the redeemed children of God and the angels of heaven (John 11:52; Romans 8:21-23). Jesus Christ is going to be the very life and existence of the new order of the universe. Nothing is going to exist without Him, for the life is in Him and from Him the life will flow (Colossians 1:17).

This is more than just a position that Christ possesses. It is the very nature of His person, for He is more than just a man; He is God almighty manifested in the flesh. Without this revelation the church will never be as effective as she needs to be in her mission. For not only do we find the fullness of creatures and creation in Christ, but also the fullness of the Godhead bodily (Colossians 2:9). The church finds her completeness in Christ because He is the fullness of God Himself (Colossians 2:10). If Christ were not God, then the church would have no hope of finding her completion through salvation in Him. But because He is God almighty manifested in the flesh, we can claim that the redemption He has purchased gives us a hope beyond this life. That future hope is an eternal life of ruling and reigning with Him.

d. The Restoration of Unity

This restoration of unity, which will come when Jesus asserts His rightful authority as the true Head of the church, actually affects two spheres of life: "both which are in heaven, and which are on earth; even in him," that is, the heavenly and the earthly.

The heavenly sphere of angelic beings are now under His control, including all principalities and powers (Colossians 2:10; I Peter 3:22). They have all been made subject to Jesus because He is more than a second person in a trinity. Jesus Christ is God manifest in the flesh, and because He is God, He rules in the heavenly sphere with power and might.

The earthly sphere of creation (material earth) and creatures (redeemed children) is also under His control. Redemption has not only adopted us and made us acceptable, but it has also given us life beyond the natural life. We can have a place in a heavenly kingdom in Christ and participate in the complete restoration of the universe.

Verse 9 has presented problems to some theologians who have misinterpreted it to mean that Christ would restore Lucifer and his angels to their first estate and would also restore those who had never believed and received the Holy Spirit. This false doctrine is called universalism. When the text says, "He might gather together in one all things in Christ," however, the term "all things" must be qualified by the last three words in the verse: "even in him." The "all things" of heaven and earth must be "in him" before they are allowed the privilege of being restored. Before an individual can be "in Christ," he must first be baptized into Christ by one Spirit (I Corinthians 12:13). Therefore, the statement that all things will be restored must be qualified by saying, "All things that are in Christ by redemption through His blood" will be restored. This redemption cannot be bequeathed to anyone who does not believe and who has not been sealed with the Holy Spirit (Ephesians 1:13). Thus the doctrine of universalism cannot be substantiated.

e. An Inheritance

Verse 11. The knowledge of God's will is a gift worthy of our praise. The list of possessions continues, however. Paul included not only a knowledge of His will but also "an inheritance." We are more than just partakers of "the mystery of his will"; we have also "obtained an inheritance." We can now share the wealth of all that Christ has secured by His sufferings.

What good is it to know the will of God and not be equipped to fulfill it? Now, through Christ, "in whom we have" an inheritance, we can be joint heirs with Him in all the wealth, wisdom, power, promises, and glory that He Himself has gained (Romans 8:17). God desires not only that we know the will of God, but that we are able to cash in on the substance of our inheritance to fulfill His will.

The parallel passage to this verse is Colossians 1:12: "Giving thanks unto the Father, which hath made us meet to be partakers of the inheritance of the saints in light." We can now partake of the necessary benefits that will enable us to fulfill God's eternal purpose. "For all things are yours," and Christ has promised to "freely give us all things" (I Corinthians 3:21-22; Romans 8:32).

Without this inheritance it would be impossible to fulfill the task God has sent the church into the world to accomplish. However, we now have everything that we need to make God's plan work in us and through us because "we have obtained an inheritance." This inheritance is best defined as the right to claim Christ's power, position, and person to enable us to fulfill our daily walk. That daily walk will lead to the eternal fulfillment of Christ's purpose. Jesus Christ has made Himself personally responsible to meet our needs—not so we can live a life of prosperity and ease, but that we might help Him bring to pass His ultimate goal of creating a family of sons.

The phrase "obtained an inheritance" comes from the Greek *kleroo*, which means a "lot or portion obtained by casting lots," showing that this inheritance was given freely. It was given without the help of the individuals' knowledge or ability, but by a sovereign choice or will. That sovereign choice was the predetermined will of God. God chose, by the "riches of his grace," to adopt us and make us acceptable in His sight.

We will receive our future inheritance when He decides, at the right time, to "gather together in one all things in Christ." We shall not only partake of His grace but also of His glory: "To an inheritance incorruptible, and undefiled, and that fadeth not away, reserved in heaven for you" (I Peter 1:4). This glory has not yet been revealed but is reserved for a future time (Ephesians 1:14; Revelation 5:10).

86

Some have interpreted this portion of verse 11 to mean, "in whom also we have become the inheritance of God," conveying the idea that the church itself is the portion of God. This concept appears in the Old Testament: "For the LORD'S portion is his people" (Deuteronomy 32:9). God considered Israel to be His portion or lot. (See also Deuteronomy 4:20, 9:29; Zechariah 2:12.) The New Testament similarly describes the church as a gift to be presented to Christ (Ephesians 5:27). In John 17:9, 11, 24 Jesus talked about "those whom thou hast given me," which means that Jesus considered the church to be His inheritance. The church is Christ's body, Christ's building, and Christ's bride (Ephesians 1:22-23; 2:19-22; 5:22-23).

These passages reveal that the church, by the grace of adoption, has received a place in God's heritage that He formed long ago when He called Israel in the Old Testament. Our value to God is equal to a costly inheritance that He purchased with His own blood. Now we can claim that we are Christ's portion and inheritance, which He received for His suffering at Calvary. I Corinthians 3:22-23 says, "Whether Paul, or Apollos, or Cephas, or the world, or life, or death, or things present, or things to come; all are yours; and ye are Christ's; and Christ is God's."

Both interpretations of Ephesians 1:11 are viable because neither compromises any truth previously revealed. Not only are we Christ's inheritance, but He is ours.

God determined in eternity past that this inheritance would be "predestinated according to the purpose of him who worketh all things after the counsel of his own will." When God decides to do something, whether it be judgment or redemption, He will invariably bring to pass exactly what He had previously determined to do. He will never violate His holiness or human free will, however. God will commit no injustice to bring about His will but will join all the forces of His attributes to work out His purpose. God can take the very plans of Satan, turn them around, and use them to help bring His eternal purpose to pass. Sin itself is no barrier for God's predetermined purpose because He can turn it around also and use it to aid His plan (Romans 8:28).

f. Predestination

Predestination is mentioned twice in the first chapter of Ephesians, the first time in verse 5 and the second time in verse 11. In the first instance, being predestinated is "according to the good pleasure of his will," and in the second instance it is "according to the purpose of him who worketh all things after the counsel of his own will." These two phrases reveal important information about the doctrine of predestination:

1. God has predestined the church to an ultimate good.

2. He will work that good regardless of the obstacles sin and Satan place in front of Him, providing that the church will cooperate with Him by having faith in His plan and receiving His Holy Spirit of promise.

Based on the good pleasure of God's will, adoption is predestined as the means of bringing a family of children into God's inheritance, allowing the Gentiles the privilege of becoming heirs to the throne. Based on the purpose of God, who works all things according to His own will, the church's inheritance was predestined.

Nothing is said about individuals being chosen unconditionally to be saved or lost. This was never Paul's purpose for proclaiming to the church the doctrine of predestination. His purpose was to open the understanding of the church to the plan of God in redemption, by adopting children into His family and securing for the adopted an inheritance. God's mercy purchased the privilege of adoption, and adoption allows us to partake of His inheritance both now and in the future.

God has taken upon Himself the sole responsibility of working this plan out exactly as He designed it. God "worketh all things after the counsel of his own will." The word "worketh" (Greek: *energeo*) means "to energize." The literal translation is "in-working." The Lord possesses the ability to take a dead situation, energize it, and mold it in order to fit it into His plan. He can change circumstances to fit His perfect will. This ability of God works unseen in many cases, but those of us who have received a full understanding and knowledge of His will know that everything that happens has a certain path that leads to the sovereign throne of God.

God does not work all of His will according to the chronology of time. The monotonous succession of days, months, and years do not always reveal the actual working of God. He possesses His own timetable by which He brings to pass His redemptive purpose.

God's work has always had a redemptive and restorative purpose. In order to bring about the ultimate restoration of the universe, God must judge all sinners who have not repented. Satan and every one of his demons must be judged along with unrepentant humans. Only after the judgment of sin can God "bring in everlasting righteousness" (Daniel 9:24).

All the working of God, all His energy, is focused on bringing to pass "the counsel of his own will." No plan has been formulated outside Himself. God's sovereignty is indisputable.

How could God be a trinity of persons if, when He took counsel to formulate His eternal purposes, He took counsel of His own will? Some people use Genesis 1:26 to try to prove a multiplicity of persons in the Godhead. According to them, when God said, "Let us make man in our image," He addressed other members of the Godhead and took counsel with them concerning the creation of man. They place emphasis on the pronoun "us." It does not allude to persons, however, but to God's majesty. His will possesses such power and is so vast that the singular form is not enough to express the immensity of its reach and capabilities. Therefore, God, in referring to "his own will," used the plural pronoun "us" in Genesis 1:26 to call our attention to His vastness and majesty.

The New Testament proclaims that Jesus Christ is, without dispute, the one who created all things (John 1:3; Colossians 1:16). Yet the Old Testament gives Jehovah God sole possession of the right to the title of Creator (Isaiah 42:5; 44:24). This comparison can lead to only one sound conclusion: Jesus Christ of the New Testament is Jehovah God of the Old Testament manifested in flesh. By the "counsel of his own will" God almighty determined to become flesh in order to redeem humanity. Everything He worked out in the Old Testament was done to bring Israel to the fullness of time, so that Messiah could be born and reconciliation could be made between God and man.

Verse 12. God's plan has progressed according to the

predetermined will and has been accomplished by the holy working or energizing of His power to the end "that we should be to the praise of his glory." Redemption's effect in our lives is to create salvation and holiness, with the end result that our lives become a testimony that praises God's glory for what He has accomplished. Redeemed humanity, with spotless lives untainted by the world, are the means God uses to garner praise for His majesty and to glorify His name. God made a name for Himself by delivering Israel from Egypt, but His name shall be made more glorious by securing eternal salvation for His people, not just for the Jews but for the Gentiles as well.

God's glory is the revelation of His consistent determination to fulfill His Word and to bring His promises to pass. Our God is "Faithful and True" (Revelation 19:11). His faithfulness to execute all His divine directives produces in the church her righteousness and victory. This victory worked out in the church through His exceeding great power is the very reason we will become praise to His glory (Ephesians 1:19). The greatest revelation of God's character is not found in His judgments, but in His gospel of redemption. Redemption, and the family of children it will produce, is the true glory of God (II Corinthians 4:4-6; I Timothy 1:11).

Paul identifies the "we" in this verse as those "who first trusted in Christ." The word "trust" (Greek: *proelpizo*) means to "hope in advance of an expected benefaction." Those who first trusted in Christ were the Jewish believers. The next verse also includes Gentile converts, referring to them as "ye."

There are two reasons why the Jews were the first

who trusted in Christ. One, they were given the oracles of God, and by those they first held the hope of a coming Messiah (Acts 28:20; Romans 15:12). Two, the Jews possessed the knowledge of the gospel of Jesus Christ before the Gentiles (Romans 1:16; 2:9).

During the beginning years of the early church, only Jews and Jewish proselytes received the Holy Ghost. Not until Acts 10 were Gentiles acknowledged as heirs of the promise of the Father, and even at that the Jewish Christians still had difficulty accepting them as equals (Acts 15). Peter had to be moved by a divine vision even to go to Cornelius's house and preach to him the message of Jesus Christ (Acts 10:9-20). Even after he went by the direction of the Holy Ghost, the rest of the church questioned his actions in Acts 11. Only after he made a tremendous effort to explain what had happened did they realize and accept this new direction the Holy Ghost was taking.

In Ephesians 1:12 Paul assured the Jewish Christians that their stand for Jesus Christ as the true Messiah was going to be to the praise of God's glory. All Jews were zealous for the glory of the one true God, and Paul made it perfectly clear that by their trusting in Christ, especially their being the first to trust in Him, they would forever be a mighty testimony to the greatness of God's glorious gospel.

4. Sealed by His Spirit (1:13-14)

(13) In whom ye also trusted, after that ye heard the word of truth, the gospel of your salvation: in whom also after that ye believed, ye were sealed with that holy Spirit of promise, (14) which is the earnest of our inheritance until the redemption of the purchased possession, unto the praise of his glory.

Verse 13. It is quite evident from Luke's account of early church history as recorded in the Book of Acts that the Jews were the first to receive the gospel. However, the plan of God also made possible the inclusion of the Gentiles in His inheritance. "In whom ye also trusted" makes clear that the Gentiles were not second-class members of the body of Christ. They owed the Jews respect as the originally chosen people of God, and God used the Jews as a channel to convey His eternal salvation to the Gentiles. But the Gentile believers were children of God by adoption, with exactly the same rights as the Jews.

Because the Gentiles deposited their faith in Jesus Christ and His redemptive plan, they were adopted and accepted. Being adopted and accepted by grace allowed them the privilege of claiming to be the sons of God. This sonship gave them an inheritance along with the Jews. Paul described their faith as trust, which is the placing of one's confidence and life in the value of Christ's promises, knowing "that he is able to keep that which I have committed unto him against that day" (II Timothy 1:12).

The Gentiles did not deposit their faith in Jesus Christ by accident. There was a prearranged plan to make this happen. Their trust developed "after that ye heard the word of truth, the gospel of your salvation." This phrase reveals God's plan for bringing about the salvation of humanity through His church. Of course, Ephesians has already made clear that without the work of Jesus Christ at Calvary there would be no adoption or spiritual blessings. He is solely responsible for all our benefits. By His own predestined will, however, He has chosen the church to help fulfill His eternal purpose to create a new spiritual family. Here, Paul revealed the method that the church is to use to help facilitate this plan of God. First comes the hearing of the Word, then comes the believing, and finally, the sealing of the Holy Spirit.

If the world is ever going to know Jesus Christ as Lord, the church must carry the gospel to them and preach "the word of truth." The church cannot preach anything it wants. It must preach the truth. Hearing the truth will bring conviction to sinners. Many will repent and believe the gospel. After they repent and believe the gospel, they will be sealed with the Holy Spirit of promise. This is God's method, and the historical accounts of Acts show it to be the means God uses to convert sinners.

The truth is "the gospel of your salvation." Jesus Christ referred to Himself as "the truth" (John 14:6). The gospel is simply proclaiming Jesus. The preaching of Jesus Christ is the only truth or gospel that can save people from their sins. I Corinthians 15:1-4 describes the gospel as the death, burial, and resurrection of the Lord Jesus Christ. Only when this truth is preached will there be any saving faith. God has chosen "by the foolishness of preaching to save them that believe" (I Corinthians 1:21). Without the preached Word of God, a sinner cannot hear with faith, for "faith cometh by hearing, and hearing by the word of God" (Romans 10:17).

God's plan is that those who are saved must hear this gospel truth from the mouth of a God-sent preacher: "For whosoever shall call upon the name of the Lord shall be saved. How then shall they call on him in whom they have not believed? and how shall they believe in him of whom they have not heard? and how shall they hear without a preacher? And how shall they preach, except they be sent?

as it is written, How beautiful are the feet of them that preach the gospel of peace, and bring glad tidings of good things!" (Romans 10:13-15). Preaching is still God's method of bringing sinners to Christ, and that preaching must be "the word of truth, the gospel of your salvation."

Three laws must be applied if a person is going to trust God unto salvation:

1. the law of hearing
2. the law of believing
3. the law of sealing

We have already discussed the law of hearing, but hearing the word of truth alone will not bring salvation. "The word preached did not profit them, not being mixed with faith in them that heard it" (Hebrews 4:2). Faith must follow hearing. The word must be mixed with faith if the saving power of Jesus Christ is to be released.

Moreover, we cannot separate faith from repentance. "Jesus came into Galilee, preaching the gospel of the kingdom of God, and saying, The time is fulfilled, and the kingdom of God is at hand: repent ye, and believe the gospel" (Mark 1:14-15). Repentance must accompany faith. If preaching does not convict the sinner's heart, then it is possible the preacher is not preaching "the word of truth." A person must not only believe that Jesus Christ died for his sins, but he must be sorry for those sins that nailed Him to the cross.

After the hearer mixes faith with the Word, God sets His royal seal upon that faith. God's witness of sincere faith is the seal of the Holy Spirit of promise. "After that ye believed, ye were sealed with that holy Spirit of promise." Scholars have pointed out that the phrase "after that ye believed" literally means "having believed." A person who receives the Holy Ghost receives it as a logical progression of his faith. He must first hear the gospel preached; then he can choose either to accept or reject it. Once he accepts and believes the gospel, he will receive the Holy Ghost.

The disciples of John the Baptist in Acts 19 faced this choice. Paul asked them "Have ye received the Holy Ghost since ye believed? And they said unto him, We have not so much as heard whether there be any Holy Ghost" (Acts 19:2). The literal translation of Paul's question is, "Have ye received the Holy Ghost having believed?" If Paul believed that they already had the Holy Ghost but were ignorant of the fact, he would have simply explained to them that they already had the Holy Ghost instead of laying hands on them to receive the gift. They believed but had not yet received the Holy Ghost. Therefore, Paul proceeded to lay hands on them, and they received the Holy Ghost.

A person must first believe and then as a direct result of believing receive the Holy Ghost. A decision of faith and receiving the Spirit can happen simultaneously, but the two are not synonymous. Often a person receives the Spirit at a later time when his understanding is enlightened as to the availability of this experience and his need for it. In every case in the Book of Acts where people received the Holy Ghost, they heard, they believed, and then they received the Holy Ghost (Acts 2:1-4, 37-47; 10:44-48; 19:1-6).

Jesus Christ stated specifically that if anyone wanted the gift of the Holy Ghost he should ask for it in order to receive it (Luke 11:9-13). After a person has heard and believed, he will be sealed with the Holy Ghost and be endued with the power from on high (Luke 24:49). He will know that he has received this seal of the Spirit by the sign of speaking with other tongues as the Spirit gives the utterance.

The Book of Acts gives us several examples of people receiving the Holy Ghost and describes this experience as the fulfillment of God's promise. In every case they spoke with tongues. When the Jews believed, they received the Holy Ghost with the evidence of speaking with other tongues (Acts 2:4). When the Gentiles believed, they received the Holy Ghost with the evidence of speaking with other tongues (Acts 10:46; 11:15). When the disciples of John the Baptist, who were believers but did not yet have the Holy Ghost, received full understanding and exercised faith accordingly, they also received the Holy Ghost with the evidence of speaking with other tongues (Acts 19:6).

The Holy Ghost comes as a result of genuine faith. The Spirit will come when the believer asks sincerely and from a repentant heart.

Paul proceeded to describe the Holy Ghost with three metaphors:

1. as a "seal"
2. "that holy Spirit of promise"
3. "the earnest of our inheritance"

The concept of a seal is not new to New Testament thinking. Paul and other writers mentioned it in various ways (John 3:33; Romans 4:11; 15:28; I Corinthians 9:2). The prophetic books use the word especially to show that the prophecy is for an appointed time (Daniel 12:4; Revelation 22:10).

The seal of the Holy Spirit secures three benefits for the believer. First, it marks his faith as genuine. Whenever a king sent a document to one of his distant provinces, the proof of the authenticity of the document was the king's seal. The Holy Ghost's habitation of the heart confirms one's faith. It is God's stamp, showing that He is at work. The way God writes His perfect law in our hearts is through the Spirit (Romans 8:9; II Corinthians 3:3). The Corinthians' conversion was the seal of Paul's apostleship, marking it as genuine (I Corinthians 9:2). The Holy Ghost is the seal of our conversion, also marking it as genuine. God has given His witness, and that witness is the Spirit of God in our hearts, shedding abroad the love of God (Romans 5:5; 8:16; I John 5:8-10).

The second benefit of the seal of the Holy Spirit is proof of ownership. The seal of the Holy Ghost proves whom we belong to. The practice of sealing merchandise, branding animals, and marking other types of property to prove ownership is ancient. The Ephesians would have been well acquainted with seals because Ephesus was the cultural and commercial center of that part of the world. Many merchants brought their wares to the city by ship and sealed their cargo to prove their ownership in order to sell it in the marketplace for a profit. Similarly God wants to show the world and the devil to whom we really belong. We are God's property because He purchased us with His own blood and gave us His Spirit.

The third benefit of the seal of the Holy Ghost is to secure protection. Whatever has been sealed has been sealed to preserve against thievery, spoiling, and molestation. In Revelation 7:3 the 144,000 were sealed before God could pour out His judgment, so they would not be hurt. Jude 1 declares that we are "preserved in Jesus Christ." As long as the believer remains filled with the

Holy Ghost he is protected from the attacks of the devil. No outside force can separate him from the love of Jesus Christ, because he is protected by the seal of the Holy Ghost (Romans 8:35-39).

The Holy Ghost is also identified as "that holy Spirit of promise." That the Holy Ghost was promised, even in the Old Testament, is beyond dispute. Isaiah revealed, "For with stammering lips and another tongue will he speak to this people. To whom he said, This is the rest wherewith ye may cause the weary to rest; and this is the refreshing: yet they would not hear" (Isaiah 28:11). Ezekiel prophesied that the indwelling Spirit would cause the believer to walk in the statutes and in the ways of God (Ezekiel 36:27; 37:14). In Joel 2:28, God proclaimed the outpouring of the Holy Spirit upon all flesh, and Peter declared the fulfillment of this promise in Acts 2:16-18. John the Baptist prophesied that when Messiah came He would baptize with the Holy Ghost and with fire (Matthew 3:11). Paul referred to this prophecy in Acts 19:4. Jesus Christ also promised that the Comforter, who is the Holy Ghost, would come to His disciples and made it plain that all His disciples would be recipients of this promised blessing (Luke 11:13; John 7:38-39; 14:16, 26; 15:26).

Paul wanted to identify exactly what he was referring to and confirm that the Holy Spirit was the "holy Spirit of promise," "the promise of the Father" (Luke 24:49; Acts 1:4; 2:33; Galatians 3:14). The Holy Ghost was indeed promised by the prophets of the Old Testament, by John the Baptist, and by Jesus Christ Himself. The apostles received the promise and began to preach everywhere that all who believed could also receive it. Without a doubt, anyone today who truly believes in the Lord Jesus

Christ can receive the same Holy Spirit that the apostles received with the evidence of speaking with other tongues.

Verse 14. Paul described the Holy Ghost as "the earnest of our inheritance." The word "earnest" means a "down payment that secures the complete payment at a later time." The Holy Ghost is a foretaste of what Christ has prepared for us in the heavenlies. Without the power of the Holy Ghost in our lives, regardless of our knowledge and understanding of God's purpose, we could never hope to fulfill His orders. God desires to impart prudence to us to help establish a daily walk that we need to fulfill His purpose in the earth. The gift of the Holy Ghost is a necessity in that daily walk.

We must remember that redemption has done more than just rescue us from sin and adopt us into the family of God; redemption has also secured for us an inheritance that we are to use to overcome the world and the devil. The earnest payment of that inheritance is the Holy Ghost. The Holy Ghost is just the first installment that secures the final payment. In II Corinthians 1:22, Paul explained that our seal is the earnest of the Spirit: "Who hath also sealed us, and given the earnest of the Spirit in our hearts." Throughout Paul's writings he represents the Holy Spirit as something every believer experiences to prepare for the return of the Savior, when He will redeem all creation (Romans 8:23; II Corinthians 5:5).

The four works of redemption revealed in the first chapter of Ephesians are:

1. the rescue, which is the work of forgiveness;

2. the adoption, which is the acceptance into the family of God;

3. the sealing, which is the earnest payment of our

inheritance—the gift of the Holy Ghost; and

4. the final payment, which is redemption reaching its fullness by setting us free from all bondage caused by sin.

The earnest of our inheritance is simply a means to a greater end, and that end is "the redemption of the purchased possession." This phrase refers to the final deliverance when our bodies will be changed and "fashioned like unto his glorious body" (Philippians 3:21). This deliverance is more than just being set free from the curse of the law and being restored to the favor of God. It is the redemption that will come when Jesus returns for His bride, and even now our souls are longing for His Second Coming (Luke 21:28; Romans 8:23; I John 3:2).

Our rescue from sin by Christ's blood is not complete until we allow our lives to be changed into the image of Jesus Christ Himself (II Corinthians 3:18). However, this change will not culminate until Jesus returns in glory. Without the adoption of sons and the acceptance that is secured through adoption, and without the Holy Ghost as the earnest of our inheritance, it would be impossible to produce this change in our lives. But when the final day comes and the final payment is made, not only will our inheritance in Christ be fully revealed, but Christ will also receive His inheritance, which is the church. The complete fullness of His eternal purpose will be known to all.

What God has begun, He is also able to finish. Redemption was finished legally at Calvary, but our actual experience is yet to come. The final consummation of all God's redemptive work will be seen in a blood-bought church standing before Him as sons of God in absolute perfection, robed in white, which is the righteousness of the saints (Revelation 19:8).

Paul identified this redeemed body of sons in this verse as a "purchased possession." The phrase "purchased possession" is translated from the Greek word *peripoiesis,* which means the "act of acquiring." God is in the process of acquiring sons and incorporating them into His purpose. This process is not yet complete and will not be completed until the last soul is saved. This makes evangelism absolutely necessary.

The legal aspect of Calvary's purchase is finished, but the purpose for Calvary is not. The unfinished task is the evangelization of our world, to create an entire family of sons that will live unto the praise of His glory. Until that purpose is complete, Jesus Christ will not return to the earth to set up His kingdom.

God's purchased possession is a church of Jews and Gentiles who have become one in Jesus Christ, a people who belong to Him personally. This truth is brought out in the Old Testament, as well as by the other writers of the New Testament. Psalm 74:2 speaks of God's people as "purchased of old," and uses this truth as the basis for asking God to remember them and restore Israel to her former glory. God, described His people as a "peculiar treasure" (Exodus 19:5; Psalm 135:4), a "peculiar people" (Deuteronomy 14:2), and a collection of jewels (Malachi 3:17). He gave these descriptions to Israel to build their faith in the inheritance they had received from Him. They were to act on that inheritance by calling on God in prayer, utilizing the power of God's opinion of them to defeat the enemy and establish God's claim upon the earth that He, and He alone, is God.

This same truth was bequeathed to the New Testament church as the apostles attempted in every way to build the faith of the saints in their new-found experience with Jesus Christ. Paul and Peter called the church a "peculiar people" (Titus 2:14; I Peter 2:9). Paul wanted to give the Ephesians this knowledge so they could use it in their daily walk in overcoming the world to build a testimony to the name of Jesus Christ. His farewell speech to the Ephesian elders expressed this truth beautifully as he charged the elders to tend carefully to the flock that God had purchased with His own blood (Acts 20:28). God has too much invested in the church to allow a wolf to destroy what He has bought with His own blood.

We do not know exactly what the final payment of our redemption holds for us. It is beyond words or thoughts: "But as it is written, Eye hath not seen, nor ear heard, neither have entered into the heart of man, the things which God hath prepared for them that love him" (I Corinthians 2:9). We do know that God has prepared for us "an inheritance incorruptible, and undefiled, and that fadeth not away, reserved in heaven for you" (I Peter 1:4).

Three times in this long sentence Paul used the expression "unto the praise of his glory." Each time the revelation of Christ's redemption becomes more clear and shines more perfectly unto the final day of His second coming. We are to praise His glory because of our adoption, we are to praise His glory because of the inheritance we have received from God, and we are to praise His glory because of the final payment of our redemption, when we are to be glorified with Christ (Romans 8:17).

The glory of Christ's redemption is revealed in that it covers eternity past, present, and future. In the past, God made a choice to adopt a family of sons. Now, He is using the church to convey His inheritance to the world. In the future, He shall return for His bride, and together we shall be glorified. Considering all that God has done, we cannot help but live to the praise of His glory and await the day when we shall be able to praise His glory forever.

Notes

[1]Dale, 25.

[2]Ruth Paxson, *The Wealth, Walk and Warfare of the Christian* (Old Tappan, NJ: Fleming H. Revell, 1939), 26.

[3]Warren W. Wiersbe, *Be Rich* (Wheaton, IL: Victor Books, 1976), 14.

[4]William Barclay, *The Letters to the Galatians and Ephesians*, rev. ed., *Daily Study Bible Series* (Philadelphia: Westminster Press, 1976), 80.

[5]Tucker, 48.

[6]Foulkes, 48.

[7]Moule, 48.

[8]Foulkes, 52.

B.

Prayer for the Bride's Enlightenment
(1:15-23)

1. The Revelation and Knowledge of Christ (1:15-19)

(15) Wherefore I also, after I heard of your faith in the Lord Jesus, and love unto all the saints, (16) cease not to give thanks for you, making mention of you in my prayers; (17) that the God of our Lord Jesus Christ, the Father of glory, may give unto you the spirit of wisdom and revelation in the knowledge of him: (18) the eyes of your understanding being enlightened; that ye may know what is the hope of his calling, and what the riches of the glory of his inheritance in the saints, (19) and what is the exceeding greatness of his power to us-ward who believe, according to the working of his mighty power.

Verse 15. After Paul praised God for the many blessings and possessions that Jesus Christ has secured for the bride at Calvary, he focused his attention on praying for the Ephesians' enlightenment. A knowledge of spiritual possessions is not enough to bequeath them to the church. There must come a spiritual enlightenment that makes known not just the blessings that are available, but the Blesser Himself.

Paul's ultimate purpose for revealing these possessions is to develop a Christ-like character in the saints.

105

To ponder the possessions brings praise to the lips, but to realize the full impact of their purpose and meaning, requires prayer. Without prayer there can be no fulfillment of the purpose. The word "wherefore" connects the prayer of verses 15-23 with the revelation of the riches possessed in Christ in verses 3-14.

True revelation does not bring spiritual pride but a spirit of supplication and intercession. As David, the man after God's own heart, said of the great promises of God given to him, "For thou, O LORD of hosts, God of Israel, hast revealed to thy servant, saying, I will build thee an house: therefore hath thy servant found in his heart to pray this prayer unto thee" (II Samuel 7:27). Prayer must be found in the heart in order to acquire the possessions.

It is most likely that Paul heard of the growing faith and love of the saints in Ephesus through Epaphras (Colossians 1:7). It may seem strange that Paul would use this terminology, considering the amount of time he spent in Ephesus. But we must remember that several years had passed from the time of his visit to the time of his writing and that the church had grown considerably in size and number. Therefore, when he received the report from Epaphras of the mighty growth, not only numerically but also spiritually, he wrote to express his appreciation for the church's spiritual development.

This verse reveals the two fundamental graces that result from possessing the riches of God's grace: "faith in the Lord Jesus Christ, and love unto all the saints." These are the infallible proofs of true conversion and revelation. No other foundation is more secure than true faith in Jesus Christ, and from it springs love for all the brethren.

The fragrance of true faith in Jesus as Lord and Savior must prevail in our lives, and we will express that faith by showing love to all the saints. If the love is not present, the profession of faith is a lie. Faith and love are interdependent. We cannot separate them; if we could, they would become ineffective. "Faith . . . worketh by love," and "the love of God is shed abroad in our hearts by the Holy Ghost" (Galatians 5:6; Romans 5:5).

One can possess religion without possessing Christ. Possessions are great, gifts are wonderful, and blessings are sweet, but nothing is as great as possessing Jesus Christ Himself, along with the virtue He manifested on this earth. God's purpose in revealing the possessions is to establish our faith in Christ and see that faith finds its greatest expression in love for the brethren.

Verse 16. These fundamental virtues that were growing and developing in the lives of the Ephesian saints caused Paul to "cease not to give thanks for you, making mention of you in my prayers." His first action after praise for the bride's possessions was prayer. He practiced prayer without ceasing, which means that in every case where it was appropriate and needed, he prayed for this church. By his life as well as his writings Paul challenged all believers to offer up prayer and thanksgiving continually (Romans 12:12; Ephesians 6:18; Colossians 4:2; I Thessalonians 5:17-18).

Without thanksgiving, prayer is incomplete. Paul taught this principle in Philippians 4:6: "Be careful for nothing; but in every thing by prayer and supplication with thanksgiving let your requests be made known unto God."

Jesus Christ illustrated the same principle when He

raised Lazarus from the dead. Before He called Lazarus out of the tomb, He prayed, "Father, I thank thee that thou hast heard me. And I knew that thou hearest me always: but because of the people which stand by I said it, that they may believe that thou hast sent me" (John 11:41-42). Resurrection power comes after thanksgiving and prayer. Paul understood this spiritual truth and applied it in order to see the glorious possessions of the bride.

Verse 17. Paul's prayers were never aimless or without focus. They always had a specific purpose. One of the great studies of the New Testament is the prayers of Paul for the churches.

Paul's greatest desire was for the church to attain its full stature in Christ so she could carry out the mission that Jesus had left for her to do. Here he specifically prayed that God would grant the church "the spirit of wisdom and revelation in the knowledge of him." Colossians 1:9 is a parallel passage.

Like verse 3, verse 17 speaks of "the God of our Lord Jesus Christ" and also calls Him "the Father of glory." This description does not imply that Jesus Christ is a lesser deity, but it shows that Jesus Christ was a true man and that only through Him can we come to know God. Through Him we can know God on a personal basis.

Jesus Christ is the Lord of glory (I Corinthians 2:8; James 2:1). The glory of God is revealed in the face of Jesus Christ (II Corinthians 4:6). Yet Acts 7:2 identifies the God of the Old Testament who talked with Abraham as the "God of glory."

The God of glory formed the child Jesus in the womb of Mary and manifested Himself in that Son to reveal Himself to humanity. By manifesting Himself in human form He provided Himself as a sacrifice upon the cross. The Spirit of God in Christ did not die, but the physical body of Jesus Christ died on the cross.

The glory of God is God revealing Himself to humanity. Jesus Christ is the perfect revelation of God's nature and character, and thus He is the glory of God.

God's character could not be better displayed than through the gospel of Jesus Christ. God's way of salvation as offered to humanity through Jesus Christ is His glory.

Paul prayed that the God of glory would give the church "the spirit of wisdom and revelation in the knowledge of him." The pronoun "him" refers specifically to Jesus Christ, for there is no better way to know God than to know the express image of God, who is Jesus Christ. Other scriptural passages likewise express a desire to know God through Christ. Paul wanted to gain "the excellency of the knowledge of Christ Jesus my Lord" (Philippians 3:8). Peter stated, "According as his [God's] divine power hath given unto us all things that pertain unto life and godliness, through the knowledge of him [Christ] that hath called us to glory and virtue" (II Peter 1:3).

We should notice that God's gifts are directly connected to the knowledge of Jesus Christ. Having a knowledge of the possessions is not good enough; we must possess a knowledge of Christ. The more we come to know Jesus Christ personally, the more we will possess His attributes and His inheritance. Relationship is definitely a priority of redemption.

The word "spirit" refers to our receiving wisdom and knowledge from the Holy Spirit. It means more than a state of mind or an attitude of faith; it describes the power of God that leads to a better understanding of the church's mission in this earth.

Paul's prayer is for a spiritual process that will revolutionize the believer's entire life. The focus is not on the spiritual attributes themselves, but on Jesus. The Holy Spirit is the revealer of all truth, and Jesus Christ is the truth (John 14:6; 16:13-14). Eternal life comes through knowledge of God, and particularly as God is revealed in Christ (John 17:3).

Enlightenment comes through prayer for a revelation (Greek: *apokalupsis*) of wisdom of Him. This revelation is literally a taking off of the cover or a manifestation of God's ultimate intention. This ultimate intention is revealed through wisdom (Greek: *sophia*), discussed earlier in verse 8, and through knowledge (Greek: *epignosis*), which means complete or full knowledge. We know only in part now, but one day our knowledge will be complete (I Corinthians 13:9-12). Until that perfect day comes, God has promised to give us the knowledge of God as we need it to apply to everyday situations.

Knowledge is good, but we need wisdom to know when, where, and how to apply it to get the maximum benefit.

The New Age movement is crying out, "Know thyself," but the church still heralds the message of Paul the apostle to "know God," not just His possessions, but Him personally. We can only do so by knowing Jesus Christ through the power and influence of the Holy Spirit.

a. The Hope of His Calling
Verse 18. The Holy Ghost plays a vital part in mak-

ing known the riches of a personal relationship with Jesus Christ, for verse 18 goes on to say, "The eyes of your understanding being enlightened. . . ." The word "understanding" is sometimes rendered as "heart," meaning "the seat of intelligence and will."[1] The understanding includes the total inner person, which needs illumination by the Spirit of God. Our eyes must be enlightened, not only to the riches of Christ but how to use them properly in order to function as Christ has planned.

Sin in general, and ingratitude particularly, darkens the mind's eye to spiritual things (Matthew 13:15; Romans 1:21; Ephesians 4:18; 5:8). A Christian cannot take advantage of the joys of conversion unless he overcomes unthankfulness through a spiritual enlightenment of his place in God's purpose and God's grace toward him. This illumination of the spirit gives confidence to the believer to endure the afflictions that may lie ahead (Hebrews 10:32).

Only the Holy Ghost can open the understanding to receive the spiritual things God has made available to us (I Corinthians 2:10-14). God needs to shine His light of grace into people's darkened hearts to remove their blindness so they might see their place in His purpose (Isaiah 42:6-7). This spiritual awakening will not only make the church realize her place but will give her the necessary tools to carry out her mission.

The first and foremost mission of the church is to know God, and Paul stated what we need to know about God and His plan: "that ye may know what is the hope of his calling." This calling is God's call to man—not "your calling" but "his calling." This call involves the past, present, and future, for God's purpose reaches back to the

111

beginning of time and then reaches to the future. We did not choose Him; He chose us to perform His work. Jehovah called Israel to be His people in Abraham, the father of the faithful (Genesis 12:1-3). He extended this calling through Isaac and Jacob (Genesis 26:1-5; 28:13-15). The Gentiles are also included in the call, with Israel being the means God used to convey the call to them (Isaiah 62:1-2). Jesus Christ is the promised seed that inherited all the blessings of Abraham, Isaac, and Jacob, and He issues a call to all the world to respond to Him by faith that they too may enjoy His inheritance (Ephesians 1:18).

b. His Inheritance in Us

Paul's prayer included more than a spiritual calling of holiness and purpose. We also need to receive the knowledge of the inheritance God has in us. God has always desired a family of sons to realize His purpose. He desires to have fellowship with that family, and that fellowship is His wealth of glory. "For the LORD'S portion is his people; Jacob is the lot of his inheritance" (Deuteronomy 32:9).

Not only do we possess in Him the riches of His grace, but He possesses in us the riches of His glory. We are His inheritance, bought and paid for by the blood of Jesus Christ. The purpose of God for the church far supersedes the need to save us from our sins. That is a preliminary necessity. But it is only a means to an end. The ultimate end God desires is to create a family of sons who will bear the praise of His glory to the whole world. This holy purpose finds its beginning in redemption and then proceeds to a divine call that bears a hope of present and future blessing. It then finds its end in creating out of sinful humanity an authentic community of believers with whom the Lord can fellowship.

The believers in this community are at one with each other and at one with Christ, the former being a result of the latter. Without this harmony God's purpose will not be accomplished.

c. His Exceeding Great Power

Verse 19. In addition, God's purpose will not be accomplished without a generous supply of His power. There must come a supernatural endowment of power to accomplish His holy purpose. All the knowledge in the world will not effect a change in one's life without the power of the Holy Ghost working vibrantly within. Christians who possess a form of godliness but deny the power thereof are only shadows of the true substance of Christ. We cannot attain God's purpose and plan without the "exceeding greatness of his power." We must know about it, but we must also know it by experience, or possess it. The two are not the same. The scriptural way to realize and receive this power is to be baptized with the Holy Ghost (Acts 1:8).

God has always exceeded His own mark of excellence. The word "exceeding" in this verse comes from a Greek word *hyperballon,* which means "to throw beyond the usual mark." Four other times in Scripture Paul used the word *hyperballon*:

1. In II Corinthians 3:10, he referred to the glory of the new covenant that "excelleth."

2. In II Corinthians 9:14, the "exceeding grace" abounded in the Corinthians because of their liberality.

3. In Ephesians 2:7, the riches of God's grace go beyond the usual or expected.

113

4. In Ephesians 3:19, we see "the love of Christ which passeth knowledge."

In each case God's exceeding greatness is seen working in the life of the believers to make their lives richer by His grace and love.

God set a mark of excellence in delivering Israel from Egypt. He set a second and greater mark in restoring the Jews from Babylonian captivity (Jeremiah 23:7-8). He set a third and even greater mark by resurrecting Jesus Christ from the dead. The resurrection is a new standard of power that works life in the heart of the believer. Because of the resurrection, the church can function within her calling and become for God the inheritance He deserves.

This power is bestowed upon us by the "working of his mighty power." The word "working" comes from the Greek word *energeo*, which literally means "the inworking." The power of God comes by a process of God's working His pleasure and will within us (Philippians 2:13). God's greatest mark of excellence goes beyond even the standard of power set by Christ's resurrection, by a glorious transformation of sinful humanity that brings life, holiness, and purpose. The result of transformation, is that the individual is equipped to do God's will (Romans 12:2).

God works within us to effect the change necessary for us to receive our inheritance (Ephesians 3:7; 4:16; Colossians 1:29). This working takes place in two ways, as shown by the two different uses of the word "power" in this verse. The "exceeding greatness of his power to usward who believe" uses the word *dunamis*, which means "miraculous power." The "working of his mighty power" uses the word *kratos*, which means "dominion, strength, or might." For us to be equipped to fulfill God's purpose, we must first experience the miracle of salvation, and then we need the impartation of strength and dominion in our daily lives. Christ must reign as Lord in the life of the believer to give him strength and dominion over satanic forces that will oppose his new-found life in Christ.

First comes the miracle of salvation, then comes daily strength from the lordship of Jesus Christ. Both are necessary in order for us to accomplish God's eternal purpose today. We need redemption to retrieve us from our faults, and we need daily strength to bear the burdens required if Christ is to be exalted in the earth. "Finally, my brethren, be strong in the Lord, and in the power of his might" (Ephesians 6:10).

2. The True Power of the Resurrection (1:20-23)

(20) Which he wrought in Christ, when he raised him from the dead, and set him at his own right hand in the heavenly places, (21) far above all principality, and power, and might, and dominion, and every name that is named, not only in this world, but also in that which is to come: (22) and hath put all things under his feet, and gave him to be the head over all things to the church, (23) which is his body, the fulness of him that filleth all in all.

Verse 20. The exceeding greatness of Christ's power is working a great recovery process in us, bringing us out of sin and translating us into the kingdom of the Son of God. This power was manifested at the resurrection of Jesus Christ. Indeed, the recovery process from sin that is at work in our lives is possible because of the resurrection of Jesus Christ. It works in us because it first worked in Jesus, securing victory over death.

115

The hope of our calling, the riches of the inheritance, and the exceeding greatness of His power are all made possible because of the resurrection. Christ displayed His love for us at Calvary, and His humiliation met the demands of God's justice (Romans 5:8). But the greatest demonstration of His power was seen at the resurrection. That power now works in us a "newness of life" (Romans 6:4).

When we view Jesus as God incarnate, we understand that He raised Himself from the dead (John 10:18). When we consider Jesus as man, however, we understand that His work of redemption needed the approval of God. The resurrection was a testimony of God's approval and acceptance. For this reason the Scriptures say that God raised Jesus from the dead, and in this sense, the resurrection is proof of Christ's worthiness (Acts 2:24; 3:15; 5:30; 10:40; Romans 1:4; Galatians 1:1; Hebrews 13:20; I Peter 1:3).

Jesus' exaltation encompassed more than resurrection. It also gave Him the privilege of inheriting the throne of God. God has given Him a place in the heavenlies by which to rule "and set him at his own right hand in the heavenly places." This means Jesus now reigns from a position of authority and power. At first the disciples did not realize the importance of Christ's going away. It was expedient, because without the ascension Christ's government could not be established (John 16:7; Acts 2:33; I Corinthians 15:25; Revelation 5:6).[2]

Christ's resurrection and ascension establish the authority of Christ in redemption. The effective preaching of the gospel must include both elements, and they are prominent in the apostles' preaching. In Acts 2, on the

Day of Pentecost, Peter proclaimed Christ's resurrection as the fulfillment of Psalm 16:10 and His ascension as the fulfillment of Psalm 110:1.

The position of Christ's authority is described as being at the right hand of God. As F. F. Bruce has explained, "When the biblical writers spoke of the right hand of God, they knew as well as we do that God has no material body, and that His right hand is a figurative expression for the place of highest honour and authority."[3] This term is not geographical, but it reveals the authority of Jesus as the executor of God's will. His position at the right hand reveals His authority, and His place in the heavenlies reveals His deity. His authority does not simply extend itself in the earthly realm, but also in the heavenlies.

The authority Christ won through His humiliation, resurrection, and ascension is evidence that He is more than just the head of the church on earth; He is also the head of all God's creation. This authority extends to three worlds: heaven, hell, and the earth. The angels worship Him, the demons fear Him, and the church adores Him. Therefore, redemption's greatest promises and privileges are available to all who believe on Jesus Christ because of His resurrection and exaltation.

Verse 21. Jesus Christ is enthroned "far above all principality, and power, and might, and dominion." His empire extends beyond the earth and reaches into the heavens. Upon this earth there are different forms of government and authority—not only human powers, but also demonic spirits. Jesus Christ reigns supreme over these authorities, both worldly and heavenly. The terms "principality, power, might, and dominion" do not have to be distinguished as to their precise meanings, but collectively

117

they teach that Jesus Christ is higher than all government, whether natural or supernatural, whether human or angelic (Colossians 1:16, 2:15; I Peter 3:22; Revelation 5:11-12). The reason His authority supersedes all other forms of human and angelic governments is because of the redemptive work He accomplished at Calvary.

This work distinguishes Him above all other humans: "Wherefore God also hath highly exalted him, and given him a name which is above every name" (Philippians 2:9).

Jesus alone has the power of redemption. Only in the name of Jesus can sins be forgiven and washed away (Acts 4:12; 22:16). His name is invested not only with forgiveness, but also with the authority by which Christ rules the universe. The people of God can rely upon this authority to overcome evil spirits that would hinder the work of God in their lives (Mark 16:17-18; Luke 10:19).

Jesus possesses this authority now "in this world, but also in that which is to come." The "world," or *aion,* means "age." This present age is still under the influence of evil spirits that control people and governments. One day, however, Jesus Christ will fulfill the complete purpose of God by destroying the influence of evil and removing it forever from the earth. This redemptive purpose began at Calvary and even now progresses toward the culmination of all things (I Corinthians 15:25-28). When the second coming of Jesus Christ ushers in the final age, He will reveal Himself as both Creator and Redeemer and ultimately do away with all evil.

Verse 22. The enthronement of Jesus Christ after His humiliation at Calvary reveals that God has also "put all things under his feet." This present age does not now see "all things put under him" (Hebrews 2:8). The last enemy

118

of the church is death (I Corinthians 15:26). Jesus has already conquered death by His resurrection. The church has not yet experienced victory over death but will realize it at His Second Coming (I Thessalonians 4:16-17).

God originally gave Adam dominion over the works of God's creative hand. His fall in the garden hindered the full realization of this dominion, however (Psalm 8:6; Hebrews 2:8). Man cannot realize the ultimate intention of God's purpose because of sin. Yet Jesus Christ, who is called the last Adam, has realized this destiny. When He appears the second time, without sin unto salvation, He will impute this dominion to the church. Through the church Jesus Christ will reign supreme. (See I Corinthians 15:45-50; Hebrews 9:28; Revelation 20:6.)

As a result of Christ's redemptive work, God "gave him to be the head over all things to the church." Colossians 2:10 says that Jesus Christ is the "head of all principality and power." He has power and authority over all spiritual governments that follow Satan as their prince (Ephesians 2:2). Revelation 1:5 says that Christ is "the prince of the kings of the earth," which means that He rules over all human governments. Above all else, we see Christ in Ephesians 1:22 as the head of the church. The headship of Christ over the church is not implemented by institutional involvement, but by a personal relationship with Christ as Lord and Savior. Unity results from this relationship, so Christ can utilize the church as His body to fulfill His purpose (Colossians 1:18, 24).

For the first time in Ephesians we see the Greek word for church, *ecclesia*, which means "the called out ones." It is also used eight other times (Ephesians 3:10, 21; 5:23, 24, 25, 27, 29, 32).

Verse 23 speaks of the church as Christ's body. We are a body of people who have been called out from our sins, from this world, and from our respective places in life in order to fulfill our destiny in taking dominion over evil.

With this *ecclesia*, Jesus Christ has established a vital relationship, a harmony that pulsates with His very life and power. By His power the church is able to execute the will of God effectively and defeat Satan in this present world.

In I Corinthians 12 Paul pictured the church as the body of Christ in the context of unity among the various members of the church. Later, in Ephesians and Colossians, Paul developed the idea of Christ as the supreme head from which the church realizes all its spiritual life and vitality. "And he is the head of the body, the church: who is the beginning, the firstborn from the dead; that in all things he might have the preeminence" (Colossians 1:18). Colossians presents Christ as preeminent in creation. In Ephesians, the emphasis shifts to the effect that preeminence has on the church.

The body is made up of both Old and New Testament saints, who find their completeness in Christ. Jesus is the recognized head of the saints of both testaments. The Old Testament saints are not complete without those of the New, and the New Testament saints are not complete without recognizing their connection with those of the Old (Hebrews 11:40).

Because we are Christ's body, we are the instruments that He uses in the earth to preach His gospel, live His life, and work His works. The church cannot consider herself the body of Christ unless she allows Jesus to use her as His instrument—an instrument of righteousness, healing, and life. The vital union between Christ and His church is seen when the church allows herself to be used for Christ's glory. Without this union the church is nothing more than an institution, devoid of life and power. With this union the church becomes the most powerful receptacle of God's glory.

When the church realizes this vital union and relationship we literally become "the fulness of him that filleth all in all." The word "fulness" (Greek: *pleroma*) bears testimony that God has chosen to realize His ultimate purpose through Christ and through the church. *Pleroma* means "a receptacle filled." God's plan for the ages does not stop with Jesus Christ. Without Christ it would be impossible, but God's plan is not complete without including total redemption for the church.

Jesus Christ instituted the church as the vehicle by which He would channel His grace and glory to the universe. This is the reason the church needs to stay full of the Holy Ghost. The world has no other channel by which the fullness of God's grace can be conveyed to them. We are the receptacle that holds the grace of God, and it is our responsibility to deposit this grace into the lives of every person we meet.

The word *pleroma* is used in other Scripture settings to mean that which fills up a torn garment (Matthew 9:16), filling baskets with bread (Mark 6:43), the fullness of the earth (I Corinthians 10:26, quoting Psalm 24:1), and the fullness of the Godhead (Colossians 1:19; 2:9). Whatever fruit is produced in the earth or in the church by the loving attention of the Master Farmer belongs exclusively to Him. Our fullness and fruitfulness are totally dependent on Christ pouring Himself into us. The fullness of the church depends totally on her ability to receive from Christ, her Head, the blessings that she can use to bless others (II Corinthians 1:4).

We experience Christ's fullness as He pours Himself into His church. The very nature of Jesus demands that He pour out of His inheritance. Allowing the church to share in this inheritance gives as much pleasure to Christ as it does to the church.

The greatest privilege of the believer is to be the receptacle that catches the glory, the grace, and the goodness of the Lord, and in turn pour it out to the world. This emptying of ourselves so others may enjoy the goodness of God through us will become our greatest joy. Too many believers are selfish with the blessings of God and hoard them for themselves. If Christ's ultimate joy and fullness is to pour Himself out into His church, then our greatest joy will be to do the same for others.

This fullness of Christ that is poured into the receptacle called the church will ultimately fill the whole universe. It "filleth all in all." God's plan includes more than redemption. It will also include the complete restoration of all things. God will become "all in all" (I Corinthians 15:28).

Jesus Christ is the cause of all things (John 1:3), the fulfillment of all God's virtues, and the divine ideal of what His creation was originally intended to be. Though sin has scarred creation, Jesus can rescue it. He rescues the sinner through the power of His resurrection, but the believer receives power to live the new life when he becomes a partaker of His exaltation.

We are seated with Christ in the heavenlies (Ephesians 2:6), and we have become "partakers of the divine nature, having escaped the corruption that is in the world through lust" (II Peter 1:4). Escape from corruption is necessary, but God's plan for the church is progressing toward completion, when each believer will be given his rightful place in the kingdom to come. Every spiritual revelation and experience we receive in this life brings us a little closer to the grand finale of redemption, when God shall be "all in all."

Notes

[1]Bruce, 39.
[2]H. C. G. Moule, *Studies in Ephesians* (Grand Rapids: Kregel Publications, 1977), 61.
[3]Bruce, 43.

C.

The Bride's New Condition
(2:1-10)

1. Our Miserable Condition before Conversion (2:1-3)

(1) And you hath he quickened, who were dead in trespasses and sins; (2) wherein in time past ye walked according to the course of this world, according to the prince of the power of the air, the spirit that now worketh in the children of disobedience: (3) among whom also we all had our conversation in times past in the lusts of our flesh, fulfilling the desires of the flesh and of the mind; and were by nature the children of wrath, even as others.

Verse 1. In the first chapter of Ephesians, Paul defined the possessions that belong exclusively to the church and offered praise to God for the work of Calvary that secured them. Then he prayed that the church would receive the fullness of the blessings. According to Paul, the church has a right to claim these blessings because of Christ's resurrection from the dead, which is the supreme display of God's power. This display replaced any former standard of power that God set in the Old Testament under the old covenant with Israel.

In the second chapter of Ephesians Paul began to describe the awful condition of sinners and why they need these possessions. Our condition prior to conversion demands nothing less than a personal resurrection from the spiritual deadness of sin. Without Christ's resurrection this would be impossible.

The word "quickened" means "to make alive." Because Jesus is the head and we are the body, His resurrection life enables us to be made alive. As long as we maintain this relationship with Christ as the head, we can claim His life as ours. This is the reason Paul felt compelled to pray for the church's understanding to be enlightened—so believers could awaken to the purpose of affecting the lives of sinners around them. Those who allow God's purpose to be realized in them can become active agents in helping sinners to be converted.

A sinner is "dead in trespasses and sins." The word "trespasses" comes from the Greek word *paraptoma,* which means "slip or fall." The word "sins" comes from the Greek word *hamartia,* which means "something that misses the mark." Missing the mark means to be less than one could be. The word is used in the context of an archer aiming at the bull's eye and missing his target. God has designated a certain mark of attainment, and to miss that mark is considered sin.

Because we have slipped and fallen, and because we cannot be what God wants us to be, even with our best efforts, we are spiritually dead. The word "dead" is a true description of the unconverted. They may be alive physically, but they are dead spiritually. Sinners have no way of ever doing what is pleasing in the eyes of God. They are lost and without hope unless they experience a personal quickening from the Lord Jesus Christ.

Not only is a sinner dead, but he is disobedient, depraved, and doomed to spend eternity without God. This miserable condition exists because of Satan, the world, and the flesh. These three enemies work to the destruction of humanity. Divine judgment is the only rightful verdict for such a condition. However, our possessions have secured a place of safety and refuge from the wrath of God. Our deliverance from judgment makes us responsible for influencing the lives of unbelievers with the true message of salvation.

Verse 2. "The course of this world" compares to Galatians 1:4: "this present evil world." The world has its own standard and custom and persecutes those who do not conform to it. We who have been redeemed belong to a different order—a new world not governed by the prince of this world, but by the Lord Jesus Christ. Sin derives its power from the world order that presses people to conform to its wishes and desires. Romans 12:2 gives us the antidote for this malady: "And be not conformed to this world: but be ye transformed by the renewing of your mind, that ye may prove what is that good, and acceptable, and perfect, will of God."

The world follows "the prince of the power of the air." Lucifer leads this present evil age, persecuting the believer and holding the sinner in his condition. He blinds people with lies so they cannot see the true light of the gospel. "In whom the god of this world hath blinded the minds of them which believe not, lest the light of the glorious gospel of Christ, who is the image of God, should shine unto them" (II Corinthians 4:4).

The word "air" refers to the kingdom that Satan rules, the kingdom of the fallen angels (Revelation 12:7-17). These spirits inhabit the earth and are under the control and authority of Satan.

Satan not only presides over the "air," but is also "the spirit that now worketh in the children of disobedience." The spirit of the age works within the hearts and minds of people to cause their disobedience to God. Without a powerful encounter with Jesus Christ, they cannot be loosed from the awful condition of bondage.

Satan is not like God. He is not an omnipresent spirit, but he is a spirit who influences attitudes everywhere. He uses spiritual means to manipulate people, bringing them into agreement with his purposes and thereby causing disobedience to God.

Verse 3. Paul reminded the Ephesians that they too had once been caught in Satan's web of deceit, and he included himself in this reference. In King James English the word "conversation" is broader in scope than just the words one speaks; it refers to one's entire conduct. Human behavior is affected by Satan's dominion. The spirit that works in the unbeliever causes his conduct to yield to the "lusts of our flesh, fulfilling the desires of the flesh and of the mind."

The "flesh" refers to the innate sinful nature of fallen humanity. The "mind" refers to our thoughts and imaginations. Sinful humans are ruled by their passions and will do whatever comes to their imagination. Satan, knowing this innate deficiency, influences these passions and uses them for his evil intentions. People have always desired the forbidden. Satan tempts us with the forbidden, even though the consequences are devastating for us. Because he is led by the devil, the sinner continues down the road of his indulgence into destruction. He cannot help himself because he is dead—he has no feeling, no life, and no power. He must be made alive by the Holy

Spirit before this terrible bondage can be broken.

Man's miserable condition is the result of his fallen nature. Because of this nature all people are sinners and all are under the wrath of God. We "were by nature the children of wrath, even as others." (See also Romans 3:23; 5:12-21.) The carnal nature is the enemy of God (Romans 8:7).

In short, disobedience comes as a result of the fallen human nature, which is inherently evil. The sinner's daily conduct is ruled by the lusts of the flesh and desires of the mind. Adam's fall in the Garden of Eden caused this state of affairs. Paul wanted the Ephesians to view their former condition in the light of God's viewpoint. He wanted them to see their former deadness, which would create a greater appreciation for God's mercy and a greater desire to help others who also suffer from the control of sin and Satan.

2. Our New Condition after Conversion (2:4-10)

(4) But God, who is rich in mercy, for his great love wherewith he loved us, (5) even when we were dead in sins, hath quickened us together with Christ, (by grace ye are saved;) (6) and hath raised us up together, and made us sit together in heavenly places in Christ Jesus: (7) that in the ages to come he might shew the exceeding riches of his grace in his kindness toward us through Christ Jesus. (8) For by grace are ye saved through faith; and that not of yourselves: it is the gift of God: (9) not of works, lest any man should boast. (10) For we are his workmanship, created in Christ Jesus unto good works, which God hath before ordained that we should walk in them.

Verse 4. The wrath of God, though justified in its

129

coming against sinful humanity, is not the final word. God also possesses mercy. God's mercy is brilliant in its glory when seen against His judgments. "The wrath of God, however, is not the whole picture. It provides the background against which His mercy and love stand out in all their radiance."[1]

God is rich in mercy. This is the reason redemption is possible. Human sinfulness has not bankrupted heaven; God's cup of mercy is new every morning. "It is of the LORD'S mercies that we are not consumed, because his compassions fail not. They are new every morning: great is thy faithfulness" (Lamentations 3:22-23). The gospel of Jesus Christ is an invitation to drink from this well of mercy that never runs dry, and once someone drinks of it he will never thirst again (John 4:14). H. C. G. Moule called mercy "the ultimate motive for redemption."[2]

"God did not lack in resources for such a task, nor did He have to go outside Himself to perform the miracle of regeneration."[3] He possessed every attribute necessary to bring about our redemption. Contained within His character are the inherent qualities of love and mercy that provide salvation to all who believe. "In His mercy, He does not give us what we do deserve; and in His grace He gives us what we do not deserve."[4] Mercy withholds the judgments, and grace imparts salvation.

God extended His mercy to us because of "his great love wherewith he loved us." God's love determines the riches of His mercy. His love and affection for us (the pronoun "us" refers to Jews and Gentiles alike) moved Him to open His treasury of grace to provide salvation. Love commanded mercy to hold back judgment, and mercy released grace to accomplish the work of regeneration that has made every believer a new creature in Christ Jesus (John 3:16; I John 4:8-9; Romans 5:8).

Verse 5. The taint of sin in our lives did not hinder God's love toward us. The ultimate display of His love for humanity came when Jesus died for us. His sacrifice at Calvary revealed His true love for us, because it was given even though we were still sinners (Romans 5:6-8). We were dead in sin because the life of Jesus did not dwell within us. Christ appeared to abolish this death and has brought to light the glorious truth of immortality and life through the gospel (II Timothy 1:10).

Paul coined a new word, *synzoopoiro* ("quickened"), which means "make alive with, resurrect with." It also appears in Colossians 2:13. It refers to a birth, a new life. Our new life with Christ came as a result of our union with Him in a holy covenant. In His earthly ministry, Jesus caused resurrection by His spoken word (Luke 7:11-17; 8:49-56; John 11:41-46). This was a physical resurrection that restored life to the individual. But *synzoopoiro* is more than that. It is a complete new life caused by a relationship or a union with Christ Jesus. It becomes effective, not only by what Christ says to us, but by how we respond in faith to Him. (See Acts 2:1-4; Acts 10:44-48; Acts 19:1-6; Romans 10:10.)

Not only are Jews and Gentiles made one in Christ but we are joined with Christ in one body, He being the head (Ephesians 1:19-23). This union cannot take place until we die to sin through repentance and water baptism (Acts 22:16; Romans 6:1-8; Colossians 2:12-13; II Timothy 2:11). We were dead *in* sin, but now we can be dead *to* sin, and through the resurrection of Jesus we live a new life to the praise of God's glory (John 14:19; Romans 8:10).

After stating the power of Christ's resurrection and its effect on the believer, Paul explained, "By grace have ye been saved." "The perfect tense (Gk. *este sesosmenoi*), expresses a present state resulting from a past action."[5] Salvation results from the finished work Christ accomplished at Calvary (Romans 3:24-26). "The first movement in salvation is not from men to God, but from God to men. This wondrous redemption was planned and executed in the heart of God in the eternity of the past, before even the world was."[6]

Our salvation is past, present, and future. The past act of God's eternal wisdom, which decided before the foundation of the world to provide a sacrifice for sins in Jesus Christ, has redeemed us by the blood of the Lamb (Hebrews 9:26; I Peter 1:18-20; Revelation 13:8). Salvation is also present, working in us deliverance that will build a testimony of glory to the name of Jesus (I Corinthians 1:18; 15:2; II Corinthians 2:15). But salvation is also future, for we are waiting for the redemption of the body (Romans 5:9; 8:23-25; 13:11; I Peter 1:5).

When we contemplate our deliverance from the penalty of sin and its consequences (God's wrath), then we can appreciate the power of forgiveness. We are no longer under the condemnation of our past, nor do we have to fear God's wrath. We are free from the "law of sin and death" by the "law of the Spirit of life in Christ Jesus" (Romans 8:1-4).

Verse 6. God raised Jesus from the dead, and now we are raised with Him. We are raised up from our past deadness to a new position in the heavenlies. This is the progression of salvation through the grace of Jesus Christ. We were dead in sin, then through repentance and baptism we were dead with Christ and buried with Christ. Through the power of the resurrection, activated by the Holy Spirit, we have been quickened with Christ, have been raised with Christ, and are sitting with Christ. We have rescue through the blood, restoration through the resurrection, and now rulership with Christ in the heavenlies. "The verbs 'quickened,' 'raised,' 'made to sit,' are all in the aorist [simple past] tense; they express what God has already done for His children in Christ."[7] This fact does not eliminate our responsibility to gain control over our self-life, but it gives us hope that because of what God has already done we can be victorious in Christ.

Our citizenship is now in heaven; therefore our conduct needs to reflect that position (Philippians 3:20). The new life we have received demands a new way of living. In Ephesians, the quickening power has seated us in the heavenlies as an accomplished fact, whereas in Colossians the believer seeks things above as a result of the quickening power of Christ (Colossians 3:1-2). Regardless of our position in Christ, we must gain rulership over our self-life. The self-life must be dethroned and Christ enthroned. That takes the process of sanctification and a daily walk with Christ.

We have already gained acceptance and access to the heavenly places because of our union with Christ. Later we shall be glorified with Him (Romans 8:17). There is an interval between the acceptance stage and the glorification stage: the relationship stage that develops through our fellowship with Him. We are not left in the graveyard of our sins but are given a new spiritual condition with new privileges and positions. Even though we dwell physically on the earth, we are spiritually seated above in heavenly places. Circumstances do not dictate that position; our union with Christ does (Romans 8:37-39; II Corinthians 2:14).

Verse 7. Paul turned the focus from redemption to the ages that will come after this one. Eternity is now in focus. God's eternal purpose is for the church to be an example of God's grace, now and forever (I Timothy 1:17; Jude 25). God's purpose now includes forgiveness, rescue, enlightenment, restoration, relationship, and rulership through union in Christ Jesus. But His purpose in the ages to come is for the church to display the wisdom and glory of God's grace as shown in what Jesus Christ accomplished for us. Our new life and citizenship in God's kingdom demands that we rule over the self-life now, but our citizenship includes a loftier plan that will give us a place in God's new order.

Jesus Christ has shown us great kindness in allowing us to share in His coming kingdom. The word "kindness" comes from the Greek word *chrestotes,* which means "love in action." Dormant love produces nothing, but the love Jesus has given to us sets into motion all His purposes, redemptive and restorative (Romans 2:4; 11:22; Titus 3:4).

In chapter 1 we learned that the resurrection was the exceeding greatness of God's power, the ultimate display of His omnipotence. When He raised the church from the deadness of their sins to share in the exaltation of Jesus Christ throughout the ages, it was through the exceeding riches of His grace, the ultimate display of His love. Every privilege Christ's redemption purchased has been given to us with this purpose in mind: that in every succeeding age all the universe would know that God's ultimate motive is grace.

Verse 8 expounds the parenthesis of verse 5. God has designated the vehicle of faith to appropriate His grace. The death of Jesus at Calvary secures salvation (eternal life) for all who believe in Him. God has given everyone a measure of faith (Romans 12:3), but each person must deposit that faith in Christ to receive the benefits of God's grace. Once faith is put in Christ, Jesus releases His grace, and His grace releases the resurrection power that changes the life of the believer (Titus 3:5).

Grace refers to God's freely bestowed blessings, His favor toward undeserving humans, His divine workings in us. Grace secures salvation, including the entire process from forgiveness of sins to the infilling of the Spirit and the catching away of the saints. The entire process of salvation is rightfully named the gift of God, and in particular, the baptism of the Holy Ghost is called the gift of God (John 4:10; 7:38-39; Acts 2:38; Romans 5:15; 6:23). Simon Peter referred to the Samaritans receiving the Holy Ghost as "the gift of God" when he rebuked Simon the sorcerer's desire to purchase it with money (Acts 8:20). The gift of God is freely given to those who place their faith in Jesus Christ. Every believer can claim all the spiritual blessings stated in chapter 1 because of grace (Romans 3:22-26; Galatians 2:16; I Peter 1:5).

Salvation is an accomplishment of the sovereign will of God's grace and purpose: "Who hath saved us, and called us with an holy calling, not according to our works, but according to his own purpose and grace, which was given us in Christ Jesus before the world began" (II Timothy 1:9). Every ounce of faith we possess can be attributed to God's graciousness (Romans 12:3); everyone who repents owes the gift of repentance to God's kindness

(Acts 5:31; II Timothy 2:25). Salvation comes, not by what we can do, but by what we let God do in us, "for it is God which worketh in you both to will and to do of his good pleasure" (Philippians 2:13).

Our part in receiving salvation is to deposit faith in Jesus Christ (John 1:12). "This faith is defined best as turning to God with a sense of need and weakness and emptiness and a willingness to receive what He offers, to receive the Lord Himself."[8] "Let a man be abandoned by God, and he is absolutely hopeless. It is the voice of God that arouses, that awakens, that causes a man to think and enquire; it is the power of God that gives strength to act; it is the same power which makes provision for the need of the new life."[9] We can claim no part in salvation except to yield to God and let Him work His good pleasure in us.

Verse 9 explains further that God has eliminated human works as a means of salvation so He could eliminate human pride. Pride was the cause of Lucifer's fall in the beginning. The pride of life is still a deadly sin that corrupts all it touches (Proverbs 8:13; 11:2; 13:10; 16:18; I John 2:16). Since salvation does not come by our works, we must give all glory to God (Romans 3:20, 27-28; 11:6). We are to glory only in the cross of Jesus Christ (Galatians 6:14; I Corinthians 1:29-31; Philippians 3:3).

God will not allow anyone to boast. The language here may imply that part of God's purpose in bringing salvation as He did was to exclude human pride. Our salvation was accomplished by God, offered as a gift, bestowed by grace, and received by faith. Therefore, our only true glory is the kindness of Jesus Christ.

Verse 10. Our new condition received by union with

Christ through faith was created by God's own sovereign act of kindness and power. Regardless of yesterday's mistakes and the past condition of the sinner, the grace of Jesus Christ has caused a new condition to replace the old. Verse 10 describes this new creation as God's "workmanship," which comes from the Greek word *poiema*, meaning "the act of creating, work of art, or masterpiece." From this word we get the English word *poem.* Human redemption is God's poetry, a work of art that God has penned for all the universe to read and rejoice in, for every principality and power to witness His masterpiece of grace and power.

Salvation produces a new creation that overcomes sin, that is "holy and without blame" (Ephesians 1:4), a new person created in the likeness of Jesus Christ (II Corinthians 5:17). We acquire the likeness of Christ through the process called sanctification, and God has promised to oversee this work until it is finished (II Corinthians 3:18; Ephesians 4:24; Hebrews 12:1-2). The past only emphasizes that the resurrection power of Jesus Christ has worked a new condition in the life of the believer. What he was before is no longer relevant (Galatians 6:15). He maintains his new condition by a constant refreshing and renewing, which comes through hearing the Word of God and submitting to the work of the Holy Spirit (Ephesians 5:26; I Thessalonians 2:13; II Thessalonians 2:13). God equips us to live the new life that grace created. Sin marred the first creation of God, but grace restored what was lost, and now we are a new creation "in Christ."

In Ephesians 2:6–10 the Greek phrase for "in Christ" occurs three times, linking this passage with John 15. There Jesus emphatically stated that we cannot have life apart from complete union with Himself (John 15:1-5).

Salvation is God's work alone and not ours, but God's new creation demands good works. Good works are not the cause of salvation, but they are definitely the result. The preposition "unto" comes from the Greek word *epi*, which makes good works an inseparable part of the work of redemption. Redemption's objective is to change us into the image of Jesus Christ (Romans 8:29; II Corinthians 3:18).

God prepared and designed His redemptive work so that it would cause us to do good works. It is no accident that once a person is redeemed, he experiences a complete change in his way of life. Jesus taught, "Let your light so shine before men, that they may see your good works, and glorify your Father, which is in heaven" (Matthew 5:16). We are to "abound to every good work" (II Corinthians 9:8) and to be "fruitful in every good work" (Colossians 1:10). These "good works" are the crowning result of God's salvation in our lives.

God's work of redemption is a finished work, but His purpose also includes the unfinished task of restoring to humanity dignity and dominion (Ephesians 4:7-16). God has promised to work in us what is well pleasing in His sight (Hebrews 13:20–21). Experiencing resurrection power is a prelude to total restoration of all things.

Notes

[1]Bruce, 49.
[2]Moule, 71.
[3]Paxon, 55.
[4]Wiersbe, 44.
[5]Bruce, 50.
[6]Paxon, 55.
[7]Bruce, 50.
[8]Foulkes, 75.
[9]C. Brown, *St. Paul's Epistle to the Ephesians: A Devotional Commentary* (1911), 48, as quoted in Foulkes, 75-76.

D.

The Bride's New Privileges

(2:11-22)

1. The Gentiles' Old Position (2:11-12)

(11) Wherefore remember, that ye being in time past Gentiles in the flesh, who are called Uncircumcision by that which is called the Circumcision in the flesh made by hands; (12) that at that time ye were without Christ, being aliens from the commonwealth of Israel, and strangers from the covenants of promise, having no hope, and without God in the world.

Verse 11. Paul asked the Gentiles to remember their former position before conversion, not to bring them into condemnation but rather to cause a spirit of thanksgiving for their new position through Jesus Christ. Remembering what we were before Christ came into our lives is one way of helping us to see the power and importance of redemption.

The national heritage of the Gentiles hindered their entrance into the covenant promises of Israel, but their new-found faith in Christ removed those hindrances to allow for a better circumcision—one of the heart. Redemption made possible their individual salvation, but it also united the opposing factions of Jews and Gentiles into one body that would live to the praise of God's glory.

The Gentiles were also hindered from participating in the Jews' salvation because of the way the Jews viewed them. They were called the "Uncircumcision." The Jewish people could not perceive God's true purpose. They could not picture themselves being used by God to bring about the salvation of the Gentiles, whom they considered as "dogs" because they did not have the external sign of the Abrahamic covenant (circumcision). Their viewpoint became so radical that typically they would not even go inside the house of a Gentile, lest they be defiled (Acts 10:28). They could not bless a Gentile or lend help to him. This philosophy was not God's original intention for Israel. The Abrahamic covenant clearly outlined the principle of evangelism, stating, "In thee shall all families of the earth be blessed" (Genesis 12:3).

In the beginning, everyone believed in one God. Due to the sins of their imagination people began to drift away from that belief into polytheism. God, seeing this tendency, called Abraham out of the nations to make of him a nation that would be God's showpiece to the whole world. He wanted to use Israel to save the world, but their self-centered attitude impeded this work.

God made a covenant with Abraham and chose circumcision as the seal of this covenant (Genesis 17:10-14). But it was a fleshly covenant. Many Israelites became proud of this sign even though it was not enough to cleanse their hearts. They became intoxicated on their own uniqueness and developed an attitude of disdain for everyone who was not born a Jew. Even though they corrupted God's purpose through complacent arrogance, the purpose remained the same. God wanted the world to have a witness that there is only one God, and His witness was the nation of Israel (Isaiah 42:5-6; 49:6).

Since the external sign of circumcision could not change the heart of Israel, God intended to replace it with a more proficient method of dealing with the wicked human heart (I Corinthians 7:19; Galatians 5:6; 6:15). The circumcision made without hands on the heart through water baptism and the baptism of the Holy Spirit is the seal of the new covenant. This seal signifies God's ultimate purpose of redemption: unifying all races and nations into one church (Romans 2:25-29; Colossians 2:11-12; I Corinthians 12:13.)

Verse 12. As a nation Israel never allowed God to use her to bring to pass His ultimate intention. "At that time," the Gentiles who should have been enlightened by the salvation of the Jews were without Christ. They did not even possess the hope of a Messiah, for Israel withheld all the promises from the Gentiles that a Messiah would come with great redemption.

Because they lacked hope, the Gentiles viewed life as cyclic, feeling that everything that has been will be again. They had no ultimate goal to reach.

Hopelessness stems from being "without God in the world." The Gentiles had to face life, in all of its cruelty, alone, with no one to turn to, no one to pray to, and nowhere to find rest. They were "aliens from the commonwealth of Israel." The word "commonwealth" here means "citizenship." All conquered peoples greatly coveted Roman citizenship because of the liberties and freedoms it granted. The Gentiles, being aliens from the spiritual citizenship, had no sense of belonging to anything important or eternal. What hopelessness—never belonging, never a part, and never included!

This horrible condition is best described by saying that the Gentiles were "strangers from the covenants of promise." The word "covenants" is plural, for on many occasions God renewed and expanded His covenant with Israel. It started with Abraham and was renewed with Isaac and Jacob (Exodus 2:24; Leviticus 26:42; Psalm 105:10). God extended His covenants with Israel and enlarged them to include His ever-progressive purpose. God's purpose is never stagnant but always progresses toward an ultimate end that promises greater things. The Gentiles did not have the privilege of belonging to God's covenant. They were "aliens" and "strangers." They had no concept or part in the theocratic government that ruled Israel; therefore their position was hopeless. Then came Jesus!

2. The Gentiles' New Privileges (2:13-22)

(13) But now in Christ Jesus ye who sometimes were far off are made nigh by the blood of Christ. (14) For he is our peace, who hath made both one, and hath broken down the middle wall of partition between us; (15) having abolished in his flesh the enmity, even the law of commandments contained in ordinances; for to make in himself of twain one new man, so making peace; (16) and that he might reconcile both unto God in one body by the cross, having slain the enmity thereby: (17) and came and preached peace to you which were afar off, and to them that were nigh. (18) For through him we both have access by one Spirit unto the Father. (19) Now therefore ye are no more strangers and foreigners, but fellowcitizens with the saints, and of the household of God; (20) and are built upon the foundation of the apostles and prophets, Jesus Christ himself being the chief corner stone; (21) in whom

all the building fitly framed together groweth unto an holy temple in the Lord: (22) in whom ye also are builded together for an habitation of God through the Spirit.

a. The Blood Makes Peace

Verse 13. They who were "without Christ," empty and hopeless, have now been "made nigh" through the "blood of Christ." "Now" is used to contrast the former condition and the present privileges. The redemption of Jesus Christ possesses power to break any barrier, even if those barriers have existed for centuries. But only "in Christ Jesus" can this be accomplished; nothing else will work. The blood's power to make nigh those who were afar off can only work if the believer is "in Christ."

Sin created a great gulf between man and God, but the blood of Christ has bridged this gap. Not only were the Gentiles separated from God but also from the covenant privileges that the Jewish people, the covenant people, enjoyed.

The rabbis considered the Gentiles to be "far off" because they were denied access to the redemption provided by the sacrifices. Yet they could be made nigh by becoming proselytes. They then received limited privileges. But "now," through the blood of Jesus Christ, all the privileges are available and a better means of being "made nigh" has been established. Becoming a proselyte to Judaism was good enough for limited access, but being washed in the blood of the Lamb gives unlimited access to God's person and presence (John 3:16; 12:32; II Corinthians 5:19; I John 2:2).

Jesus Christ is the mediator—the go-between—the "daysman" (Job 9:33), who purchased by His death the

Gentiles' access to all the privileges. He offered His sinless life as a ransom for those who were afar off (Isaiah 53:11-12; 57:19). He has destroyed the barrier that separated the Gentiles not only from God but also from the Jewish people. Redemption creates harmonious fellowship between God and man and between warring factions of humanity.

Verse 14. Many of the covenant people of God had developed an innate dislike over the years for what they called "Gentile dogs." The Mosaic law itself made a clear distinction between Jew and Gentile. A wall of partition was created that could not be broken down without supernatural help.

Jesus became that help. He became "our peace." Jesus has become the focal point of love in which both opposing factions find common ground for fellowship. In Him all the nations of the world are made into one body, one functional organism that lives to bring glory to Jesus (John 17:11; I Corinthians 10:17; 12:13). The Jewish people could no longer use their law as a wall to keep out the Gentiles. The Gentiles could no longer use their dislike of the Jews as an excuse not to have fellowship with them. God dissolved the national barriers in order to create a new thing, the church of the living God. Peace can be achieved inwardly, but experiential peace must be revealed relationally with all mankind (Galatians 3:28; Colossians 3:11).

The "middle wall of partition" could refer to the wall that separated the court of the Gentiles from the court of the women in the temple Herod built.[1] No Gentile was allowed past that wall; the penalty for violation was death. Paul was falsely accused of bringing a Gentile past this barrier and was placed in prison (Acts 21:28-34).

Human arrogance has built barriers to keep out others. The sectarian spirit of our age has fostered hostility that has thrust our world into conflict on many occasions. The Jews were not exempt from this human trait. The arrogance and hatred for others that some of them displayed kept people from experiencing the blessing of redemption (Matthew 23:13-15). They should have allowed their privileges to be a light to the Gentiles, but instead they became a barrier. Jesus, through the shedding of His blood on the cross, removed those barriers; therefore, He became "our peace."

Verse 15. Paul described this "wall of partition" as the enmity or hatred that existed between Jews and Gentiles. This enmity was created because of the "law of commandments contained in ordinances." Jews allowed their law to affect their attitude toward Gentiles. This same attitude existed in Gentiles toward outsiders. Therefore, they needed a common ground in order to make peace. Jesus Christ is that place of reconciliation. Both parties were guilty of sin, and both had to be cleansed by the blood of Jesus.

Before this enmity could be dealt with, the ordinances that were the cause of it had to be removed. The ceremonies and regulations could never bring about a change of heart, which was required to remove the enmity. The law of Moses was good, but it did not have the power needed. Moreover, it became misused by many Jews who tried to make it the basis of salvation and who added to it manmade traditions.

Consider the Pharisees who added to the Mosaic law their personal traditions and made it virtually impossible for anyone except their elite group to be saved. Only one thing could remove this barrier, and that was the death of Jesus Christ. Through His death He abolished the ordinances that were against us (Colossians 2:14, 20).

"In his flesh" does not refer just to the earthly ministry of Jesus through miracles, healings, and teachings. It refers more to the vicarious work of redemption accomplished by His death, burial, resurrection, and ascension (I Corinthians 15:1-8). He provided "in his flesh" a body to be offered as a sin sacrifice, thereby removing the enmity by forgiving the sins of all who repent and believe (Colossians 1:20–22).

The law of Moses was a schoolmaster to bring people to Jesus Christ (Galatians 3:24-25). It was a shadow and type of things to come, pointing to Christ, who would give everyone the right to hear the gospel (Acts 10). Jesus fulfilled the law by the sacrifice of Himself and replaced it with something better, also Himself (Matthew 5:17).

Though the ceremonial law was abolished (Colossians 2:16–17), the moral law was strengthened (Matthew 5:21-48). Because His death abolished the ceremonial law, Jesus made peace between the opposing factions by removing the cause (enmity caused by the law) and made "one new man."

The word "make" means "to create." The word "new" comes from the Greek word *kainos,* which means "a new thing."[2] God has promised a new privilege for the believer—a new thing, not a revised world with its old systems remodeled, but a new world with a new man. This new man is the new citizenry of believers, a corporate body made up of people from every race, creed, color, and nationality joined together in Christ.

Each individual receives the privilege of becoming a new man with divine forgiveness and peace, but he also receives the privilege of being incorporated into the church (Ephesians 4:13). Jesus has promised that a new man will be created in the individual and then incorporated into a body that will function as the church, a new citizenry of believers.

b. Reconciliation by the Cross

Verse 16. Through His death, Jesus provided reconciliation for both Jews and Gentiles. The Gentiles were not in need of the Cross any more than the Jews were. "For all have sinned, and come short of the glory of God" (Romans 3:23). Both needed the Cross. The Cross provides for the individual believer complete forgiveness of his sins and acceptance into the new body. When the Jews and Gentiles are reconciled to God, they will be reconciled to one another.

The reason the reconciliation of God is so powerful is because the Cross was not merely an expression of God's sympathy for man's plight; it is a true sacrifice that met the demands of God's holiness on behalf of a sinful world. The Cross was "an altar work" that "executed the enmity"[3] (Romans 5:10; II Corinthians 5:18-20).

Sin created the enmity between God and man. The Cross executed sin and put to death the enmity once and for all so that now man is reconciled to God. But God's redemption does not stop there. He continues His reconciliation until man is reconciled to man. Reconciliation (Greek: *apokatallassein*) means to bring estranged friends back together. It is God's purpose that the church become a glorious model of oneness among the people of the earth by making friends out of enemies. What peace treaties and peace conferences cannot accomplish, the blood of Jesus Christ can (I Corinthians 10:17; Colossians 3:15).

Jesus Christ mediated peace at the Cross, removing the barriers and walls, reconciling both Jew and Gentile to God and then to one another. He created a new thing—the church—and is both foundation and head, author and finisher of our faith.

Verse 17. Jesus came in the flesh with a mission of peace. Through His death He made peace, which gives every preacher the authority to declare that peace. We can now preach peace to Gentiles and Jews alike, and both are in desperate need of it.

Jesus came to declare that we can attain peace with God through His sacrifice (Luke 2:14; 4:18-19; Acts 10:36). He first came to the covenant people, Israel (those who were nigh), and then to the Gentiles (those who were afar off). This verse quotes from Isaiah 57:19: "Peace, peace to him that is far off, and to him that is near, saith the LORD; and I will heal him."

In Acts 2:39 Peter similarly referred to those who were "afar off," declaring that repentance, water baptism in Jesus' name, and the infilling of the Holy Ghost was the message of peace to all, giving universal scope to the gospel call. Because we have experienced this peace and realize this truth, we are now commissioned to go forth as ambassadors of peace and preach "the gospel of peace" to those who do not have it (Romans 10:15).

c. Access to God

Verse 18. Only through Jesus Christ can Jews and Gentiles gain access to the presence of the Father. Access is one of the most precious privileges. It cannot be denied, even to the Gentiles. Because of the vicarious work of the Cross both Jews and Gentiles have equal footing before the Father.

The word "access" comes from the Greek word *prosagoge*. The word evokes many descriptive pictures of this wonderful privilege. We can see someone bringing a sacrifice to God, ushering another person into the presence of God, introducing an ambassador into a national assembly, or introducing a speaker to an audience. But the most accurate word picture for the meaning of the text is the duty given to a *prosagogeus* of the Persian court, which was to introduce people who sought an audience with the king.[4]

Jesus has given us access to the Father by introducing us not just to the presence of God but to a state of grace where we have perpetual favor with God. In Romans 5:2 our access is "into the grace wherein we stand," and Ephesians 3:12 uses the word "access" also. We have found favor with God and now have access to Him to make our petitions known. Peace provides access, and access provides power in prayer.

Before Christ, a Gentile had a limited access to God, primarily by becoming a Jewish proselyte. Now, however, both Jews and Gentiles have much greater access to God's presence and power through the Spirit of God. Calvary purchased the right for all to be filled with the Holy Spirit, and the Holy Spirit makes all the privileges available. The Jews needed the Holy Ghost and so did the Gentiles (Acts 1:8). Jesus declared Himself to be the "door" and "the way" (John 10:7; 14:6). Because He opened the way as our forerunner (Hebrews 6:20), we now have the privilege to receive His Spirit, the Holy Ghost, giving us access to the Father.

One of the greatest privileges the Holy Ghost has bestowed upon Jew and Gentile alike is the right to call God our Father (Romans 8:15; Galatians 4:6). The Jews were somewhat familiar with this term because of the Old Testament references to God as the father of Israel (Psalm 103:13; Isaiah 9:6; 63:16). The Gentiles were unfamiliar with this term in reference to God because their gods were harsh and vengeful. They did not relate to these gods as a father. When Jesus declared God to be our personal Father, He revealed God as benevolent and approachable, one who would not turn away from the cries of those in need of His mercy.

d. Fellow Citizens of the Same House

Verse 19. Now that the Gentiles have peace with God and access to God as their Father, they are no longer "strangers" (Greek: *xenoi*) and "foreigners" (Greek: *paroikoi*). Strangers and foreigners are people who live in the same country with native-born citizens but do not share in the privileges and rights of citizenship. All that has changed for the Gentiles, to whom Paul was referring when he said "ye." Now they are "fellowcitizens" (Greek: *sympolitai*), which means "a native of the same city or town." Through the apostolic, new-birth experience, the Gentiles became native-born citizens.

The entire work of Calvary, which provides possessions and privileges for those who believe, serves to build the divine institution of the church. God's ultimate goal is to produce a spiritual family of sons, and He uses the church as His means to accomplish His goal (Galatians 4:26).

Paul described the church first as a city with a citizenry that is comprised of people from all nationalities. Their natural heritage is no longer a barrier, thanks to Calvary. All have received a new name because they have been born again and are first-class citizens of the city of God with all the rights and privileges of native-born citizens. (See Psalm 87:5–6; John 3:3–7; Revelation 3:12.) The Gentiles, because they belong to this new kingdom, now possess the "blessing of Abraham" through the Spirit (Galatians 3:14).

The church is also a family or "household" (Greek: *oikeioi*). The corporate church is the "household of faith," and individual members are the "children of God" (Galatians 3:26; 6:10). The house of God is made up of both Jews and Gentiles, all of whom were in need of being born again and receiving the "adoption of children" (Ephesians 1:5).

Verse 20. Paul finally described the church as a building. God built it as His masterpiece (Psalm 127:1; Ephesians 2:10); however, He used people to help Him lay the foundation, namely the apostles and prophets.

The apostles' names are on the foundation stones of the New Jerusalem. (Revelation 21:14). While the foundation of the church is Jesus Christ (I Corinthians 3:11), the apostles and prophets of the New Testament were "eyewitnesses of His majesty" (II Peter 1:16). They saw the works of Jesus from the beginning (Acts 1:21-26), and they had a personal revelation of Jesus Christ that others did not have (Matthew 16:16-18). God used them to help establish and confirm the saints of the first century, and their writings in the New Testament are the only authoritative revelation of Jesus Christ that we have.

The apostles and prophets laid the foundation. Their doctrine and revelation of Jesus are the foundation upon which the church is built. Any deviation from their doctrine is error. The foundation they laid was none other than Jesus Christ.

The prophets spoken of here are not the Old Testament prophets, but New Testament prophets that God used to help give direction to the church in times of need (Acts 11:27-28; 13:1; 15:32; Ephesians 3:5). Along with the apostles, they helped to confirm the saints and served as master builders (I Corinthians 3:10).

Though Jesus Christ Himself is the foundation, not just any teaching about Him will work. Some believe the wrong thing about Jesus (Matthew 16:13-14). What we know and say about Jesus is important (Matthew 16:15-18). The only place we can go to find the true revelation of Jesus Christ is the Word of God. The apostles and prophets (which probably include the writers of the New Testament who were not a part of the original twelve apostles) wrote the report of Jesus' ministry and revealed the significance of that ministry. Their revelation about Jesus is the only true revelation and the only foundation for our faith. For this reason Paul spoke of the church as being built on them, with Jesus being the chief cornerstone.

"The corner-stone is cut out beforehand, and not only bonds the structure together when at last it is dropped into place, but serves as a 'stone of testing' to show whether the building has been carried out to the architect's specifications."[5] The chief cornerstone ties the whole building together, making it truly complete. Each stone is dependent on the one stone to make a complete building.

Jesus holds this distinct position of honor in the building. Each saint who is built upon the foundation of the true revelation of Christ finds his place of usefulness in God's purpose in direct relationship to Jesus Christ (Colossians 2:7). Jesus identified Himself as the stone the builders rejected but which has now become the chief cornerstone (Mark 12:10). In doing so He referred to Old Testament prophecies (Psalm 118:22; Isaiah 28:16).

Peter likewise referred to this prophecy in preaching that salvation only comes in the name of Jesus (Acts 4:11-12). He later taught that our salvation is directly connected to our making Christ the chief cornerstone (I Peter 2:6-7). When we allow Jesus to be the foundation and rock of testing, to ensure the exactness of our fitting into the building, then and only then can we be a part of God's building. The fact that Jesus is the chief cornerstone should make Him precious to us. The more precious He is to us, the more vital a union we achieve in Him.

Verse 21. Only as a person finds His place in the church will he ever grow into a "holy temple in the Lord." Without a relationship with Jesus Christ as Lord he will never realize the fullness of his potential.

"All the building" (Greek: *oikodome*) can refer either to individual buildings or individual parts and phases of the whole building process. Paul either referred to individual churches or to the whole superstructure of the universal church. The context indicates the latter reference, speaking of the one church under development through various phases. However, this does not exclude application to the local church, nor the individual saint. The building process has to start with the individual and then progress to the local church and into the universal church.

By His own wisdom God designed the church to progress through a building process that is not complete in one phase but develops over several phases of maturity. We are God's building (I Corinthians 3:9), and He will see that what He has started gets finished (Hebrews 12:2).

God has chosen various means to help complete the process. One such means is the ministry of edification. The word *oikodome* is translated as "edifying" in Ephesians 4:12, 16, 29. By the saints' ministry of building up one another, the building comes closer to completion, though it will not be complete until Jesus returns to set up His kingdom. The church is still progressing toward His ultimate purpose, both in numbers and in maturity.

The individual matures as well as the church. Without the individual maturity of the living stones that make up the building, the church would never progress. God matures the individual by his relationship with other saints and with Jesus Christ (Ephesians 4:15; I Peter 2:5).

The term "groweth" actually refers to organic growth, bringing the metaphor into a higher realm of meaning. This building is more than a concrete entity; it is a living organism. Saints are living stones (I Peter 2:5) and members of a living body (I Corinthians 12:12, 27). The church is a living, vibrant entity that ever grows into the fullness of what Christ wants us to be.

Before this growth can be complete, individual believers must allow themselves to be "fitly framed together" (Greek: *synarmologeo*), which means to "make a living union of various parts." Ephesians 4:16 uses the same word in reference to the church as a body. The church is growing constantly in size and in maturity, spiritually and numerically. Individuals achieve growth as they draw closer to God and to other saints. Only as individual saints find their proper gifts in the church and begin to function in those gifts will the church be able to grow. Adding to the church sons and daughters who are born again of water and Spirit is still the prime directive of those who are fitted in God's building.

We must develop a twofold relationship. We must first build a relationship with Jesus Christ and be established "in the Lord," and then we must build a relationship with other saints. With this union, the church becomes a glorious temple for God to inhabit. The word "temple" (Greek: *naos*) means "inner chamber" or "the place where God meets His people in the spirit." As a man, Jesus provided a physical tabernacle for God to dwell in (John 1:14; 2:19-21). Now the church is the earthly tabernacle through which God reveals Himself to others.

This occurs as believers are one "in the Lord." There is no life or growth outside of Jesus Christ, "for without me ye can do nothing" (John 15:5). We experience true life as we find our proper place in His building and in relationship to Him, sharing with other saints, without division, the glorious fellowship of the Spirit. (See Philippians 2:1-3.)

Verse 22. "Ye also are builded together" describes the union between Jews and Gentiles. "Ye" refers to the Gentiles who have been grafted into the tree of Israel (Romans 11:17-24). They are joined together with the Jews and now share in the same privileges and access to God's presence, creating as it were a new habitation totally different from the former. This union between opposing factions creates a holy "habitation of God through the Spirit." Together they become God's habitation, a place for

157

God to manifest Himself to the world.

God does reveal Himself through individuals, but He also manifests His presence in a very special way in the joining together of the body of believers (I Corinthians 3:16; II Corinthians 6:16). God's presence is a sanctuary where people find not only peace but joy and "pleasures for evermore" (Psalm 16:11). Wherever a sacrifice is offered and accepted by God, it becomes a place where He puts His name, His blessings, and His promises (Exodus 20:24). Jesus has offered the supreme sacrifice, and through it He has created a new temple where Jews and Gentiles can enjoy the same identity.

They can do so only "through the Spirit." No one can call Jesus Lord except by the Holy Spirit (I Corinthians 12:3).

Jews and Gentiles together form the habitation, but the structure will not be complete until Jesus returns to catch away His bride. Then all will be joined together as one. There will be no Jew or Gentile, bond or free, but all will be perfectly one in Christ "for an habitation of God through the Spirit."

Notes

[1]Barclay, 112.
[2]Ibid., 116.
[3]Moule, 81.
[4]Barclay, 117.
[5]Bruce, 57.

E.

The Bride's Revelation of the Mystery
(3:1-13)

In Ephesians 1 Paul identified the bride's possessions as the riches of God's mercy. In chapter 2 he explained that the possessions belong to Jews and Gentiles alike. As a result of the peace of the Cross, they were reconciled to God and to one another, forming a habitation through which God could manifest His mercy in ages to come. These truths, stated so clearly in the first two chapters of Ephesians, are the true cause Paul was in the ministry. He considered it his personal responsibility to convey these riches to the Gentiles.

1. Paul, a Prisoner (3:1)

(1) For this cause I Paul, the prisoner of Jesus Christ for you Gentiles.

Verse 1. "For this cause" introduces a prayer that Paul did not actually begin until verse 14. To possess the riches of God's mercy requires prayer. But before Paul could pray, he had to explain the revelation and describe his personal responsibility to declare it. Verses 2-13 are parenthetical verses inserted to give more light on the revelation of the grace of God and Paul's responsibility to carry that grace to the Gentiles.

"I Paul" is an expression of self-realization as the purpose of his ministry weighed heavily upon him. (See II Corinthians 10:1; Galatians 5:2; Colossians 1:23.) He felt the weight of his calling and took it very seriously (I Corinthians 9:16). Paul's apostleship to the Gentiles was a burden of serious responsibility, with serious consequences. He was imprisoned due to the hatred of Jews for his message of Christ and of equality to the Gentiles (Acts 21:17-34; 22:21-24; 26:12-23).

Paul's imprisonment was not a source of bitterness or resentment. He called himself the "prisoner of Jesus Christ." (See Ephesians 4:1; II Timothy 1:8; Philemon 1, 9.) Neither Jewish hatred nor Gentile imprisonment could stop his apostolic ministry, because he viewed his imprisonment as an advantage in furthering the gospel rather than a hindrance (Ephesians 2:13; Philippians 1:14).

Paul took his mission very seriously and accepted the consequences of imprisonment as the will of God for his life. He could do so because his motive was true. He did it "for you Gentiles." His imprisonment was the direct result of his love for the Gentiles and his passion to see them experience the riches of God's grace. The cause outweighed the consequences because he was held captive by the magnificent obsession of ministering the gospel of Jesus Christ.

2. The Mystery Made Known to Paul (3:2-5)

(2) If ye have heard of the dispensation of the grace of God which is given me to you-ward: (3) how that by revelation he made known unto me the mystery; (as I wrote afore in few words, (4) whereby, when ye read, ye may understand my knowledge in the mystery of Christ) (5) which

in other ages was not made known unto the sons of men, as it is now revealed unto his holy apostles and prophets by the Spirit.

Verse 2. The words "if ye have heard" (Greek: *eige*) have been the cause of controversy. How could the Ephesians, having known Paul and his ministry as well as they did, have only heard about the gospel that he preached? The answer is that this "does not necessarily imply that they might not have heard; it is quite probably a rhetorical way of reminding them of what they knew already."[1]

Paul wanted them to remember that God had given him his mission and ministry as a "dispensation" (Greek: *oikonomia*), meaning "stewardship" or "house management." (See also I Corinthians 4:1-2; 9:17; Colossians 1:25; I Peter 4:10.) God's grace transformed Paul from a persecutor of the church into a messenger of the very revelation he had persecuted. Because of his relationship with Jesus Christ, God had imparted a revelation to him, and it was his responsibility to dispense this revelation to the Gentiles. God gives the grace but expects people to manage the communication of that grace.

Paul considered the salvation and calling he experienced on the road to Damascus and in the city (Acts 9) to be the grace given to him. God's revealing light brought him into fellowship with Jesus Christ and the saints and gave him an apostleship to carry the same grace to the Gentiles (Romans 15:15-16; I Corinthians 3:10; Galatians 2:9). His message was that the Gentiles have the same privileges and possessions in Christ as the Jews and those privileges are by God's grace (Acts 13:43; 14:26; II Corinthians 9:8). Jesus commissioned him "to open their eyes, and to turn them from darkness to light, and from the power of Satan unto God, that they may receive for-giveness of sins, and inheritance among them which are sanctified by faith that is in me" (Acts 26:18). To Paul, there was no higher calling or privilege.

The dispensation of grace given to Paul was given "to you-ward." It was given to him so he could give it to the Gentiles. Paul's apostleship was a gift to the Gentile world. Without his voice declaring the grace of God, many would never have had the opportunity to know Jesus Christ in His saving power. Because of that, Paul did not mind being a prisoner of Christ and giving his whole life to preach the gospel to every creature.

Verse 3. Paul received the message of grace by a special revelation from God and not by the human instrument of teaching. The apostles who were with Jesus during His earthly ministry were not the agents God used to convey this revelation, although they confirmed it. Paul's first encounter with Jesus was on the road to Damascus, but he received many other revelations while in Arabia after his conversion (Galatians 1:11-12; 16-17; II Corinthians 12:1, 7).

The revelation of the mystery unfolded in several phases throughout Paul's writings. He placed emphasis on different aspects of the redemptive process, revealing that all make up the mystery of Christ. A "mystery" is a sacred knowledge withheld from unbelievers but known to believers. It was hidden in times past but now is made manifest. The means God used to reveal these truths to Paul are described best in Acts 9 and Galatians 1-2, but the content of the revelation is the focus in this verse.

"As I wrote afore in few words" is Paul's way of

pointing out the significance of the previous verses in which he described so beautifully the "exceeding riches of his grace." He then proceeded to enlarge upon their significance in this chapter.

Verse 4. Paul told the Ephesians that after they had read what he had written they would understand the knowledge he possessed of the mystery of Christ. He did not say this to boast of his intellect, but he did want the Ephesians to recognize the revelation's divine authority, as a result of the gift of God. When they understood the mystery's divine origin, they could readily accept its authority.

The mystery as defined in Ephesians has a different emphasis than in Colossians. In Colossians the focus is "Christ in you, the hope of glory" (Colossians 1:27). This hope is what Christians have to look forward to, because of the indwelling Christ. On the other hand, in Ephesians the "mystery of Christ" is the Gentiles being "made partakers of his promise in Christ by the gospel" (Ephesians 3:6). The inclusion of the Gentiles in the redemptive purpose of God is a mystery that was kept from the foundation of the world but is now manifested through Paul's revelation. There is no contradiction between Colossians and Ephesians, but rather a perfect harmony when we understand that each revelation is a building block to make up the complete message of salvation. In Colossians, Christ Himself is the focus, while in Ephesians the redemptive work He accomplished is the highlight. Christ and His work can hardly be separated; they are one and the same.

Verse 5. The fullness of the truth of the New Testament church (one new body made up of Jews and Gentiles on equal ground) was not revealed to the Old Testament prophets (Romans 16:25; Colossians 1:26). In previous ages, the "sons of men" or "generations of men," meaning the people of the Gentile world, had no clue as to the coming of Christ and His mission. (See also Ephesians 2:12.) Even the Old Testament prophets possessed only a shadow of that truth (Isaiah 49:6). Paul quoted from the three ancient divisions of the Old Testament (Law, Prophets, and Writings) in Romans 15:9-12 to prove that his revelation was not a new idea but was foreshadowed in the prophetic writings of the Old Testament.

The fullness of the truth about the church did not come until the Spirit revealed it to the holy apostles and prophets of the New Testament. The word "now" shows that Paul referred to the New Testament apostles and prophets who gave us the New Testament canon (Ephesians 2:20). His use of the word "holy" to describe their position does not give them any cause for exaltation. As in Ephesians 1:4, the word "holy" is *hagios,* which simply means they were hand-picked, set apart, and consecrated by God to do specific work. Any person consecrated by God for a specific work is considered holy, and that includes all believers.

It is important to realize that this revelation did not come because of some special holiness in the apostles or prophets, but it came "by the Spirit." Ephesians 2:18, 22 states that the Spirit gives access to the Father. By His Spirit God inhabits His holy temple, created through the joining together of believers in Christ. Access, habitation, and revelation are all works of the Holy Ghost. Without the Spirit's enlightenment, there could never be a heavenly vision or revelation of God's truth in its fullness

(Revelation 1:10). Intellectual knowledge alone does not produce salvation. "Easy believism" does not provide the possessions or the privileges of God's grace. We must be baptized with the Holy Ghost as the apostles themselves were on the Day of Pentecost (Acts 2:1-4).

3. The Fellowship of the Mystery (3:6-13)

(6) That the Gentiles should be fellowheirs, and of the same body, and partakers of his promise in Christ by the gospel: (7) whereof I was made a minister, according to the gift of the grace of God given unto me by the effectual working of his power. (8) Unto me, who am less than the least of all saints, is this grace given, that I should preach among the Gentiles the unsearchable riches of Christ; (9) and to make all men see what is the fellowship of the mystery, which from the beginning of the world hath been hid in God, who created all things by Jesus Christ: (10) to the intent that now unto the principalities and powers in heavenly places might be known by the church the manifold wisdom of God, (11) according to the eternal purpose which he purposed in Christ Jesus our Lord: (12) in whom we have boldness and access with confidence by the faith of him. (13) Wherefore I desire that ye faint not at my tribulations for you, which is your glory.

a. The Gentiles As Fellow Heirs and Partakers

Verse 6 explains the full revelation of the mystery received by the apostles and prophets. The truth that Paul sought to proclaim to the whole world is the inclusion of the Gentiles into the body of Christ—joining them together with the Jews and giving them access to God as Father with equal rights. The Gentiles, as discussed earlier in

Ephesians 2:12, were "without Christ," "without God in the world," "strangers," and "aliens," but now, through Christ, they are "fellowheirs" (Greek: *sunkleronomos*). Though they did not have a right to the inheritance of faith by natural birth, they have received the right through a spiritual birth. Union with Christ entitles everyone to the blessings of the Abrahamic covenant (Galatians 3:29). The law of the natural birth no longer applies, but the "law of the Spirit of life in Christ Jesus" (Romans 8:2). This law makes the Gentile just as much a child of God as any Jew born to Abraham's house: "and if children, then heirs; heirs of God, and joint-heirs with Christ" (Romans 8:17).

Fellow-heirship opens up a way for the Gentiles to belong to the "same body" (Greek: *sussomos*), meaning that they have achieved brotherhood with the Jews in a living unity. A new community has been formed, totally separate and diverse from any other. According to Charles Hodge, the word "fellowheirs" was coined by Paul. It is a new word to describe a new thing—one body made up of individual members acting in cooperation and harmony with the other members for the mutual benefit of all (I Corinthians 12:12-31).

Paul's background, steeped in Jewish tradition and Phariseeism, would have hindered his viewpoint on this matter. His attitude toward the Gentiles had to be revolutionized for him to be able to carry the gospel to them. He was able to do this through the revelations given to him by Christ.

Now that the Gentiles are fellow heirs and of the same body, they are made "partakers [Greek: *summetochos*] of his promise in Christ by the gospel." They share in the same inheritance of faith and promise of life given because of union in Christ (II Timothy 1:1). All these promises, possessions, and privileges can only be found through union with Christ. Paul pointed this out many times in Ephesians, repeatedly calling our attention to what we gain "in Christ." Without Christ the Gentiles have nothing at all, but with Him they are partakers of all that He has to offer.

Again, Paul affirmed that these truths are transmitted by the effective communication of the gospel of Jesus Christ. Without preaching there can be no salvation. People find Christ "by the gospel." Paul established churches through the preaching of the good news of peace in Christ (I Corinthians 4:15; Romans 16:25-26). The "foolishness of preaching" is absolutely necessary to convey the truths of the mystery (I Corinthians 1:18, 21). What good is it to have a revelation and no means to communicate its beauty to others? God, who is rich in mercy, gave us the glorious privilege of preaching the gospel to everyone so all could be saved. Through the power of preaching, people can realize their condition, be converted, and begin to enjoy every privilege and possession that is available in Christ (Romans 10:8-15).

Verse 7. Paul's ministry was his work and service to God, given to him by divine favor and produced by divine power. He considered his apostleship to be the greatest gift God could give him. This gift was the grace of God as expressed in his conversion and commission. Paul was made a "minister" (Greek: *diakonos*), meaning a man whose life is taken up in his work. Paul's life was taken up in the work of sharing the riches of Christ with the Gentiles.

167

Making a minister out of Paul, who was once a persecutor of the church, required not only God's mercy but also "the effectual working of his power." This power was not merely the supernatural circumstances surrounding Paul's conversion but the inward change created by the indwelling Christ. He experienced a change of heart and mind due to the exceeding greatness of God's power that worked mightily in him.

Paul made other references to this divine inworking (Greek: *energeia*) to teach that conversion is not merely an intellectual acceptance but is an act of God's power (Ephesians 1:19; Philippians 3:21; Colossians 1:29). Whether it be conversion or the work God calls one to do after conversion, it takes the power of God to produce it. Mercy is not enough to make a ministry. It must be coupled with the power of the Holy Ghost to be completely effective. (See I Corinthians 15:10; II Corinthians 3:5; 4:1; 12:9-10; Philippians 4:13; Colossians 1:11.)

Verse 8. The "saints" are the people of God who make up the church due to a divine call (Romans 1:7; I Corinthians 1:2). Paul not only considered himself to be the least of the apostles (I Corinthians 15:9), but the least of any of God's people, because of his persecution of the saints and consent to the stoning of Stephen. His persecution of the church was against Christ as well, and to him that was the worst sin one could commit (I Timothy 1:13-15). What grace it was for him to experience the love of Christ and His forgiveness, not only in conversion but also in a holy calling to "preach among the Gentiles the unsearchable riches of Christ." No wonder he considered the "grace given" to be the "unsearchable riches of Christ."

The word "unsearchable" (Greek: *anexichniaston*)

means "not to be tracked by footprints."[2] It does not mean no one can discover the riches of Christ, but that no one can discern them by human ability. They are a gift from God and cannot be exhausted. They are limitless.

Paul used the same word in Romans 11:33 to describe God's ways as "past finding out." It was beyond Paul's comprehension that after he had so maliciously caused havoc in the Christian church, God would bestow such grace upon him. Human reasoning cannot fathom why God would convert such lowly men and turn them into flaming evangels for His cause. How unsearchable are His riches!

Christ and His riches are available to the believer. The bride can receive, through anointed preaching, all that makes Jesus "the satisfying portion of the soul."[3]

b. The Manifold Wisdom of God

Verse 9. Throughout the ages of God's dealings with humanity prior to the coming of Christ, the mystery of the gospel was hid. The Old Testament prophets foretold Christ's coming in the flesh, but the fact that His coming and death would open the door to the Gentiles was unexpected. So Paul, through his revelation and preaching, opened to the world the vibrant truth that God had removed the barriers between cultures. Paul's message was not new in the sense of God newly deciding to admit Gentiles into His redemptive purpose, for God had planned to do so from the very beginning.

Paul also wanted to illuminate the minds of people after they had been converted by showing them their part in the mystery. The word "fellowship" comes from the Greek word *koinonia*, which means "partnership." Every believer has a part to play in revealing this mystery to the world. Our salvation is in Christ Jesus, but we also possess a stewardship of the mystery: to reveal in public what had been "kept secret since the world began" (Romans 16:25).

It was Paul's responsibility to share this message with the world, but he also desired to help others see their stewardship in this sharing. God used Paul to "make all men see" (Greek: *photizo*). He used him to throw light upon the mystery, to reveal God's full purpose of redemption, and then to get others to share in partnership.

There is a close connection between redemption and creation. Redemption's blessing came to light by Him "who created all things." The King James Version attributes the work of creation to God through Christ, while modern translations, relying on the critical Greek text, omit the reference to Christ. Either way, the statement is accurate, for Jesus is God manifested in the flesh. Nothing less than the power of God almighty can create the world, and nothing less than God almighty can redeem fallen humanity. It takes the creative power of God to make a broken life new again.

Verse 10. Paul's mission to make known the mystery was threefold:

1. to preach Jesus to the Gentiles and convert them to Christ
2. to enlighten all as to their part in God's purpose
3. to manifest to the angels the "manifold wisdom of God"

Redemption effects justification, forgiveness, adoption, acceptance, and access in the life of believers to create the church. The church is God's masterpiece, and

He wants all the universe to see it. "Principalities and powers" includes both good and evil angels (Ephesians 1:21; 6:12; Colossians 1:16; 2:15). The angels would like to look into the plan of redemption but they cannot (I Peter 1:10-12). God desires to teach these "heavenly," or supernatural, beings, especially Lucifer, a lesson concerning His character.

Jesus Christ is the wisdom of God (I Corinthians 1:24, 30). Through Him God created the church, which reveals to the angels God's character and nature as seen in redemption.

God's wisdom is called "manifold" wisdom (Greek: *polupoikilos*), which means "many colored" or "various in character." Even though the angels may have been created on a higher plane than humanity (Hebrews 2:7), they still do not know all there is to know about God. So God has chosen the church as His means of revealing the many-colored aspects of His nature and character. He is weaving a pattern from variously colored threads, creating a masterpiece for all the universe to look upon and stand in awe at His infinite wisdom.

Verse 11. At the final stage in God's great plan, He will present the church for all heavenly beings to see. His "eternal purpose" (Greek: *prothesis*, used of the showbread that was set for or exposed before God) is to be "purposed" (Greek: *poieo*), or "made to happen," in Christ Jesus. Through Him and Him alone can this purpose be worked out. The thought was originally formed *in* Him, and *through* Him it became a reality for Jew and Gentile alike. Beginning with the Incarnation on to His exaltation, Jesus Christ, the anointed Messiah, is Lord of all. God "hath saved us, and called us with an holy calling, not according to our works, but according to his own purpose and grace, which was given us in Christ Jesus before the world began" (II Timothy 1:9).

c. Boldness in Christ

Verse 12. Christ's accomplishments at Calvary purchased the church's privileges. We can now come before the throne of grace with boldness (Greek: *parrhesia*), or "outspokenness," to pour out our petitions to Him (Hebrews 4:16; 10:19). Our boldness is based on the "access" we have with "confidence" (Greek: *pepoithesis*), or "total reliance." All believers possess the privileges of boldness, access, and confidence, based on the fullness of the revelation of the mystery. We can now walk in and out before God in prayer because we have been accepted through the blood. Without fear of rejection we can fearlessly speak out "by the faith of him"—faith in the person, the blood, and the love of Jesus Christ.

Verse 13. After Paul revealed all the privileges in Christ and stated his special involvement in sharing them with the Gentiles, some of the saints may have wondered, Why then is Paul in prison? Why isn't he at liberty to preach throughout the world? Paul let them know that his "tribulations" were due to his preaching the gospel to the Gentiles and demanding that they have the same access as the Jews. His bonds were really their "glory," because through them the gospel was still being propagated.

Paul wanted the Ephesians to know that the reason he could endure the afflictions and face the hardships was because he knew the One in whom he had believed. Access, with confidence, gave him the power to continue.

Paul desired to show the Ephesians that he did not view his imprisonment as a defeat but as a victory. Because it was God's will for him to endure it, he accepted it willingly. Through his imprisonment he was actually glorifying God, and he wanted the Ephesians to glory in it as well. (See II Corinthians 4:7-12; 12:9-12; Philippians 1:12; Colossians 1:24.)

Notes

[1]Bruce, 59.
[2]Moule, 90.
[3]Hodge, 59.

F.

Prayer for the Bride to Receive Fullness
(3:14-21)

1. The Riches of His Glory (3:14-18)

(14) For this cause I bow my knees unto the Father of our Lord Jesus Christ, (15) of whom the whole family in heaven and earth is named, (16) that he would grant you, according to the riches of his glory, to be strengthened with might by his Spirit in the inner man; (17) that Christ may dwell in your hearts by faith; that ye, being rooted and grounded in love, (18) may be able to comprehend with all saints what is the breadth, and length, and depth, and height.

Verse 14. Earlier in this epistle Paul prayed for the Ephesians to receive a revelation of their possessions (Ephesians 1:16-23). He attempted to renew this prayer in Ephesians 3:1 but detoured to show further the fullness of the mystery. He resumed the prayer in verse 14 and intensified it by adding, "I bow my knees unto the Father of our Lord Jesus Christ." The normal Jewish posture of prayer was to stand, but here we find Paul on his knees before God. The cause—that they might receive the fullness of God's wealth and riches—demanded earnest prayer.

After showing his special place in sharing the secret

175

of God's plan for the Gentiles and after addressing the trials the Ephesians were experiencing due to his imprisonment, Paul intensified his efforts to bring about their spiritual enlightenment as to the fullness of God's will for them. The passion with which he prayed was not uncommon to Paul. He knelt to pray at his departure from the Ephesians elders in Acts 20:36 and with the disciples at Tyre in Acts 21:5. Strong feelings surged through Paul as he prepared himself to seek God on behalf of the Ephesians to conclude what he started in the first chapter.

Many manuscripts omit the phrase, "of our Lord Jesus Christ" from verse 14, and so do most modern translations.

Verse 15. The Greek word for "family" in this verse is *patria*, referring to the lineage of the family on the father's side. This may be the reason why the phrase "of our Lord Jesus Christ" has often been omitted from verse 14; some may not accept that in Jesus Christ every family is named. In any case both God's heavenly family of angels (Hebrews 12:22-23) and His earthly family of believers bear His name, and the supreme name by which God has revealed Himself is Jesus (Philippians 2:9-11).

God is the one from whom all fatherhood comes, but He is also the author of our salvation and has revealed Himself by a name before which even the angels of heaven must bow in submission: "That at the name of Jesus every knee should bow, of things in heaven, and things in earth, and things under the earth" (Philippians 2:10). (See also Acts 4:12.) No other name gives more power to prayer than the name of Jesus. We have power in prayer through our relationship with God as our Father and through God's redemptive plan as signified by the name of Jesus Christ. (See John 14:13-14; 15:16; 16:23-24, 26.)

a. Strengthened with Might

Verse 16. Empowered by a relationship with God as Father and enabled by the name of Jesus, Paul made his request. The request has four parts. This verse deals with the first one: that God would give to the Ephesians out of the abundance of His riches the strength to possess what is capable of being possessed. He gives in proportion to all His wealth, not just out of His wealth (which could be a meager gift), but from His abundance (Romans 5:17). God will give abundant strength from His royal bounty.

If the Ephesians were going to bear the burden of Paul's imprisonment, accept their partnership in the mystery, and receive the fullness of the blessings, they would have to be "strengthened with might by his Spirit in the inner man." The word "strengthened" (Greek: *krataioo*) means "to empower" or "to make capable." They had to be empowered with "might" (Greek: *dunamis*), which means "miraculous power" or "the ability to perform miraculously." God enables His church with miracle power, equipping them with His Spirit. Without the Spirit the church cannot function as God intends. Paul called on the Corinthians to "be strong" (I Corinthians 16:13), and he also said of himself, "I can do all things through Christ which strengtheneth me" (Philippians 4:13). He was a personal recipient of the strength mentioned and expected every believer to be so empowered.

"But ye shall receive power, after that the Holy Ghost is come upon you: and ye shall be witnesses unto me both in Jerusalem, and in all Judaea, and in Samaria, and unto the uttermost part of the earth" (Acts 1:8). The purpose for the power is to make us partners in the mystery by being a witness of His salvation. God will enable us

177

to do so if we will allow our inner man to receive this strength.

The "inner man" is the seat of the will. A person's will must be submitted *to* Christ before it can be strengthened *by* Christ. The inner man must be renewed every day (II Corinthians 4:16) and fed by the Word of God (Romans 7:22). Thus, refreshed and renewed, the believer can possess the fullness of Christ.

b. Rooted and Grounded in Love

Verse 17. Paul continued his petition to God on behalf of the Ephesians by asking, secondly, "that Christ may dwell in your hearts." This petition is actually a result of the first one being answered. If people are strengthened by the Holy Ghost in the inner man the natural result will be Christ's setting up a permanent residence in their hearts whereby they will experience a daily manifestation of His presence. Though a person has been saved and filled with the Spirit, he still needs the manifested presence of Christ in his daily life. Asking for this indwelling does not change the fact that he received an initial experience, but God is interested in more than just a one-time experience. His interest includes the daily manifestation for which the apostle asked, with the concern of a father who desires that his children receive all that God intends.

Paul interchangeably referred to the Holy Ghost and Jesus Christ as the Spirit that dwells within the believer. Many commentators have balked at this freedom because Paul did so without explanation. But Paul had a fundamental revelation of the fullness of the Godhead dwelling in Jesus Christ bodily (Colossians 2:9).

The Holy Ghost and Jesus are the same God. Jesus spoke of the Holy Ghost as being sent at His request and then explained the fulfillment of this request as Himself coming to dwell within the believer (John 14:16-18). Jesus Christ dwells within the believer through the Holy Ghost, for the Holy Ghost is the Spirit of Jesus Christ (Romans 8:9-10). Through the revelation of the oneness of the Godhead being manifested to us in the body of Jesus Christ, the believer finds enrichment as he realizes a deeper dimension of Christ's dwelling in him. This indwelling provides for a strong daily walk with Jesus.

Only "by faith" can this indwelling take place. Faith is the responsibility of the individual who desires the indwelling of Christ through the Spirit. "Without faith it is impossible to please him" (Hebrews 11:6). Paul knew that Christ's ultimate goal is to develop the faith of His people. The extent of Christ's indwelling depends upon the level to which they allow Him to develop their faith.

This faith is not just the initial act of believing the gospel. It is also the enduring faith that can withstand trials and temptations. The Ephesians needed faith to stand when their hero was locked behind bars with no divine intervention to release him to continue the preaching of the gospel. This faith has a goal: for the believer to be "rooted and grounded in love." It is not just an intellectual acceptance of historical facts, nor an intellectual decision to make Jesus Lord. It is a life-changing experience and an ongoing process.

Being "rooted" is an agricultural term that refers to the biological growth of plants and trees. This imagery is common in the Scriptures, especially in the Old Testament, which likens those who delight in God's law and

179

put their trust in the Lord to a tree planted by water (Psalm 1:2-3; Jeremiah 17:7-8). Only through love can a person become rooted and receive the nourishment he needs to continue growing in the Lord. By spiritual roots he becomes a partaker of "the fatness" (Romans 11:17), which is actually God's own nature (II Peter 1:4).

Not only must we be rooted, but we are also to be grounded in this love. Being "grounded" is an architectural term that refers to the solid ground upon which a firm foundation is built. Love is the foundation from whence faith springs into action to claim all the possessions that grace has purchased. Without love our desire to claim what Christ has made available would only result in our consuming these blessings according to our lusts. We need the true love of God to eliminate greed and replace it with a firm foundation. Love for God, His purpose, and His people is the only foundation upon which to build one's heart as a holy place where Christ can dwell.

c. Comprehending the Love of God

Verse 18. Two key words reveal the intent of Paul's request as he moved to the third part of his petition:

1. "Able" (Greek: *exischuo*) means "to have full strength."

2. "Comprehend" (Greek: *katalambano*) means "to take eagerly, to possess or to seize."

God has provided a redemption of vast and far-reaching dimensions. We now have, through the indwelling of Christ, the full capability to seize what is rightfully ours. Paul's request may seem bold, but he knew the power of his God and knew that no request is too great for Him to grant.

180

If we are going to possess these dimensions of God's love, we will only be able to do it "with all saints." As we interact with one another we begin to realize our full potential. It is impossible for us to gain the fullness of God's presence and power alone. We need to find our place in the local church in order to grow to fullness. Only as ministers expound the Word to us and only as we have fellowship with other saints will we be able to seize the bounty of what Christ's love for us has measured out.

The Holy Spirit was given to Jesus without measure (John 3:34), for He was God incarnate. But to us God has measured the dimensions of His redemption. His love for us motivated this measure. As we will see in the next verse, the actual measure will increase until it includes the fullness of God Himself.

What do these measurements mean? First, Paul prayed that the saints possess "the breadth" of God's purpose. How wide is God's reach? Can it not include the whole world? Every nation, every tongue, every kindred, and every race are included in God's kingdom. It spans ethnic barriers, oceans, and national barriers. His reach is broad enough to include all of suffering humanity. God told Abraham to walk through the land and determine his own borders by his own vision and walk (Genesis 13:17). We can determine exactly what the measure will do for us by our own faith in Christ and love for the saints.

Next, Paul prayed for the saints to seize "the length." How long will this redemption last? In John 3:16 Christ promised every believer "everlasting life." Isaiah 9:7 gives insight into the longevity of Christ's kingdom: "Of the increase of his government and peace there shall be no end, upon the throne of David, and upon his kingdom, to

181

order it, and to establish it with judgment and with justice from henceforth even for ever. The zeal of the LORD of hosts will perform this.'' How long? Forever!

Third, Paul prayed for the saints to possess "the depth." How far down can God reach to redeem lost humanity? Not only can He reach any nationality or race, but He can take the vilest sinner, cleanse his way, and make him brand-new. The purpose of redemption is to take the sinner and make him a saint.

Finally, Paul prayed for the saints to take "the height." How high can one person go in Christ Jesus? We are made to sit in heavenly places, but what is the real extent of the glory that awaits the bride of Christ in the age to come? Philippians 3:21 says Christ "shall change our vile body, that it may be fashioned like unto his glorious body, according to the working whereby he is able even to subdue all things unto himself." John said, "Beloved, now are we the sons of God, and it doth not yet appear what we shall be: but we know that, when he shall appear, we shall be like him; for we shall see him as he is" (I John 3:2).

2. Filled with All the Fullness of God (3:19)

(19) And to know the love of Christ, which passeth knowledge, that ye might be filled with all the fulness of God.

Verse 19. Some things concerning Jesus Christ can only be known in the Spirit. Regardless of our intellectual prowess, we cannot fully discern the love of Christ. We must offer prayer so that we can experience the love of Christ in its richness. Only by experiencing His love for us can we know the riches we have received. Therefore, Paul prayed that the Ephesians might "know the love of Christ, which passeth knowledge."

This love passes knowledge, because it can only be really known by a wretched sinner who has been pulled out of sin and made a saint by grace. The rational faculties of man fail to understand the depth of God's love for humanity. One can understand it only by a personal encounter with the Savior. Angels cannot perceive this love, nor the carnal mind, but a sinner can.

Why did Paul pray for the Ephesians? Why did he want them to comprehend with all saints the depths of Christ's redemption and His love for them? Because it is through this spiritual awakening that they would be "filled with all the fullness of God." Paul's prayer was bold in claiming the fullness of God Himself for the bride of Christ. But God so loved the church that His redemptive purpose includes bestowing this fullness. The measure we have received from His love and His Spirit is progressing toward an ever-increasing revelation of God's fullness, which comes through the indwelling of the Holy Ghost. The purpose of the Holy Ghost is to give to the saints a greater understanding of Christ's love for His church. Because of this love we can attain "unto the measure of the fulness of the stature of Christ" (Ephesians 4:13). As a result of this prayer we can be "complete in him, which is the head of all principality and power" (Colossians 2:10).

3. Paul's Prayer Directly to God (3:20-21)

(20) Now unto him that is able to do exceeding abundantly above all that we ask or think, according to the power that worketh in us, (21) unto him be glory in the church by Christ Jesus throughout all ages, world without end. Amen.

Verse 20. Paul ended his prayer with resounding praise for the immense power of God. Paul knew that his God would be able to transcend anything one could ever ask or think. Every possession that had been revealed to the Ephesians earlier in the epistle and all the riches given in grace to the saints are nothing compared to what God can do. He can do "exceeding abundantly" (Greek: *huperekperissos*), or "superabundantly." God can do more than the imagination can fathom. Praise is definitely in order for all situations.

Prayer reaches greater power with God when it ends with praise to the King for His ability to supersede anything that we can ask for or think. When praise concludes prayer, it adds an extra dimension of power that moves the heart of God. Other examples in the New Testament where praise concluded prayer are Romans 16:25-27 and Jude 24-25. Both prayers ask for the preservation of the saints. Paul emphasized the power of thanksgiving when coupled with one's requests (Philippians 4:6).

Paul took this statement one step further because he knew that the power to accomplish this "exceeding abundant" work is not remote but in the heart of the individual saint. "The power that worketh in us" is the power God uses to bring to pass His purpose and will in our lives, not only to enjoy the riches His grace has secured but also to live a holy life and walk in His ways, which the next part of the epistle discusses. Paul wanted the Ephesians to know that the deposit of Christ's presence in them through the Holy Ghost is the very power God uses to work "superabundantly." He wanted to awaken them to their potential and allow it to work the reality of God's purpose in them. Christ must dwell in us, and when He does He imparts the same power that raised Jesus from the dead (Ephesians 1:19-20). It is the power of the resurrection, and every saint contains this power through the indwelling of Christ.

Verse 21. "The Western text reverses the order, so as to read 'in Christ Jesus and in the church'; some later uncials omit 'and,' thus yielding the A.V. reading, 'in the church by Christ Jesus.' But the best authenticated reading presents an ascending order of worth: in the church, which is the body of Christ, and in Christ Jesus, who is Head of His Church, let God be glorified."[1]

God's greatest glory is seen in the redemption of Jesus Christ. God alone deserves the glory for what the love of Christ has accomplished. When we see the crowning diadem of God's riches for the church, which is to be filled with all the fullness of God Himself, then we can only stand aside in awe and declare along with Paul, "Unto him be glory." No one can glory in such a feat. Only God deserves the praise and the honor.

The glory will continue beyond this present age. In every succeeding age, continuing into eternity, the Lord will receive glory and honor for the redemptive purpose, which has no end. There is no better way to end this first part of the epistle to the Ephesians than to give God glory for all His spiritual blessings in Christ. There is no better way to end than with an "amen"—let it be so.

Note

[1]Bruce, 70.

III.

THE BRIDE'S WALK IN CHRIST
(4:1-6:9)

A. The Walk of Unity (4:1-16)
   1. Walking Worthy of the Vocation (4:1-3)
   2. Seven Unities to Keep (4:4-6)
   3. Ministry of Christ to the Church (4:7-10)
   4. Fivefold Ministry Given to the Church (4:11)
   5. Purpose of the Ministry (4:12-16)
      a. Equipping the Saints for Service (4:12)
      b. Gaining the Fullness (4:13)
      c. Ridding the Body of False Doctrine (4:14-16)
B. The Walk of the Believer (4:17-32)
   1. Not Walking As the World (4:17-19)
   2. Putting Off the Old Man (4:20-22)
   3. Putting On the New Man (4:23-24)
   4. Putting Away Evil Conduct (4:25-32)
C. Walking As Dear Children (5:1-21)
   1. Following God's Example (5:1)
   2 Christ's Love at Calvary As Our Example (5:2-5)
   3. Walking As Children of Light (5:6-21)
      a. Pleasing God (5:6-13)
      b. Awaking to God's Will (5:14-17)
      c. Being Filled with the Spirit (5:18-19)
      d. Giving Thanks with Submission (5:20-21)

D. The Walk As It Relates to Relationships (5:22-6:9)
   1. Husbands and Wives (5:22-33)
   2. Parents and Children (6:1-4)
   3. Masters and Slaves (6:5-9)

A.

The Walk of Unity

(4:1-16)

1. Walking Worthy of the Vocation (4:1-3)

(1) I therefore, the prisoner of the Lord, beseech you that ye walk worthy of the vocation wherewith ye are called, (2) with all lowliness and meekness, with longsuffering, forbearing one another in love; (3) endeavouring to keep the unity of the Spirit in the bond of peace.

Verse 1. The word "therefore" marks a transition from a discussion of the wealth of the believer to the walk of the believer; it connects duty with doctrine. Without a proper relationship with Jesus Christ as Lord, the riches will not be used to glorify God but will instead be abused and consumed upon the lusts of the flesh. Riches gained in Christ cannot profit the believer unless he accepts the responsibility to conduct himself in a manner that brings glory to God.

Paul appealed to the Ephesian saints to adjust their behavior to bring honor to the vocation for which God had called them. He used the circumstance of his imprisonment to add emphasis to the appeal for them to continue developing their relationship with God. If he could live for God in prison, they could walk worthy of the riches they had gained in Christ. With a phrase he often used—

"I . . . beseech" (Romans 12:1; I Corinthians 1:10)—he made his entreaty, through love, to motivate the saints to become what redemption originally designed for them to be: faithful saints.

This verse embodies the apostle's ultimate objective in ministry: "that we may present every man perfect in Christ Jesus" (Colossians 1:28). His every appeal was to bring the believer into a closer walk with Christ, to gain the image of Christ, and to reveal Christ to the world. Every Christian is called into this vocation, expected to serve the Lord faithfully after receiving salvation. Paul made the same request of the church at Thessalonica, "That ye would walk worthy of God" (I Thessalonians 2:12) and the church at Colossae, "That ye might walk worthy of the Lord unto all pleasing" (Colossians 1:10). He thus emphasized the truth that a Christian's behavior affects the honor of God in the eyes of the world. Proper conduct and right conversation make the gospel more attractive to the unbeliever: "Let your conversation be as it becometh the gospel of Christ" (Philippians 1:27).

Verse 2. Once Paul established that the saints need to walk worthy of their vocation, he described four virtues necessary to accomplish it:

1. "Lowliness" or "humility" (Greek: *tapeinophrosune*) was despised by the Gentiles because they considered it a sign of weakness. The Greek viewed humility as a quality befitting a slave or a prisoner. But to a Christian true humility is total dependence on God, where one could actually be called a slave or a prisoner of God. True humility does not devalue a person but acknowledges the sovereignty of God. Jesus introduced true humility to the world and set the standard by which to measure

all humility: "For I have not spoken of myself; but the Father which sent me, he gave me a commandment, what I should say, and what I should speak" (John 12:49).

2. "Meekness" (Greek: *praotes*) means gentleness or self-control. The word evokes the picture of an animal that has been tamed and properly trained, obedient to its master's command. The power that works in every believer tames the sinful nature. The Holy Spirit properly trains people for more effective service. Without self-control the believer will not be obedient to the Master's command. Only total dependence on God and obedience to God produce a worthy walk.

3. "Longsuffering" (Greek: *makrothumia*) means both persistence and patience; the ability to endure and the patience to wait. Enduring the hardships of trial and testing until God brings deliverance is a necessary quality for every believer. However, we must couple endurance in life with patience in relationships. In this verse longsuffering means patience with other people's faults and shortcomings. Without longsuffering it would be impossible to possess the final virtue in Paul's list.

4. "Forbearing one another in love." All of these virtues find their foundation in love. The root is love, and the fruit is a worthy walk. Love is *agape*, a word the Christian writers gave a richer meaning. It means unconquerable love, always giving and never expecting a return.

Lowliness and meekness define our relationship with God, which is dependence and obedience. Longsuffering and forbearance define our relationship with other saints in the church. How we treat others affects our relationship with God. Appropriate behavior toward other members of the church helps to promote the gospel.

Verse 3. When love is the basis for ministry and service, the result is peace. Peace is the benefit of possessing the four virtues of verse 2. The bond of peace can be broken if every member of the church does not consciously seek to maintain it.

Knowing this, Paul admonished the Ephesian saints to endeavor to keep the unity of the Spirit. The word "endeavouring" comes from the Greek word *spoudazo*, which means to make every conceivable effort, to give diligent care or prompt, zealous effort. Only by everyone's accepting that other saints have problems and make mistakes will the church maintain unity.

Unity is an operation "of the Spirit." It is a gift of the Holy Ghost to the church, but it is maintained by the love the saints have for one another. The church shows love by accepting one another's faults—not by condoning sin, but by "praying always with all prayer" that those in sin might escape the snare of the devil (Ephesians 6:18; II Timothy 2:26).

Oneness in the church can only be maintained through the loving efforts of believers who continue to forbear one another's differences and weaknesses. It is everyone's responsibility. No church, regardless of its doctrinal accuracy, can expect the Lord's full blessing unless the members promote unity in love for one another and in the bond of peace. Strife within the body taints the beauty of our Lord's death and makes His Word unattractive to the world. Our best contribution to the gospel of Jesus Christ is to maintain the unity of the Spirit.

2. Seven Unities to Keep (4:4-6)

(4) There is one body, and one Spirit, even as ye are

called in one hope of your calling; (5) one Lord, one faith, one baptism, (6) one God and Father of all, who is above all, and through all, and in you all.

Verse 4. The apostle next presented seven unities that bond the church together. The first unity is the one body or one church created of all the nations and peoples of the world.

This one body is produced by one Spirit, which is the Holy Ghost working within the body to produce all the foregoing virtues. "For by one Spirit are we all baptized into one body" (I Corinthians 12:13).

This oneness is also a product of the one hope for which all Christians live, which stems from their common calling: "Ye are called in one body; and be ye thankful" (Colossians 3:15). The shared purpose, as well as the new birth, unites the body. It includes the hope of future salvation that will be revealed at the second coming of Jesus Christ: "Beloved, now are we the sons of God, and it doth not yet appear what we shall be: but we know that, when he shall appear, we shall be like him; for we shall see him as he is" (I John 3:2).

Verse 5. The Holy Ghost joins the saints together in one body, and the one purpose gives the body a focus, but the one Lord gives the church one commander. Through His directives the church receives her orders to carry out the daily purposes of Christ's kingdom. The Greek word *kurios,* translated "Lord" in this verse, was used for the Roman emperor, giving him the place as master of all things. Paul used the word to describe Jesus, because He is the true emperor and master of the church and universe. Only as the church receives instruction from Jesus Christ as the Head, communicated through the Holy

Ghost, will the one purpose be accomplished.

One Lord who is ruler and master provides for the church one faith, as revealed in the Scriptures. The word "faith" can refer to the act of believing or to the essence of one's doctrine. Some think that the essence of one's doctrine is not important, but it is important to God what one believes. God will justify both Jew and Gentile by the faith they have in Christ Jesus (Romans 3:30), but the church is also urged to "earnestly contend for the faith which was once delivered unto the saints" (Jude 3). Having faith is important, and so is having "the faith," a set of beliefs. Paul expected the Colossians to be "stablished in the faith" (Colossians 2:7). He also referred to the "joy of faith" (Philippians 1:25).

So faith is both a virtue and a set of beliefs. A particular aspect of those beliefs that Paul wanted the Ephesians to remember is that there is one baptism. Through this baptism, each individual believer was placed into the one body. "One baptism" cannot be limited to either water baptism or Spirit baptism; they constitute the same baptism. Evangelical scholar F. F. Bruce explained that baptism of water and the reception of the Holy Spirit work together in the conversion experience:

> It must be remembered that in New Testament times repentance and faith, regeneration and conversion, baptism in water, reception of the Holy Spirit, incorporation into Christ, admission to church fellowship and first communion were all parts of a single complex of events which took place within a very short time, and not always in a uniform order. Logically they were distinguished, but in practice they

were all bound up with the transition from the old life to the new.[1]

We must not separate water baptism and Spirit baptism in the plan of God, because both are part of the complete new birth. "Jesus answered, Verily, verily, I say unto thee, Except a man be born of water and of the Spirit, he cannot enter into the kingdom of God" (John 3:5). The phrase "born of water" refers to water baptism, and the phrase "of the Spirit" refers to Spirit baptism. John the Baptist's baptism by water was incomplete without the further Spirit baptism promised by the Messiah Himself (Acts 1:5; 11:16). Moreover, after the coming of the Holy Ghost, Paul commanded the disciples of John the Baptist to be rebaptized in the name of the Lord Jesus and laid hands upon them to receive the Holy Ghost (Acts 19:4-6). The apostles proclaimed the one baptism of water and Spirit throughout the Book of Acts (Acts 2:38; 8:16-17; 10:44-48). God uses baptism of water and Spirit to place the believer into Christ and make him a member of His body, the church (Romans 6:3-5; I Corinthians 12:13; Galatians 3:27).

Verse 6. The concept of God as Father was alien to the Gentile world, but Christians who are in Christ Jesus and have realized sonship know God as their Father. Paul expressed His benevolence by three different phrases, describing His care for those who belong to Him. First, He is "above all." God's throne exists above all rulers and principalities (Colossians 1:16; 2:15). He alone is in control of man's destiny. God is able to direct a person's steps. "In all thy ways acknowledge him, and he shall direct thy paths" (Proverbs 3:6). God's watchful care over His people, to ensure their safe passage from this world to the next, is a testimony of His true fatherhood.

The second expression used to describe God's benevolence is "through all." As provider for all our needs, He is able to meet any difficulty the believer may face during stormy trials on earth. God's all-sufficient grace provides a reservoir of strength that believers can count on because of the sonship they have received by the riches of God's grace (II Corinthians 12:9). His benevolent love invites us to prove Him and see whether or not His blessings can provide in such abundance that there is not room enough in our lives to contain it (Malachi 3:10). Because God is our Father, He assumes a personal responsibility to meet the church's every need according to His riches in glory (Philippians 4:19).

Finally, God is "in you all." The indwelling of God in His saints, through the Spirit, makes the church a temple for God's personal residence. The promise that God will abide with us forever is one of the many benefits of being a child of God. Jesus promised this eternal, abiding presence to His disciples in John 14:23: "If a man love me, he will keep my words: and my Father will love him, and we will come unto him, and make our abode with him." Every aspect of God's nature is available to the saints to aid their walk in everyday life.

Though God operates by various methods, it is still the same God who works out everything in our daily lives according to His eternal purpose and for the ultimate praise of His glory (I Corinthians 12:5-6). When the final word is spoken, all the glory will belong to the One who has worked out our salvation from the beginning to the end. "For of him, and through him, and to him, are all things: to whom be glory for ever. Amen" (Romans 11:36).

"One Spirit," "one Lord," and "one God and Father" reveal to us that God operates in the life of a believer in three different ways:

    1. God dwells within the believer through His Spirit;

    2. God issues commands to the believer as Lord; and

    3. God rules in the heavens as Father over all creation.

The apostle did not refer to three distinct divine persons, but to a God who manifests Himself in the life of believers in diversity of power and operation to work His eternal purpose in them, for them, and through them.

3. Ministry of Christ to the Church (4:7-10)

Verse 7. Though the church is a corporate body made up of many different members, each individual member of that community has a unique place to fill. God has provided gifts to enable each believer to function within the community successfully.

The church cannot expect to function properly unless each individual receives specific grace "according to the measure of the gift of Christ." Grace is given in direct proportion to the measure of Christ Himself. Jesus Christ is the possessor of these gifts and also the provider of them. Only as the believer possesses Christ will he be able to claim His gift of grace. The emphasis in this verse is not on the gift itself but on the giver, Christ Jesus. In His infinite wisdom, Jesus will bestow these gifts as He wills to create the maximum effect. No matter how diverse the gifts are, the same Spirit of Christ works through the same church for the same purpose. "Now there are diversities of gifts, but the same Spirit" (I Corinthians 12:4).

We find in the New Testament three lists of gifts that God has bestowed upon the church through Jesus Christ: in Romans 12:3-8; I Corinthians 12:4-11, 27-31; and Ephesians 4:11. Though the contents of the lists differ, each gift gives power to believers to be a help and blessing to the other members of the body. Gifts are not given for the sole benefit of the recipient but so the recipient may bless others.

Verse 8. This verse connects the triumphant ascension of Jesus Christ to the gifts given to the church. It is a fulfillment of the Messianic prophecy in Psalm 68:18: "Thou hast ascended on high, thou hast led captivity captive: thou hast received gifts for men; yea, for the rebellious also, that the LORD God might dwell among them." Because of Christ's ascension into the heavenlies, He now can abide in the hearts of all people through the Holy Ghost. He explained, "Nevertheless I tell you the truth; It is expedient for you that I go away: for if I go not away, the Comforter will not come unto you; but if I depart, I will send him unto you" (John 16:7).

In Psalms, the victor (Jesus Christ) received the gifts for people. In Ephesians, the victor gives gifts to people. It is all a part of the process that began with Christ's resurrection. After being raised from the dead, which set a new standard of power, Christ ascended to claim His rightful place at the throne. His exaltation secured a place for Him that carries many benefits. But instead of hoarding them to Himself, He became the benevolent bestower of gifts.

We can picture a victorious king enjoying a triumphant procession through the streets of a capital city he has conquered. Behind him is a long line of captives and gifts indigenous to that country. He is receiving the gifts from those over whom he rules. But our King Jesus, though He receives gifts, also bestows them upon His servants. "And having spoiled principalities and powers, he made a shew of them openly, triumphing over them in it" (Colossians 2:15). The captivity that He has taken captive are the souls of people who were bound by Satan but are now prisoners of Christ. "Now thanks be unto God, which always causeth us to triumph in Christ, and maketh manifest the savour of his knowledge by us in every place" (II Corinthians 2:14).

Verse 9. Paul deviated from his original description of the unities and gifts given to the church and parenthetically inserted the next two verses. His purpose was to define in greater detail the full impact of Christ's victory over Satan by bringing into focus His incarnation, death, burial, and exaltation. Paul connected the ascension to the truth of Christ's descent (His incarnation). Before Christ could be exalted He first had to descend from heaven and assume the form of man. However, His condescension went further than just His physical body. He also subjected Himself to death and was buried.

A great controversy has existed over what the "lower parts of the earth" are. The lower (Greek: *katotera*) parts can refer to death, the grave, or hades (the abode of the dead). (See Psalm 16:10; 69:15; Acts 2:25-35; Romans 10:7; I Peter 3:19.) Paul actually referred to Christ's entire mission, which began with His incarnation and continued to His ascension. Christ's victory at Calvary was

199

a complete victory that had retroactive power as well as power for all generations to come.

Verse 10. Jesus Christ, God Almighty, descended from the heavenly sphere and took upon Himself the likeness of man to oppose satanic forces here on earth. The only way God could defeat Satan as ruler of this sinful world was by making Himself vulnerable to satanic attack through the Incarnation. After Christ's overwhelming victory through His flesh, He ascended into the heavenlies to assume His rightful place as ruler of the universe. Jesus sits on the throne of the highest heaven, "far above all heavens."

The Bible speaks of three different heavens.

1. the universe where man has his existence (Genesis 2:1; Psalm 8:3)

2. the spirit world where Satan and His forces dwell (Ephesians 2:2)

3. the dwelling place of God's throne (II Corinthians 12:2).

Jesus ascended above the earth and the powers of darkness and sat on the throne of the Almighty so He can "fill all things." His ultimate purpose is to dwell in everyone who will believe on Him and to dispel all darkness from the minds and hearts of humanity.

While on earth Jesus could only dwell physically in one place at a time. By His Spirit He is omnipresent and can simultaneously bless His people all over the world (Ephesians 1:23; Colossians 2:9-10).

3. Fivefold Ministry Given to the Church (4:11)

Verse 11. The other lists of ministry gifts describe them as special endowments to believers to make them more effective in the work of God (Romans 12:6-8; I

Corinthians 12:28-31). Ephesians emphasizes the minister himself who is empowered by these gifts. The other passages treat the specific ministry imparted as a special blessing from the Lord. But in this verse, the minister himself in the exercise of his gift is considered a gift from the exalted Christ to His beloved church.

Paul listed five ministries that God has given to the church for its betterment. This passage has given rise to many questions. Do these ministries still exist today? Can people today obtain the ministry of an apostle or prophet? Which gift takes preeminence over the other, or do all stand equal?

The church's maturity and function depend on a balanced ministry. The church can function adequately in this world only when it receives instruction and help from all of these ministries.

Apostles

The twelve apostles (Greek: *apostolos*) held a special place in the forming of the New Testament church (Luke 22:30; I Corinthians 15:5; Revelation 21:14). They were Christ's ambassadors and eyewitnesses of His resurrection. The original twelve cannot be replaced because they were with Jesus in His earthly ministry and were personally picked to be His cabinet during His administration on earth. After Judas was removed from his place as an apostle, Matthias was selected to take his place. To fill this office he had to be an eyewitness of the earthly ministry of Jesus Christ, from the baptism of John until the resurrection (Acts 1:21-26).

However, there were other apostles besides the original twelve. Paul, Barnabas, James the Lord's brother,

Silvanus (Silas), Junia, and Andronicus were also considered apostles of Jesus Christ (Acts 14:14; Galatians 1:19; I Thessalonians 1:1; 2:6; Romans 16:7).

The purpose of this ministry is to take the gospel to virgin territory and establish churches. Apostles are commissioned by Jesus and empowered with His miraculous grace to accomplish the work of laying the foundation of the church in new territory. (See I Corinthians 9:1; II Corinthians 12:12.)

What a vital ministry for the church today! How many times have missionaries braved rugged conditions to establish an apostolic church on foreign soil and God has helped them with many supernatural wonders? Without apostles, the church would not expand and be established in new areas.

Prophets

As we have already stated, in Ephesians 2:20 and 3:5 the prophets referred to are not Old Testament prophets but New Testament prophets. God does endow people with the ability to give direction and warning to the church (Acts 11:27; 13:1; 15:32; 21:9-11). Agabus received a special word from God concerning Paul and what awaited him at Jerusalem (Acts 21:10). God also used him to predict a famine (Acts 11:28).

A prophetic ministry can be one that foretells or forthtells God's purpose for His church. Prophecy is not limited to foretelling the future. It can also speak encouraging words that build faith (I Corinthians 14:24-25, 29). This ministry is not lost to the church. God still speaks to and through people to give direction, warning, and edification to the church.

Evangelists

An evangelist has the ability to share the gospel of Jesus Christ with individuals who need salvation (Acts 8). Philip was an evangelist (Acts 21:8), and his ministry was noted primarily for soulwinning (Acts 8). Evangelists have a unique quality of ministering to the lost and developing a soulwinning mindset in the church.

The church needs ministries that can help reap the harvest of lost souls who are being influenced by the church. Without this ministry the church cannot grow.

Pastors

A pastor, or shepherd, is someone who cares for the flock of God. After an apostle pioneers a work, a prophet gives direction, and an evangelist increases the number, a pastor must step in and take care of those precious saints on a daily basis (Acts 20:28; I Peter 5:1-4). The pastor is to feed the flock of God with the Word (John 21:15; Titus 1:9; I Peter 5:2). Through his teaching of the Word of God, the pastor is to protect the church from false doctrine and spiritual danger. God enables people with a pastoral ministry to properly care for the local assembly on a day-to-day basis. Paul also urged pastors to do the work of an evangelist, because it is important that every overseer of the church involve himself in personal soulwinning (II Timothy 4:5). God enables people with a pastoral ministry to properly care for the local assembly on a day-to-day basis.

Teachers

God endows certain people with a special gift of explaining the Word of God. Through their diligent study and apt presentation they nourish the minds of the people with what the Lord is saying to the church through the holy Scriptures. The need for this ministry is great, because everyone needs a regular diet of the Word of God (James 1:21; I Timothy 4:16; II Timothy 3:16).

Both in English and Greek, the wording of the list of ministries links pastors and teachers closely together, indicating that the same individuals commonly fill both roles.

5. Purpose of the Ministry (4:12-16)
a. Equipping the Saints for Service (4:12)

Verse 12. The five ministries given to the church are to "perfect" the saints. This perfection (Greek: *katartismos*) means "to repair, mend, and completely furnish." It is a surgical term such as would be used to describe the repairing of a broken limb, which necessitates setting the bone back in its proper place so it can be healed. God has called ministers to equip the church with all the necessary armor and weapons from the Word so the church can accomplish its ministry. This ministry not only equips the individual believers but also sets them in their rightful place "for the work of the ministry." This means that the preaching of the Word of God should train each believer to fulfill his own ministry, to discover his gift, and to receive strength, direction, and power to accomplish God's purpose for him.

The emphasis is not on the minister himself doing the work, but on the empowered believer being equipped to do the work. It is the job of the preacher to train each saint in his own ministry, or service. As each learns his place and begins to function in his ministry, the result will be the edification, or building up, of the whole body.

b. Gaining the Fullness (4:13)

Verse 13. As the church continues to be edified by the Word, the corporate body begins to grow. Individual believers mature spiritually as they receive teaching and instruction from the ministry, and the corporate body also matures by the proper interaction of individual members. This maturation process finds its culmination in "the unity of the faith."

"The unity of the faith" is more than the initial act of believing. It is growing in one's appreciation of Christ's redemptive work and increasing in the knowledge of who Jesus Christ really is and what He has done for us through Calvary. As the believer comes to a full knowledge of Christ's redemption, he can apply that knowledge to his life. This applied knowledge causes growth and spiritual enrichment.

We cannot enjoy the fullness of this work without proper fellowship within the corporate structure of the church. As each believer comes to know Jesus personally and doctrinally, the church reaches a state of maturity where she can function with effectiveness and power in the earth.

In this context the word "perfect" (Greek: *teleios*) means "full age," while the word "stature" (Greek: *helikos*) means "the same age." The measure of a Christian's maturity is Jesus Christ Himself. When a Christian comes of age he awakens to who he really is in Jesus Christ. By following the example set by Jesus, he begins to grow in strength and power. The stature that the believer is trying to reach is no less than that of Jesus Christ Himself, but he cannot do it alone. He needs the fellowship of the others. He should not compare himself to other

Christians, however, because they do not set the standard by which to judge his progress. The example left by Jesus Christ is the example we should follow.

Reaching full stature as a perfect man involves complete function and maturity. Full stature can be both spiritual and numerical growth. When the number of believers is complete, Jesus will return.

The terms "perfect man" and "fullness of stature" are both individual and corporate. They can only be reached through a constant diet of the Word and from fulfilling one's ministry. The entire process will not be complete until Jesus returns to establish His kingdom in the earth.

c. Ridding the Body of False Doctrine (4:14-16)

Verse 14. The purpose of the ministry is to teach God's Word to the church. The Word not only produces maturity but also stability. Preaching protects from false doctrine that can ravish the work of God's purpose and redemption in a local assembly. False doctrine makes people unstable and unprofitable.

The reason God has placed the fivefold ministry in the church is to keep false doctrine from destroying the flock. Through preaching, believers can grow and "be no more children." Paul was saying to the Ephesians, "It is time to grow up." It is time to stop being "tossed to and fro" (Greek: *kludonizoma*) like the waves of the sea, driven by the winds. The word describes a boat tossed in a storm. False doctrine is like a storm that rocks the boat and endangers everyone's life.

If a church is truly mature, the people will not be moved by every wind and wave of doctrine. Some people get swallowed up by so many new ideas and religious fads that they lose sight of the important things of God.

These doctrines are propagated by the "sleight of men" (Greek: *kubeia*), which means "dice playing." These people have no fear of God, but they gamble with the souls of others. They use "cunning craftiness" (Greek: *panourgia*), which means "trickery." The only antidote to the poison of such people, who desire to deceive for their own gain, is a God-called minister who feeds the flock with the Word of God. A Bible-based ministry provides maturity and stability to the church.

Christians who are taken in by every new religious fad never really grow any roots. Because they are not truly grounded in truth, they cannot interact properly with the rest of the body. They never fulfill their ministry and become useless to God's purpose (Colossians 2:8).

Verse 15. The ministry's weapon against false doctrine is to speak "the truth in love." The minister must present the truth about Jesus Christ and His wonderful redemption in a kind, loving way. Truth came by Jesus Christ, and Jesus is the truth (John 1:17; 14:6). When believers learn of Jesus Christ in an attitude of love, the truth will cause them to grow and become like their Master.

What a person says and the attitude or motive he has when he says it reveal his maturity level. The more a person hears, speaks, and thinks of Jesus Christ, the more he grows in Him. The less a person hears, speaks, and thinks of Jesus Christ, the less he grows. The gospel should not only affect the heart but also the speech. By sharing Christ with others we show that Jesus is our Head and Master. Only by a relationship with Him as ruler of our lives will we ever be able to grow and be like Him (I John 1:6-7; 4:16-19). Only by fellowship with the truth of Jesus Christ will people be changed into His image.

Verse 16. From Jesus Christ alone comes the unity of the church. The church is joined together in Him by an invisible bond of love. The church is "fitly joined together" (Greek: *sunarmologeo*) and "compacted" (Greek: *sumbibazo*) which means unity has developed by association or affection. Association with the truth and affection for the Master join the church in one accord (Acts 2:1).

Members may come from different sociological backgrounds and have a variety of personalities, but when joined in Christ they become a part of a larger body, joined by their association with the faith and their love in the Spirit. They produce a unity that God can use to fulfill His purpose in the earth.

No one is insignificant. Each one can contribute his portion to the benefit of the whole body: "by that which every joint supplieth, according to the effectual working in the measure of every part, maketh increase of the body unto the edifying of itself in love." Each believer possesses a certain measure of ministry and has something to contribute.

The word "joint" (Greek: *haphe*) means "alignment." The word "supplieth" (Greek: *epichoregia*) means "contributes." When each believer is properly aligned and has found his place, then he is in position to make his contributions to the work of God. When the individual begins to supply his ministry to the other members of the body, it begins to increase spiritually and numerically.

Edification is a product of the love that believers have

208

for one another and the care they give to each other. The church's growth is dependent on this edification, but it cannot happen until the ministry properly trains and equips the church.

Note

[1]Bruce, 79.

B.

The Walk of the Believer

(4:17-32)

1. Not Walking As the World (4:17-19)

(17) This I say therefore, and testify in the Lord, that ye henceforth walk not as other Gentiles walk, in the vanity of their mind, (18) having the understanding darkened, being alienated from the life of God through the ignorance that is in them, because of the blindness of their heart: (19) who being past feeling have given themselves over unto lasciviousness, to work all uncleanness with greediness.

Verse 17. After Paul discussed the need for relationship between the individual believer and the corporate body, he proceeded to describe the behavior expected of each individual in the body. Without each member walking in the integrity of Jesus Christ, the corporate body would become corrupt. Paul explained in detail the attributes needed in order to please the Lord.

He began by contrasting the walk of the new life with the old one. But before he defined the details he showed that this new life with its new ways is something that the Lord Himself requests: "This I say therefore, and testify in the Lord." Paul's desire for believers to live a pure life came as a result of his relationship with the Lord Jesus. He knew what God expects, because he knew God and testified that God desires the same of all believers.

Paul made a definite separation between the world and the church by asking believers to walk differently from the Gentiles. The church's way of life should bear no resemblance to the value systems of the world. The people of the world walk "in the vanity of their mind." The reasoning of this world does not even acknowledge the existence of God. The thinking of sinners is so corrupted that they develop values with their own personal interests at heart. "Because that, when they knew God, they glorified him not as God, neither were thankful; but became vain in their imaginations, and their foolish heart was darkened. Professing themselves to be wise, they became fools, and changed the glory of the incorruptible God into an image made like to corruptible man, and to birds, and fourfooted beasts, and creeping things" (Romans 1:21-23).

Man's worship of anything other than God is vanity, something useless or worthless. The carnal man has created other gods and idols, but God expects everyone to turn from worship of the creature and worship the only true living God.

Verse 18. When people turn from worship of God to the worship of the creature, their understanding becomes darkened. They cannot perceive the existence of God; therefore they are alienated from the benefits God desires to give.

God imparts His life to every believer, but it is absent from unbelievers. Therefore, they are "dead in trespasses and sins" (Ephesians 2:1). The life that God gives to the believer is His very own life. The born-again process is not the creation of another life form separate from

God, but the infusion of God's own life into the heart of the believer.

Those who refuse to take knowledge of God are ignorant; they do not realize that without God there is no life. Ignorance of God causes a hardening of the heart. The word "blindness" (Greek: *porosis*) could actually be translated "hardened." Mark 3:5 uses *porosis* to describe the hardened hearts of those who opposed Jesus in the synagogue, and Paul used the word to refer to Israel's blindness (Romans 11:25). In both cases it refers to a group of people who refused to let God change their opinion because of misconceived theological viewpoints. They preferred to hold on to their false religious ideas than to accept life-changing truth.

When people do not worship God as Creator they shut themselves off from the life-changing power His presence brings. Therefore, the virtues of righteousness never have an opportunity to develop. Only by acknowledging God's existence and submitting to Him, can people whose lives have been broken by sin ever hope to rebuild them.

Verse 19. Refusing to acknowledge God's existence and to accept His life-changing power eventually puts people in a position where they can no longer feel. "Past feeling" (Greek: *apalgeo*) means they "no longer feel pain." When people persist in sin ultimately they no longer sense that they have done wrong. They cannot tell the difference between right and wrong, and even when they suffer the consequences for their errors they no longer recognize that they are suffering because they have sinned. "Their conscience [is] seared with a hot iron" (I Timothy 4:2).

God allows them to live a life of uncleanness, giving them over to their own way of living, but He also allows them to suffer the awful consequences of their decisions (Romans 1:24-28). Paul warned the Ephesians that once God has given them up, they would perform all manner of evil "with greediness" (Greek: *pleonexia*). This word means to possess more than what one should possess or to desire what someone else has. When people strive to have more only for the sake of having more, God considers their greed to be both immoral and idolatrous (Ephesians 5:3, 5). God wants His people to be content with their earthly possessions while desiring spiritual things (Colossians 3:2; I Timothy 6:8).

2. Putting Off the Old Man (4:20-22)

(20) But ye have not so learned Christ; (21) if so be that ye have heard him, and have been taught by him, as the truth is in Jesus: (22) that ye put off concerning the former conversation the old man, which is corrupt according to the deceitful lusts.

Verse 20. Paul made no separation between Jesus Christ's person and His teachings. If we have Christ we will keep His commandments. People who claim Christ through an "easy believism" that demands no commitment or obedience do not have the true Christ.

People cannot effectively obey Christ until they know Christ. The teachings of the apostles were a direct result of the life Jesus lived before them, not just what He taught (Acts 1:1). Christ's example provided the apostles the material with which they laid the foundation of the church, not only in doctrine but also in lifestyle and behavior.

If someone has truly learned Christ he will follow in His footsteps (I Peter 2:21). The old life must be abandoned and a new life accepted, old ways renounced and new ways adopted. This was apostolic teaching from the beginning. Paul, seeing the precedent set by those who preached before him, urged the bride to continue in this way, both in doctrine and lifestyle.

Verse 21. Some have used this verse to dispute Pauline authorship of Ephesians, since he was so well acquainted with the church at Ephesus and had spent much time there preaching and teaching (Acts 20:20-21). But Paul was not questioning whether they had heard about Jesus. He was in essence saying, "If you have heard about Jesus at all you, know very well that Jesus lived and taught an entirely different lifestyle from that of the Gentile world."

In this reference Paul used the name of Jesus without any other title attached. This was rare for Paul, but he used Jesus' name alone here to emphasize the Incarnation. Jesus was both God and man. The Spirit of God lived in the man Jesus Christ in the fullness of power and strength, and the man displayed on earth, through His humanity, all the values and attributes of God. Through His humility and life on the earth we can see the truth as a living entity.

Truth is more than a system of doctrines and facts. Truth is a person, and that person is Jesus. Jesus said of Himself, "I am . . . the truth" (John 14:6). To find truth, whether it be the truth of doctrine or behavior, we must come to know Jesus Christ in a personal relationship. We must see His example as recorded in the Gospels and proclaimed by the apostles and follow that example (John 13:15).

Verse 22. The heritage of fallen humanity is the sinful Adamic nature that has been passed down from generation to generation. This nature is corrupt, dominated

215

by sin, and must be dealt with supernaturally. Through the new birth this dominion of sin, or "the old man," is put away initially (Romans 6:2-6). However, the believer still possesses a responsibility to purify the habits, behavioral patterns, actions, and lifestyle ("conversation") that would be displeasing to the Lord. God has called all saints from the old life into a new way of life in Jesus Christ.

Paul urged the Ephesians not to gratify their own lusts, which lead to death. The reason he was so adamant about his request was that he knew that the old man is corrupt and under the sentence of death and eternal damnation. These lusts are deceitful.

The Greek word for "lusts" is *epithumia*, which means "desire, craving, longing." People who are wrapped up in their own self-gratification become arrogant in their presumptuous actions, and they desire everything to come their own way. The New Testament is firm in its resolve to condemn the pleasures of sin, for sin promises fulfillment that is transient and illusory. "But exhort one another daily, while it is called To day; lest any of you be hardened through the deceitfulness of sin" (Hebrews 3:13).

Unfortunately, those who are caught in the web of the deceitfulness of sin usually continue in their selfish path until death overtakes them. Their hearts become so hardened that they do not see the destructiveness of their behavior, not only in their own life, but to the lives of those they influence. "And with all deceivableness of unrighteousness in them that perish; because they received not the love of the truth, that they might be saved" (II Thessalonians 2:10). The only escape from this deceit is to receive exhortation from the Word and a love for the truth. Only then can the individual find deliverance.

3. Putting On the New Man (4:23-24)

(23) And be renewed in the spirit of your mind; (24) and that ye put on the new man, which after God is created in righteousness and true holiness.

Verse 23. Our minds need a continual renewing (Romans 12:2). We can overcome the world only when our minds receive fresh manna from the Word. The mind controls our actions and attitudes and must be renewed in order to function properly under the kingdom laws of the new birth. The new birth is necessary, but we must also undergo a daily process of renewing (II Corinthians 4:16). The Word of God and God-anointed preaching and teaching can renew our minds so that we can understand and follow the will of the Lord.

Without this renewal it is impossible for the new way of life to take effect. A new way of thinking will make a new way of life. A daily diet of the Word through reading, preaching, and teaching will effect this renewal process, which in turn will bring about a new form of living, higher than that of self-indulgent lusts of the old nature.

Verse 24. Putting on the new man means taking on the nature of Jesus Christ Himself. The new birth imparts a nature that is born in the image of Jesus Christ. Again, putting on the new nature begins at the new birth but must continue as a daily process. "Put ye on the Lord Jesus Christ, and make not provision for the flesh, to fulfil the lusts thereof" (Romans 13:14). (See also Colossians 3:10.)

The word "new" (Greek: *kainos*) means new in

character and in time. At one time we were bound by the old man, but after the new birth we became a brand-new person due to the power of redemption. From that point we must adopt a new way of life with a new set of principles. As our new nature gains greater control over our actions, we are gradually transformed to take on the character of Jesus Christ. It takes a constant acceptance of the new life and a conscious act on the part of the believer to turn from the old and adopt the new.

Paul mentioned two qualities to sum up the character of Jesus Christ and the New Testament believer: "righteousness and true holiness." God creates the new man in the life of the believer, and as a result he bears an image that is both righteous (in right standing) and holy (separated from sin). As we embrace the truth of Jesus and wash our minds by it, the result is a dedicated life that follows the example left by Jesus Christ, a life that is above reproach and blameless. A righteous walk of holiness is the greatest compliment one can pay the Master for His sacrifice at Calvary.

4. Putting Away Evil Conduct (4:25-32)

(25) Wherefore putting away lying, speak every man truth with his neighbour: for we are members one of another. (26) Be ye angry, and sin not: let not the sun go down upon your wrath: (27) neither give place to the devil. (28) Let him that stole steal no more: but rather let him labour, working with his hands the thing which is good, that he may have to give to him that needeth. (29) Let no corrupt communication proceed out of your mouth, but that which is good to the use of edifying, that it may minister grace unto the hearers. (30) And grieve not the holy Spirit of God,

218

whereby ye are sealed unto the day of redemption. (31) Let all bitterness, and wrath, and anger, and clamour, and evil speaking, be put away from you, with all malice: (32) and be ye kind one to another, tenderhearted, forgiving one another, even as God for Christ's sake hath forgiven you.

Verse 25. In the first part of this chapter Paul requested that the Ephesians maintain the unity of the Spirit. He showed them that the only way they could do so was by putting away the old man and putting on the new man.

Then, Paul listed some sins that must be dealt with. Each believer must make a conscious effort to put away these sins. They will not go away simply because of the new birth. There is a process of cleansing that takes time and cooperation.

This "putting away" is the same as in verse 22, but it is defined in greater detail. Paul began his list with lying. Since God is truth and Satan is a liar (John 8:44), we are to imitate Jesus and not Satan. This verse quotes from Zechariah 8:16, where the prophet exhorted the people to speak truthfully so God could bless them. Colossians 3:9 similarly states, "Lie not one to another, seeing that ye have put off the old man with his deeds."

Deceitfulness of any sort causes an offense not only to the body but also to God. The church obviously cannot function properly unless people respect one another enough to tell the truth. Outsiders must see Christ's likeness in the believer's behavior toward each other in order for them to perceive the love of God. If we can treat one another with respect by being truthful, then the church can fulfill her ultimate destiny and reveal Jesus Christ to a fallen world.

The reason Paul gave for requesting truthfulness was that each church member belongs one to another. No one member makes up the whole body, but each derives strength from the other. Lying creates a breach in the life that is transmitted from believer to believer, and the body becomes dysfunctional, so that it cannot bring glory to Jesus Christ.

Verse 26. "Stand in awe, and sin not: commune with your own heart upon your bed, and be still. Selah" (Psalm 4:4). The word "awe" in the Hebrew is *ragaz* which means "to tremble," either from fear or anger. (The Revised Version translates it as anger.) Paul quoted from this Old Testament passage in making his appeal for all believers to put away anger. Not only did Paul address the problem, but he provided the remedy. Observing the time limit stated in the Scripture helps keep anger from becoming sin. We should relax at the end of the day and recognize that continued anger will only disturb our spirit and will ultimately be destructive.

Anger is not sinful as long as it is kept under proper control and used constructively. Anger due to wounded pride or hurt feelings leads to sin, but God can use anger due to a righteous indignation against sin to help purge that sin. Jesus became angry when He saw the people's doubt in the synagogue when He healed the man with the withered hand (Mark 3:5). His objective was healing, and their tradition would not allow the flow of His benevolence. His anger obviously did not hinder the supernatural. Jesus also showed anger when He cleansed the Temple of money changers (John 2:13-17). A misuse of His Word or His house incurs the wrath of God. This type of anger is not sin.

Verse 27. Those who allow anger to possess them and who harbor ill will towards others only allow the devil an opportunity to destroy them. Giving the devil access to one's spirit through the door of anger provides him ample opportunity to further his own purpose.

Paul used the word *diabolos* here instead of *satanas*, which he used more frequently. In Acts 13:10 he used *diabolos* in his rebuke to Elymas the sorcerer. The word means "slanderer" or "accuser." When anger controls one's spirit, that person falls under the power of the devil's accusation. The devil gains an opportunity to use that person to accuse others falsely. Uncontrolled anger not only destroys the individual who harbors the anger, but it also harms the person upon whom the anger is vented.

Verse 28. Lying, anger, and now stealing need to be put away. Christians must adhere to a higher standard than that of the world in order for their witness of Jesus Christ to gain credibility. The new birth provides power to deliver the believer from these habits.

Paul followed the negative injunction with a positive solution. The former thief needs to work for his own living, setting aside a portion of his income to help the underprivileged. The motive for getting money should be to give to those who are in need. Instead of pilfering from the church, he should work to provide for his family and give to the poor. Working one's own way through life is something that Paul exemplified himself, and he expected others to follow that example (Acts 20:34; I Thessalonians 2:9; II Thessalonians 3:7-12). Jesus desired that His disciples give to the poor, and the apostles followed that injunction (Matthew 19:21; Acts 20:35).

Verse 29. Paul now turned his attention to the words

221

spoken by the Christian. Words of deceit, rage, harshness, insult, or obscenity are forbidden for any true child of God. Verbal communication is a vital link in establishing unity and providing encouragement to others. What one says definitely has an effect on the hearer, and that effect can be for evil or good. "Death and life are in the power of the tongue: and they that love it shall eat the fruit thereof" (Proverbs 18:21). It is important for every Christian to realize the power of words, because wrong speech can disrupt the unity of the Spirit, thereby thwarting the function of the church. "Let your speech be alway with grace, seasoned with salt, that ye may know how ye ought to answer every man" (Colossians 4:6). If the tongue is not bridled, then the heart is not pure (James 1:26-27).

Verse 30. Corrupt words spoken by an unbridled tongue not only destroy the hearer but also grieve the Holy Ghost. They frustrate the work of redemption that the Holy Ghost desires to accomplish in the lives of people. Words spoken in rage or deceit only serve to tear down the church, not build it up. Using hateful words and causing a brother to stumble are serious offenses (Matthew 5:22; Romans 14:15-21). The purpose of the Holy Ghost dwelling in a believer's life is to build him up and, through his words and actions, to build up others. Evil and harsh words hinder the work of the Holy Ghost in the life of the speaker and the hearer.

Any offense committed against the brethren is also committed against the Holy Spirit. Such an offense breaks the seal that has been placed on the life unto the day of redemption. What the Holy Ghost is doing is more than a temporal work—it is His job to keep us until the Second Coming. The final revelation of the sons of God is the ultimate work of the Holy Ghost (Romans 8:11, 19), and we should not frustrate that by words that are not beneficial.

Harsh words do not bring glory to Jesus Christ. Love needs to be the governing factor in the believer's speech.

Verse 31. Maintaining the unity of the Spirit is the key for the church's proper operation in the earth. Paul recapped what he had been saying by listing six vices that come from undisciplined tempers and tongues. These sins generate an ill-will toward people that makes it difficult for the Spirit of Christ to bring them to salvation. Therefore, Paul implored the Ephesians to put away these attitudes so that God's work, through the church, might prosper.

1. *"Bitterness"* (Greek: *pikria*) means "prolonged resentment" or "a slow-working deadly poison." Though the results of death and destruction are not immediate, they are inevitable. Unfortunately, many people who succumb to the "root of bitterness" end up defiling not only themselves but others as well (Hebrews 12:15).

2. *"Wrath"* (Greek: *thumos*) means "explosive anger" or "extreme passion," which has the connotation of anger that happens in a moment and is gone.

3. *"Anger"* (Greek: *orge*) here has the connotation of "habitual anger" or "longed-for revenge." As explained in verse 26, anger itself is not necessarily a sin, but uncontrolled anger or anger nursed as a grudge becomes sinful.

4. *"Clamour"* is loud, insistent speech, the kind that hurls insults and mocking refrains. Reckless accusations and rude language should never come from the lips of God's chosen people. Even Michael did not bring any

railing accusations against Lucifer but relied upon the Lord's rebuke rather than his own (II Peter 2:11; Jude 9).

5. *"Evil speaking"* (Greek: *blasphemia*) needs to be put away as well. To speak evil of others opens the door of one's spirit to demonic influences (II Peter 2:10; Jude 8).

6. *"Malice,"* or hard feelings towards others, disrupts the unity of the Spirit, hinders the function of the church, and brings about a breach that is difficult to bridge. God's fivefold ministry needs the liberty to minister the Word of God to the saints so that these vices might be purged from the body.

Verse 32. After the vices are purged, Paul armed the saint with positive replacements. God never takes away without replenishing. These are the virtues that will enable the church to function properly.

God expects His people to be kind to each other. This verse speaks of a practical kindness that is displayed by seeking the prosperity and benefit of our brother, rather than our own will (I Corinthians 10:24).

To this virtue we are to add a tenderheartedness (Greek: *eusplanchnoi*) that is seen in a person's willingness to forgive. This Greek word is used only in one other place in the New Testament, in I Peter 3:8, where it is translated as "having compassion." Paul wanted his readers to know that all acts of kindness must come from a heart of compassion for one's brother.

These acts of kindness should demonstrate our willingness to forgive one another, as Jesus forgave us (Colossians 3:13). Jesus taught this principle of forgiveness to His disciples and exemplified it in His life and death. His silent rebuke of the Pharisees' treatment of the woman caught in adultery is evidence that the Son of man came into the world to forgive sins (Luke 19:10; John 8:6). Christ's cry upon the cross, "Father, forgive them; for they know not what they do" (Luke 23:34), places upon the church a tremendous responsibility to act in the same manner. Paul added strength to his plea with the Ephesians to act as their Master had acted and forgive one another.

The Greek word for "forgive" is *charisomai* which means "to forgive a debt." God will not forgive the sins of any person who refuses to forgive (Matthew 6:15).

The chapter began with a plea for unity and ends with a request for forgiveness. No unity can be kept of Spirit or of faith, no function of the ministry can be successful, no witness of Jesus Christ can be credible, without a spirit of forgiveness based on Jesus Christ's forgiveness of us.

C.

Walking As Dear Children

(5:1-21)

1. Following God's Example (5:1)

(1) Be ye therefore followers of God, as dear children.

Verse 1. The highest standard of behavior the believer can use to pattern his life after is that of God Himself. To know God's holiness and character and to imitate Him exclusively yields the greatest harvest of fruit.

Paul charged us to be "followers of God" (Greek: *mimesis*), which means a "mime or mimic." As the preceeding verse shows, one of the greatest attributes of God that Paul desired the church to possess is forgiveness. The Greeks knew the word *mimesis* very well. It referred to the training of an orator who would study the masters and imitate them by practicing their style over and over again. As Christians, we are called by God to be His witnesses or spokesmen in the earth. What we say can add credibility to our witness or destroy its influence. When we imitate God's own behavior in spirit, character, and word we will not only forgive wrongs committed against us but will, by forgiving others, help to further God's purpose.

There is no greater example of God's wonderful attributes than those displayed in the life of Jesus Christ.

In Him God put all of His virtues on public display for us to follow.

Grace has made us "dear," or beloved, children of God. We are not God's stepchildren but bone of His bone and spirit of His Spirit, and we should behave as our Father in heaven does. Children mimic their parents, for good or for evil. A father must be careful of the legacy he leaves his children because they will act upon what they have seen their father do much more than on what he has said. Jesus acknowledged this truth when He said, "I speak that which I have seen with my Father: and ye do that which ye have seen with your father" (John 8:38). Parents can receive no greater compliment than to know that their children are following in their footsteps, living a life that is a mirror of their actions, mannerisms, and attitudes. Jesus gained honor as a beloved Son by doing what the Father had commanded Him to do (Matthew 3:17).

God is also pleased when His beloved children reflect in their actions the same glory that was reflected in Jesus' earthly ministry. We can enjoy God's approval by following in the footsteps of Jesus (I Peter 2:21) and obeying the injunction to be merciful even as the Father is merciful (Luke 6:36).

2. Christ's Love at Calvary As Our Example (5:2-5)

(2) And walk in love, as Christ also hath loved us, and hath given himself for us an offering and a sacrifice to God for a sweetsmelling savour. (3) But fornication, and all uncleanness, or covetousness, let it not be once named among you, as becometh saints; (4) neither filthiness, nor foolish talking, nor jesting, which are not convenient: but rather giving of thanks. (5) For this ye know, that no whore-

monger, nor unclean person, nor covetous man, who is an idolater, hath any inheritance in the kingdom of Christ and of God.

Verse 2. Imitating God's behavior must include a walk of love. Ephesians 4:2 deals with the walk of the believer in reference to service unto God. In this verse, the walk refers to the relationships among believers. Paul commanded all believers to walk in love due to the love Jesus Christ has for them, a love proven by the sacrifice at Calvary.

Jesus laid down His life for His friends and His enemies (John 15:13; Romans 5:10). Our love is a response to what He has already done and the love He has already shown: "We love him, because he first loved us" (I John 4:19). His expression of love should motivate us to serve our brethren in love. "Hereby perceive we the love of God, because he laid down his life for us: and we ought to lay down our lives for the brethren" (I John 3:16). Jesus Himself commanded it: "And this is his commandment, That we should believe on the name of his Son Jesus Christ, and love one another, as he gave us commandment" (I John 3:23). (See also John 13:14; 15:12.)

Because of His love we are to walk in love (Romans 5:5; 13:8). Christ expressed His love by giving Himself, and we should do likewise, sharing our love with others and forgiving one another.

Christ gave Himself so we could have the hope of eternal life. His offering satisfied the requirements of God's judgment against sin. Jesus loved us and gave Himself for us as an offering (Greek: *prosphera*) and a sacrifice (Greek: *thusia*), which was a sweet-smelling savor unto God.

229

A sweet-smelling savor simply means that Christ's sacrifice was acceptable and pleasing to God. It refers to the meal and peace offerings of the Old Testament, which were a sweet smell unto the Lord (Genesis 8:21; Exodus 29:18, 25, 41; Leviticus 1:9, 13, 17; 2:9). The meal offering is a type of absolute holiness and obedience, while the peace offering is a type of peace made between opposing forces. Because of Christ's obedience to the commands of the Father, His sacrifice was well pleasing to the Lord, and the result is peace between God and man.

As Christ's offering was acceptable to God, so we should make our lives acceptable to the Lord. When we imitate Christ and follow in His footsteps, the resulting actions will be an offering accepted by God. Paul described the gift of the Philippian Christians as a sweet smell (Philippians 4:18), and he also commented that his service to God as a minister to the Gentiles was a sweet savor. "For we are unto God a sweet savour of Christ, in them that are saved, and in them that perish" (II Corinthians 2:15). The work of redemption in our lives has produced this aroma of love that God finds so pleasing, especially when this love is manifested in a life dedicated to the cause of Jesus Christ.

Verse 3. Paul often listed vices that need to be put away from the walk of the believer (Romans 1:29; I Corinthians 5:11; Galatians 5:19-21; Colossians 3:5-9). In Ephesians 4:22-31 he had discussed a number of evils; here he addressed immorality.

Ephesus was a very immoral society. The entire Roman Empire was decadent and sexually undisciplined, but this was especially true in Ephesus. Therefore, every person converted to Christianity had to be taught to abstain from immoral practices. Even though the social environment did not promote moral values, the message of Jesus Christ radically changed the heart to allow the new behavior of sexual purity to flourish. The gospel's power does not depend on the social environment to take root and grow.

When a person is born again, he becomes a new creature, and he is expected to put away "fornication" (Greek: *porneia*), which refers to any sexual act outside the sanctity of marriage. This word is joined with "uncleanness," a more general reference to all lust and immoral behavior.

Paul then linked fornication with "covetousness" (Greek: *pleonexia*), which means "ruthless greed"—a desire that consumes people to possess what does not belong to them. Possessions give them a sense of conquest and achievement. They are consumed by a flaming passion for possessing the forbidden. The link between the sins of fornication and covetousness reveals the similarity of motive that prompts such behavior. These sins should never be named among true Christians. Not only should Christians never participate in such evils, but they should not allow them to become part of their conversation. In the Old Testament, God forbade the people of Israel even to mention the name of other gods lest doing so would entice them to follow after those gods (Exodus 23:13; Deuteronomy 12:30).

The reason Paul gave for desiring moral chastity is that we are saints (Greek: *hagios*). Saints are people whom God has called out to be His witnesses, and they are to walk in a manner that reflects His glory. Sexual impurity does not reflect the true nature of God but rather brings dishonor and thwarts His purpose. How much greater would be the witness of saints when they do not give themselves to vile language and immorality? The light of the gospel shines much brighter and has a much greater effect in the lives of those it touches.

Verse 4. Paul continued to describe the conduct and conversation that the believer should avoid. He forbade "filthiness" (Greek: *aischrotes*), which refers to any type of conduct that would bring shame to a person's reputation. "What fruit had ye then in those things whereof ye are now ashamed? for the end of those things is death" (Romans 6:21).

No communication should proceed from the mouth of a believer that does not edify the listener. If it does not build up, it should not be spoken. "But now ye also put off all these; anger, wrath, malice, blasphemy, filthy communication out of your mouth" (Colossians 3:8).

Another forbidden element of speech is "foolish talking." Speech that really says nothing should not be said at all. Finally, Paul urged the Ephesians not to jest (Greek: *eutrapelia*), from a root meaning "to turn easily." Quick-witted people can pollute any conversation by making light of sacred things. In context and connotation, "foolish talking" and "jesting" have particular reference to vulgar, suggestive, or obscene speech.

These forms of speech are not "convenient" (Greek: *aneko*), from a verb that means "to attain to" or "to reach for." These things are not what the believer is striving to accomplish in life. God has important work for the church to do, and the best way to accomplish that work is for the saints to put their speech to better use by the "giving of thanks." (See Hebrews 13:15.) The church is to turn away from *eutrapelia* (jesting) and turn to *eucharistia* (giving of thanks). A spirit of thanksgiving makes prayer effective and ministers grace to the hearer. The best use of anyone's power of speech is to bring glory to God (Colossians 3:17; I Peter 4:11).

Verse 5. Paul, desiring to drive home his point concerning immorality, made a bold statement: "For this ye know," or "be assured of this," that no one who indulges in illicit sex, lust, or greed will inherit the kingdom of God. He turned the attention of the reader from the sins to the consequences of those sins.

Some have thought that the kingdom referred to here is the millennial reign of Christ and that they would be saved but excluded from Christ's future earthly kingdom. This is not the case. The word "inheritance" (Greek: *kleronomia*) means "heirship" or "possession." Continued unrepented sexual impurity bars a person from any possession in Christ's glorious kingdom, present or future. They will be disinherited altogether.

Others have thought that this verse implies that sexual impurity is the unpardonable sin and that any indulgence in such activity would keep a person from ever being a part of the realm of Christ. But this cannot be so, considering Paul's teachings in I Corinthians 6:9-11, where he specifically stated that the Corinthians were cleansed from these sexual sins. Redemption provides a cleansing from these unclean practices. Paul urged the Ephesians to put these things away because the consequences of not doing so would cause them to be lost forever. Sexual impurity is not the unpardonable sin, but both the Old and New Testaments condemn any sexual activity outside of marriage. If not repented of, these sins will disqualify people from partaking of the possessions of the kingdom.

Paul again linked idolatry with covetousness in this verse, as he did in verse 3 and in Colossians 3:5. Any form of greed, whether for money, sex or power, becomes a form of worship, with the object of greed displacing God as the lord of one's life. God will not tolerate idol worship regardless of the form it may take, whether the idol is made by human hands or human desires.

The reference to the kingdom as being Christ's and God's does not mean there are two separate kingdoms, nor two separate persons in the Godhead. There is only one kingdom and one God. Rather Paul referred to the two phases of redemption, which are rescue and restoration. The present kingdom is where sinners are rescued by the preaching of the gospel. In the future kingdom, redemption will have paid the final debt, people will be restored to a higher level of living, and God will be all in all (I Corinthians 15:24, 28). Sexual immorality and greed will bar people from enjoying the benefits of either kingdom.

3. Walking As Children of Light (5:6-21)
a. Pleasing God (5:6-13)

(6) Let no man deceive you with vain words: for because of these things cometh the wrath of God upon the children of disobedience. (7) Be not ye therefore partakers with them. (8) For ye were sometimes darkness, but now are ye light in the Lord: walk as children of light: (9) (for the fruit of the Spirit is in all goodness and righteousness and truth;) (10) proving what is acceptable unto the Lord. (11) And have no fellowship with the unfruitful works of darkness, but rather reprove them. (12) For it is a shame even to speak of those things which are done of them in secret.

(13) But all things that are reproved are made manifest by the light: for whatsoever doth make manifest is light.

Verse 6. At this time in the church's development enemies of the truth were propagating two doctrinal errors. First, some false teachers promoted the idea that the spiritual man was unaffected by the natural man. Therefore, the sins of the flesh did not hinder the spiritual development of the individual. A second faction twisted Paul's teachings on liberty from the law to proclaim a liberty to sin. Paul refuted these notions soundly (Romans 6:1-2, 15). He solemnly warned that disobedience to the commandments of the Lord would bring the wrath and judgment of God (Ephesians 2:3). Though some judgment is reserved until the last day, today's judgment includes being shut off from the life of God and excluded from the benefits of Christ's victory.

Verse 7. In this verse Paul used the same word that he did in Ephesians 3:6 *(summetochos)* to describe the Gentiles' partaking of Christ's promises. But on this occasion Paul commanded that the Ephesians should take no part in acts of disobedience. A Christian must not take pleasure in people who sin (Romans 1:32), for those who indulge others in their sin will share their eternal damnation. A Christian cannot walk worthy of his calling unless he severs all connections with false teachers and false brethren who commit sin and try to make it look spiritual and acceptable to God.

Verse 8. The New Testament frequently compares the conflict between righteousness and sin with the contrast between light and darkness. The new kingdom, under the rulership of Jesus, is light, and all who oppose it are darkness.

Light and darkness are not compatible. They cannot coexist. One will triumph over the other. However, only light possesses energy. Darkness is merely the absence of light and therefore is easily defeated by the entrance of light. There is really no contest at all. When God's power is released, the forces of evil are easily conquered.

John described God's very nature as light, saying that in Him is no darkness at all (I John 1:5). In creation, God called light into existence by His Word (Genesis 1:3). In the same way, God has shone spiritual light into the lives of every believer (II Corinthians 4:6).

Jesus Christ is the light of the world (John 9:5). Through a personal relationship with Him, people no longer dwell in darkness but are alive unto God with a new nature that bears the image of Jesus Christ. As the believer follows Jesus, the light of life, that light illuminates a new pathway to victory (John 1:9; 8:12; 9:5). This victory is a translation from one kingdom to another, from being under the authority of Satan to accepting the authority of Jesus Christ (Acts 26:18; Colossians 1:13; I Timothy 6:16; I Peter 2:9).

The apostle boldly stated that the Ephesians were darkness prior to their conversion. Their very nature was darkness itself, and consequently, their behavior was evil and immoral. But when they were born again they became "light in the Lord." Therefore, they were to behave as "children of light" (I Thessalonians 5:8; I John 1:6-7).

Being children of the light should elicit two responses from believers. First, the inner working of truth will make them honest and open before God, not hiding anything (John 3:19-21; Hebrews 4:12-13). When people's actions and motives are evil they try to hide them. Children of the light can step into the light of deep scrutiny from the Lord without fearing His wrath because they know He will cleanse them from all evil.

Second, children of the light will shine their light to others (Matthew 5:16). The inner work of the light and the outer work of evangelism will both be a prevalent part of their lives. Whereas the inner work is a subjective work of the Spirit, the outer work is the objective purpose for the coming of the light.

Verse 9. In Galatians 5:22 Paul listed nine aspects of the fruit of the Spirit, but here he referred to three. He offered positive replacements for the evil works of darkness he had earlier forbidden the Ephesians to partake of. (In many manuscripts, the phrase "fruit of the Spirit" is inserted instead of the "fruit of the light," and most scholars today conclude from the context that this is the more likely rendering.) These three powerful elements of the divine nature—goodness, righteousness, and truth—are the natural result of light dwelling within the believer.

"Goodness" refers to moral purity. Those possessed by love's light will treat their fellow man with respect and not with evil intentions. Paul considered sexual impurity, whether adultery or fornication, to be a mistreatment of others. God's ultimate intention for our lives is good, and He expects Christians to do good to others.

"Righteousness" refers to right character. The principles of a person's character must be right if his actions are going to be right. Being right within and doing right by obeying God's Word is the natural result of the light.

"Truth" is a by-product of the light, because deceit and lies cannot exist where God's light dwells. These attributes are evil and their result is evil, but when there is truth, God's goodness can flourish.

Verse 10. If a believer is truly a child of the light, his behavior in word, deed, and motive will be pleasing to God. What is acceptable (Greek: *eurestos*) to the Lord simply means to do what is pleasing. But beyond that the believer is to determine, by diligent seeking, whether his actions please the Lord (II Corinthians 5:9). Paul knew that it would be impossible to list every evil deed that could be committed so he asked the church to weigh every action and to determine what is pleasing to the Lord.

The word "proving" can mean "to prove" or "to approve of." In this case either definition can fit. The believer must know what God accepts and what He does not accept. When believers base their approval on what they know is right and pleasing to the Lord they enter into a higher dimension of obedience that goes beyond merely following commands. (See Philippians 4:18.) They begin to walk in the Spirit. When the light shines into the heart and translates the believer into the kingdom of Christ he will no longer seek to please himself. He will want to please the Lord, which is the mark of a true Christian who submits to the lordship of Christ in truth and in light (Galatians 1:10; Colossians 1:10).

Verse 11. In Galatians 5:19-23 Paul contrasted the "works of the flesh" with the "fruit of the Spirit." Here he characterized the sinful lifestyle as darkness and unfruitfulness. Sterile lives result in death. Therefore, he commanded the Ephesians not to participate in the evil deeds of people who refuse to allow the light to change them into productive saints.

When a Christian makes up his mind to live a life of

godliness, the resulting light reproves the unrighteousness of sinners. People who delight in their sin stand condemned in the presence of a righteous child of God. If a Christian has fellowship with them in their commission of evil deeds, he will be seen as condoning their actions rather than reproving them. The Christian must disassociate himself from evil conduct, reproving it by refusing to partake of sinful activities. He should be a friend of sinners but not a friend of sin.

Light reveals the true nature of God and consequently exposes what is evil. By doing so, the light causes sin to wilt and die. The society of the world can only be healed when a righteous church rises up with righteous behavior to expose sinful humanity and cleanse it through the light of the gospel. Reproof comes not so much from speech but through a godly example lived before the sinner.

Verse 12. Even to mention certain evil deeds brings shame. For one to constantly speak of the actions of the ungodly only advertises rather than reproves sin. Speaking against sin as in Romans 1:24-32 does not violate this command. Rather, Paul referred to daily conversation, which should minister grace to the hearer. Joking about immoral activity is clearly prohibited.

Reproving sin through the silent process of a living testimony before the world will bring sinful humanity into reproof concerning their sin. When Christians refuse to partake of the sins of the world an immediate line is drawn between the righteous and the unrighteous. When the unrighteous see the joy of living a godly life, they will desire to forsake their sins and join with the righteous in their quest for glory.

Verse 13. When the light of a godly life exposes sin,

239

it brings the sinner to a decision. He is convicted of his sin and is urged to repent. God will accept his repentance, and God's light will purge his heart. As a result, the sinner will himself become a light that God can use to shine on the pathway for others to follow.

Only the power of the light can dispel darkness. As long as sinful actions remain hidden, the sinner remains a captive. A godly life becomes light for others to find their way to the cross of Jesus Christ and be delivered. Exposure of sin is therefore linked with conversion. Once reproved, the sinner can be forever set free from the works of darkness to the glory of God. (See John 3:19-21.)

b. Awaking to God's Will (5:14-17)

(14) Wherefore he saith, Awake thou that sleepest, and arise from the dead, and Christ shall give thee light. (15) See then that ye walk circumspectly, not as fools, but as wise, (16) redeeming the time, because the days are evil. (17) Wherefore be ye not unwise, but understanding what the will of the Lord is.

Verse 14. Paul drew from several passages in Isaiah to form this spiritual injunction (Isaiah 9:2; 26:19; 52:1; 60:1). Though he borrowed words from the Old Testament, it does not seem that he actually attempted to quote from any particular verse. Commentators have speculated as to why this is so. One popular theory is that he quoted a fragment of an early Christian hymn sung at the baptism of converts. The early church considered baptism to be a part of the believer's enlightenment and illumination and a vital part of the new birth.

Romans 13:11 similarly implores the church to awake from the slumber of inactivity and fulfill the purpose of

God while there is still time. Paul called upon the Ephesians to awaken that they might receive the light that only Christ can give. To live a godly life before the world will take something more than our own moral purity and good works can accomplish. We need supernatural illumination from the light of Jesus Christ.

The word "shine" (Greek: *epiphausko*) actually refers to "the rising of the heavenly body," which Matthew 28:1 and Luke 23:54 use to speak of the dawning of a new day. The acquisition of light from Christ causes the dawning of a new day in a person's life, as he becomes a new creature (creation). This statement reemphasizes the tremendous power of the new birth, which includes water baptism.

The illumination process begins with waking from the slumber of a sinful condition. Awakening leads to repentance, then baptism into the death and burial of Christ. The result is a resurrection by the power of the Spirit to walk in the newness of life. The light of Jesus shines upon the sinner not to condemn him to hell but to raise him up from spiritual death to walk in a new way of life that is better than the old.

Verse 15. We are to put away the old life in favor of the new, which demands a walk that is precise and disciplined. Ephesians 1:8 identifies wisdom as one of the possessions of the bride. In Ephesians 1:17 the apostle prayed that the bride would receive the spirit of wisdom, and in Ephesians 3:10 the result is a life that manifests the wisdom of God. This wisdom not only shows the eternal purpose of God, but it also governs everyday decisions so that God's eternal purpose may have greater impact in individual lives.

The parallel passage in Colossians 4:5 says we are to walk in wisdom so that those who are outside the church will not be able to find an occasion to condemn the church. We are to walk "circumspectly" (Greek: *akribos*), which means to walk with discipline, watching each step closely. We must be careful in our speech, take heed to our attitude, and keep ourselves morally pure so those who are watching our actions can find nothing to accuse the church.

Jesus commanded His disciples, "Behold, I send you forth as sheep in the midst of wolves: be ye therefore wise as serpents, and harmless as doves" (Matthew 10:16). Paul explained in Romans 16:19, "I would have you wise unto that which is good, and simple concerning evil." Only a wise church whose walk is precise and disciplined can deal with an evil world that is ready to persecute the church at a moment's notice.

Verse 16. Paul was aware of the danger of misusing time, especially in reference to divinely given opportunities. Israel missed her time of visitation and consequently came under the judgment of God (Luke 19:44). This same misuse of time could very well cause judgment to fall upon the church.

The parallel passage of Colossians 4:5 asks the church to take advantage of every opportunity to witness to their neighbors about Jesus Christ. Ephesians asks us to take advantage of every opportunity to show ourselves righteous by fulfilling our duties as faithful Christians. Witnessing and godly character go hand in hand. One is dependent upon the other. Only when one's character is in compliance with the Word of God can the witness be effective to change lives.

The word "redeeming" (Greek: *exagorazo*) means to "buy up," and the word "time" (Greek: *karios*) means "a special time or opportunity." Paul urged the Ephesians to buy up every available opportunity to do what was right in the eyes of the Lord so the world might see the benefit of Christ's light. "As we have therefore opportunity, let us do good unto all men, especially unto them who are of the household of faith" (Galatians 6:10).

The reason Paul made this request is "because the days are evil." This phrase could mean several things. It could simply mean that the world is watching and waiting to find fault with the church so they may persecute her. Or it could mean that lost souls must be reclaimed before it is too late. "But this I say, brethren, the time is short" (I Corinthians 7:29). We should never neglect the chance to share Jesus with the world while there is still an opportunity to convince them of the truth.

Verse 17. Paul repeated his request that the Ephesians not be unwise in their actions, but he used a different Greek word this time *(aphrones),* which means "making stupid decisions." It is possible for people to regress from their state of spiritual awareness and become lax in their moral behavior and speech. If they are going to buy up every available opportunity they must first know which ones are the best. We must have a precise understanding of God's will in order to use our opportunities to reach others.

Paul again presented to the church the absolute necessity of continuing their search for the knowledge of God and His will. Without this knowledge our decisions will eventually lead to disaster, not only for our souls, but for the credibility of the church in general.

This verse is much like verse 10. What is pleasing to God is definitely His will for the life of the believer. To find that will and allow it to guide one's life will further the cause of God upon the earth.

In Romans 12:2, Paul joined both ideas together in one verse: "And be not conformed to this world: but be ye transformed by the renewing of your mind, that ye may prove what is that good, and acceptable, and perfect, will of God." This should be the ultimate goal of every believer in his daily walk.

c. Being Filled with the Spirit (5:18-19)

(18) And be not drunk with wine, wherein is excess; but be filled with the Spirit; (19) speaking to yourselves in psalms and hymns and spiritual songs, singing and making melody in your heart to the Lord.

Verse 18. The only way to overcome the vices that Paul listed in this section is through the indwelling Holy Spirit. No matter how many virtues we seek as positive replacements, without the power of Spirit to enable us our efforts are doomed to failure.

Before Paul exhorted the Ephesians to be filled with Spirit he admonished them, "Be not drunk with wine." The first part of verse 18 is a quote from the Septuagint version of Proverbs 23:30. Overindulgence in wine was very common in the Gentile culture. Even though it was repeatedly condemned in the Old Testament, new converts to the Christian faith were predominantly Gentile and had no abstinence teaching. Paul instructed them that their former life of drunkenness was unacceptable to God.

Paul prohibited such behavior among the leaders of the church and the saints (I Timothy 3:3, 8; Titus 1:7; 2:3).

None were left out. So strong was his prohibition that Galatians 5:19-21 lists drunkenness as one of the "works of the flesh." I Corinthians 6:10 says that drunkards will not inherit the kingdom of God. A state of drunkenness disqualifies people from the benefits of the kingdom. They are not able to recognize their opportunities and therefore are unable to capitalize upon them.

Paul joined this command forbidding drunkenness with an exhortation to be filled with the Spirit. In Acts 2:13, those who witnessed the upper room experience misinterpreted the actions of the 120 as caused by drunkenness. But Peter pointed them to a higher form of enjoyment by identifying this experience as the fulfillment of the prophecy of Joel. When a person repents and believes on the Lord Jesus Christ, he will be filled with the Holy Ghost as the 120 were on the Day of Pentecost. This experience provides the power for the believer to lay down the vices of the old man and put on the new man, Christ Jesus. Even though a person makes a mental decision to serve the Lord, he still needs the power of the Spirit to grant him the privilege of overcoming sin.

The exhortation to be filled with the Spirit does not refer to a single, once-and-for-all experience but to continual and repeated action. There is a continual filling and a life that is pleasing to God as a result of this continued blessing. Christians do not need alcoholic substances to lift themselves above today's pressures. They possess a power that can lift them higher than any other substance, and without a hangover.

Actions of the flesh can only be defeated by life in the Spirit (Romans 8:9). Through the Spirit the believer becomes a habitation of God (Ephesians 2:22), receives revelation of the eternal purpose of God (Ephesians 3:5), and experiences power in prayer (Ephesians 6:18). No greater life can be lived than the life that is under the control of the Holy Ghost.

Being filled with the Spirit means being under the control or leadership of the Holy Ghost (Romans 8:14). The purpose of the glorious gift of the Spirit is to reveal Jesus Christ to us, first by convicting of sin and then by glorifying the Lord Jesus Christ (John 16:7-14).

Verse 19 gives us insight as to how the early church conducted worship services. It seems the services were characterized by much singing, rejoicing, and praise. The fellowship of the body of Christ is not through intoxication with wine, but our revelry is to be spiritual, by expressing ourselves in song and praise.

"Speaking to yourselves" actually means "to speak to one another." If we are jubilant due to God's goodness, then we should express that joy one to another. Our joyful songs are expressions of thanksgiving and exhortations to each other to offer encouragement in battles against the enemy. (See Hebrews 10:25.)

Paul listed three types of songs sung by the early church: psalms, hymns, and spiritual songs. All three are to be done by "making melody in your heart to the Lord." "Psalms" (Greek: *psalmos*) refers to the Old Testament psalms as well as New Testament psalms written and sung after the fashion of the Old. (See Luke 1:46-55, 68-79; 2:29-32.) These were a vital part of the worship service of the early church.

Along with psalms, Paul listed "hymns" (Greek: *humnos*), which to the Greeks were festive lyrics in praise of a god or hero. What greater hero than Jesus Christ, who so beautifully submitted Himself to the cross of Calvary to purchase our salvation? In reference to verse 14 we have already discussed the possible evidence of early Christian hymns. Other fragments that scholars believe could have belonged to such hymns are found in Ephesians 4:4-6; I Timothy 1:17; 2:5; 6:15; Revelation 4:11; 5:13; 7:12.

Finally, Paul introduced the third type of song in his list as "spiritual songs." These could be unrehearsed songs sung under the inspiration of the Holy Ghost. When the heart is overwhelmed with joy, the Spirit within begins to move on believers, and under the direction of the Spirit they begin to sing. Paul talked about such songs in I Corinthians 14:15: "I will sing with the spirit, and I will sing with the understanding also." All these expressions of joy and thanksgiving, whether from an old psalm, a new hymn, or a freshly given inspiration, must come from the melody of the heart in order to be pleasing to the Lord.

This verse makes it clear that singing and its uplifting power was an important part of the early church's worship service. Jesus and His disciples sang prior to His agony in the garden (Matthew 26:30). The disciples sang when their backs were against the wall (Acts 16:25). Singing was a great part of the fellowship of the believers as they rejoiced together in the goodness of the Lord (I Corinthians 14:26; Colossians 3:16; James 5:13).

d. Giving Thanks with Submission (5:20-21)

(20) Giving thanks always for all things unto God and the Father in the name of our Lord Jesus Christ; (21) submitting yourselves one to another in the fear of God.

Verse 20. "Giving thanks always for all things" seems

247

almost impossible! Yet Paul asked the church to rise above murmuring and complaining to give thanks. Again and again he beckoned the church to walk with him in the higher attitude of giving thanks (I Corinthians 14:16; Ephesians 5:4, 20; Colossians 1:12; 3:17; I Timothy 2:1; Hebrews 13:15). The apostle had discovered that the secret to a victorious life in Christ is to give God praise and thanksgiving no matter what state one is in.

Praise and thanksgiving help purify the spirit. Because ill circumstances happen to everyone, righteous or unrighteous, the key to overcoming is the response to them. If a person allows defeat in his spirit, then the circumstances will defeat him, but if he realizes that God works everything out for good, then he can give thanks regardless of the circumstances.

Paul set this example himself (II Corinthians 4:7-15; 12:5-10). In the Philippian jail, Paul and Silas prayed and then sang praises. The result was a mighty deliverance by an earthquake. Paul faced many perils in various preaching points across the Gentile world (II Corinthians 11:23-33). "None of these things move me" was Paul's response, because he knew the greatness of his God (Acts 20:24).

Thanksgiving is directed "unto God," because He is our Father. His benevolent care of His children, whether it be in charity or chastisement, is all for our good. Once we comprehend this truth the only adequate response is "giving thanks."

We are to give thanks "in the name of our Lord Jesus Christ." Through His mediatorial work at Calvary all spiritual blessings are communicated. Therefore, it is fitting that we should give thanks in His name. Not only does Christ's work at Calvary demand such praise, but also His person, because "God . . . hath highly exalted him, and given him a name which is above every name" (Philippians 2:9). Simply put, Jesus Christ is God Almighty manifested in flesh. Thus Paul instructed, "Whatsoever ye do in word or deed, do all in the name of the Lord Jesus, giving thanks to God and the Father by him" (Colossians 3:17).

Verse 21. Paul concluded this portion of the epistle with a special exhortation to mutual submission, which provides an introduction to the teaching on relationships that follows in Ephesians 5:22-6:9. The walk of the believer includes many things, from the unity of Spirit and faith, to the putting off of the old man and his ways, to putting on the new man after the image of Jesus Christ. However, none of this work can be accomplished without submission in the body of Christ. Spirit-induced enthusiasm, expressed in song, is no substitute for submission. Without submission the fivefold ministry would be helpless in instructing those who need the nourishment of the Word to live an overcoming life. Without submission, mutual encouragement would be impossible, and the body would splinter.

Paul spoke strongly against individualism in the body of Christ. Considering all the pressures we face and all the worldly influences from which we must abstain, without the fellowship of other Christians we would fall (Hebrews 10:25). The operation of the Holy Ghost in the church is for the edification of the whole body, not just for the benefit of one person. Submission is necessary for unity, the spiritual success of the ministry, and the productive operation of the Holy Ghost. Mutual submission will maintain a joyful fellowship that will nourish every member of the body.

Submission must take place in the "fear of God." "The fear of the LORD is the beginning of knowledge" (Proverbs 1:7). I Peter 2:17 commands the church, "Fear God." We perfect holiness, not through the fear of the minister, but through fear of God (II Corinthians 7:1).

D.

The Walk As It Relates to Relationships

(5:22—6:9)

1. Husbands and Wives (5:22-33)

(22) Wives, submit yourselves unto your own husbands, as unto the Lord. (23) For the husband is the head of the wife, even as Christ is the head of the church: and he is the saviour of the body. (24) Therefore as the church is subject unto Christ, so let the wives be to their own husbands in every thing. (25) Husbands, love your wives, even as Christ also loved the church, and gave himself for it; (26) that he might sanctify and cleanse it with the washing of water by the word, (27) that he might present it to himself a glorious church, not having spot, or wrinkle, or any such thing; but that it should be holy and without blemish. (28) So ought men to love their wives as their own bodies. He that loveth his wife loveth himself. (29) For no man ever yet hated his own flesh; but nourisheth and cherisheth it, even as the Lord the church: (30) for we are members of his body, of his flesh, and of his bones. (31) For this cause shall a man leave his father and mother, and shall be joined unto his wife, and they two shall be one flesh. (32) This is a great mystery: but I speak concerning Christ and the church. (33) Nevertheless let every one of you in particular so love his wife even as himself; and the wife see that she reverence her husband.

Verse 22. Paul now turned his focus to the home of the believer. If Christ is truly Lord over the believer's life, the first place this will be evident is in the home. After the individual puts away sin and possesses the true light of Christ, he can then bring the light of his new way of life into his home.

Paul began his discourse on the home by reminding the wife of her Christian duty to submit to her husband (I Corinthians 11:3; Titus 2:5; I Peter 3:1). The words "submit yourselves" are not found in the Greek but were inserted by the translators because of the context of the verse in relation to verse 21. Submission must progress beyond the general assembly of the saints and reach into the home.

We should note that Paul discussed the duties of husband and wife, not their rights. Submission is not slavery, bondage, or subjecting oneself to demeaning abuse. It is recognizing the husband's God-given authority to lead the home. When a wife submits to her husband's leadership, she honors God's plan. Leadership is not dictatorship, nor is it a license for abuse.

One must keep in mind the cultures of Paul's day. In Jewish, Greek, and Roman cultures women had a very low estate. They were despised by the male populace. Paul's theology on a woman's place in the home and church was revolutionary, to say the least, because he explained that in the kingdom of God "there is neither male nor female: for ye are all one in Christ Jesus" (Galatians 3:28). Under divine inspiration he gave a place of spiritual equality to the woman, with the same right to redemption and blessing as the man.

However, while husband and wife are coequal marriage partners, only one person can lead the home, and God intended the man to be that leader. Besides being the only way to please God, it is the only way to maintain unity and peace. The wife is to submit "as unto the Lord." This does not mean the husband takes the place of Christ, but it is the wife's duty to the Lord to submit to her husband. If the wife truly loves the Lord she will love her husband and allow him to realize his God-ordained role in the home (I Corinthians 7:3-5).

Verse 23. The love relationship of husband and wife should mirror that of Christ and the church. God has ordained a certain leadership, beginning with Christ in heaven. Christ is the head of the man, and He delegates this leadership to the man over his home (I Corinthians 11:3). Comparing marriage to the bond of Christ and the church placed a much stronger emphasis on marriage than did the society in which Paul lived, for it did not require monogamy.

The church is to be God's witness in the earth, and in order for that witness to achieve its maximum effectiveness, the relationship between husband and wife must comply with God's standard. His standard is not humiliating for the woman. As Christ is "saviour of the body," so the husband must be the protector of his bride. When Jesus Christ chose to learn obedience by the cross, He accepted His responsibility to care for the church's every spiritual need. So must a husband accept his responsibility to care for his wife, for they are "one flesh" (Genesis 2:24).

If a couple will pattern their marital relationship after the relationship of Christ and the church, then they will establish a mutual dependence that will ensure the success of that marriage. Each person must do his or her part, sharing a mutual responsibility but also enjoying a mutual benefit. This success will, in turn, lead to a more effective witness, enhancing the purpose that God has originally intended for His church. Healthy homes produce a healthy church.

Verse 24. It would not have been out of character for Paul to deviate from his discussion and elaborate on Christ's being the Savior of the body, but significantly, he did not. Instead, Paul reiterated the importance of the wife's duty, a duty no less lofty than the church's submission to Christ. The marital relationship is shown in more grandeur than ever before. The true character of the church is best seen in the relationship of husband and wife.

Paul stressed that when a woman accepts the responsibility of marriage and a family, she must also accept her role in that family. Though this by no means demeans her abilities or talents, she must put her family first. The wording of this verse receives a great deal of criticism by modern proponents of women's rights. However, their argument is weakened when we consider that this submission is a matter of choice and not force.

Verse 25. Paul did not neglect the duty of the husband. His obligation is to express unselfish love, which brings balance to the wife's submission. He must provide a loving atmosphere based on total concern for her welfare.

Submission is not possible in an abusive situation, because submission is a choice. In order for the wife to fulfill her role, she must receive a love that is higher than affection, admiration, or passion. It must be a true, unselfish love that manifests an unceasing desire to protect her and care for her well-being. The husband must have a self-sacrificing love such as Christ has for the church.

The husband's duty in a marriage is much greater because his model is much greater. Even though the church's obedience may fall short of the true ideal, Christ's love is never insufficient or inadequate. God demands that the husband love his wife no less than Christ loved the church, which He demonstrated at Calvary when He died for the church. This kind of love safeguards the relationship and preserves the wife's sense of well-being, by providing a conducive environment for her to fulfill her duty to the husband. The verse even suggests that the husband should be willing to lay down his life for the benefit of his wife and family. He should view the marital relationship as an opportunity to give rather than receive.

Verse 26. As was typical for Paul, he deviated from the topic at hand to delve deeper into the redemption truths of Christ's sacrifice for the church. He left the topic of marriage to dwell on the awesome power contained in the Cross and the true purpose of Christ's sacrifice by showing its effect on the life of the believer.

Through the Cross Jesus Christ has made the church His true possession. She now belongs to Him, totally and absolutely. When a man and woman are joined together in matrimony they claim possession of one another's lives. Jesus Christ, likewise, claims ownership of His bride.

Before He can do so the church must be free from sin. In this regard, the verse mentions two works: sanctification and cleansing. "Sanctify" refers to a continual action. "Cleanse" in the Greek is an aorist (simple past) participle, referring to a past event—literally "having cleansed." Christ's provision for His bride by His sacrifice on the cross includes both the removal of past sin and the ongoing process of separation from sin in the present. Without a daily provision of sanctification the world would swallow up the believer. This fact does not diminish the power of the past experience of repentance and water baptism, but it does show the absolute necessity of the believer's continual renewal and daily walk in the Spirit (Romans 8:4; 12:2).

Much controversy has arisen over the final clause of this verse: "With the washing of water by the word." Some say it refers to the preaching of the gospel, but it more likely refers to water baptism administered with the spoken word. There is a similar reference in Titus 3:5, when Paul spoke of water baptism as the "washing of regeneration." In the Greek here, the "word" is *rhema,* a specific statement, not the more general and inclusive *logos.* In the New Testament, the significant word spoken over the believer for his cleansing from sin is the name of Jesus invoked at water baptism. "Arise, and be baptized, and wash away thy sins, calling on the name of the Lord" (Acts 22:16).

Verse 27. The ultimate goal of Calvary is for Christ to present to Himself a church that has been totally perfected and is altogether lovely. This presentation is the church's future, her glory, and the completion of her redemption.

As verse 26 shows, without Christ's continual sanctifying process the church would never obtain this future glory. The church today is spotted and imperfect, to say the least, but this fact motivates us to glorify God for the tremendous grace He has bestowed upon His imperfect church and for the assurance of future perfection.

This future glory is the purpose of Christ's mission. Verse 26 says, "Look at what Christ has already done and is doing," while verse 27 says, "Look at what Christ shall do." These two verses, as well as Ephesians 1:14, state the theme of the entire epistle, drawing back the veil to let us view both God's present work in the church and His future promise for the church.

Christ's presentation of the church to Himself is the final part of a threefold presentation of the church. Part one occurs when the individual believer presents himself to Christ for salvation and service (Romans 12:1). The second part is what Paul considered his ultimate goal as an apostle: to present the church to Christ as a chaste virgin (II Corinthians 11:2). The work of the ministry in preaching the Word prepares the believer for the final presentation (Colossians 1:28), when Christ presents the church to Himself as a bride standing before her husband arrayed in the finest apparel, radiant in her beauty.

This glory can only result from a sovereign work of grace. "This is the LORD'S doing; it is marvellous in our eyes" (Psalm 118:23). God's work of grace will ultimately remove all spots and wrinkles. God is able to cleanse the church from sins of the spirit and of the flesh, in order that we might be holy and without blemish (Ephesians 1:4). This is impossible without His loving care and ministry of grace, but it also requires that we personally appropriate His grace on a daily basis and let it work in our lives. "Having therefore these promises, dearly beloved, let us cleanse ourselves from all filthiness of the flesh and spirit, perfecting holiness in the fear of God" (II Corinthians 7:1).

Verse 28. Paul returned to his original discourse on marriage, again stating the responsibility of the husband to love his wife. The word "so" brings with it a tremendous meaning. It says that the effect a husband's love has on his wife is similar, though in a limited way, to the effect of Christ's love upon the church. Because of her husband's love, a wife will be able to grow and flourish. His love makes something beautiful out of her life. The husband is not only responsible to take care of his wife in the natural sense, but he is also responsible for her spiritual development. If the husband will follow the example set by Jesus Christ, he will seek the best for his wife. This is not a self-love that seeks its own profit, but an unselfish love that allows the wife to reach her greatest potential.

Since husband and wife are one flesh and "heirs together of the grace of life" (I Peter 3:7), when a man's wife benefits, he benefits. Thus it is in his own best interest to love and take care of his wife. When he loves his wife unselfishly, he actually acts lovingly toward himself.

Verse 29. A man who mistreats his wife destroys himself and defeats his own purpose, ruining his own opportunities for fulfillment and happiness in life as well as hers. Consequently, he is inflicting spiritual injury upon himself.

A man nurtures himself by providing all the creature comforts his income will allow. He nourishes his body with food and his mind with knowledge in order to reach life's highest possible standard of living. In the same manner, the husband is to care for his wife. This command extends beyond his wife to include his children also (Ephesians 6:4; I Thessalonians 2:7).

This passage shows that a man's care for his family is a matter of self-preservation. If he mistreats his family, he ultimately causes his own harm and self-destruction. Therefore, a man's highest good is found in not just taking care of himself but his wife also. Jesus Christ, in His love for the church, is our model of loving provision.

Verse 30. Again, Paul emphasized the tremendous importance of the marital relationship, for it serves a greater purpose than simply enabling husbands and wives to get along with one another. It exemplifies the relationship between Christ and the church, allowing the church to become what she is intended to be. The church cannot reach her greatest potential unless its marital relationships are in proper order.

As Christians, we are members of Christ's body. As such, we are examples to the world of Christ's love, and we should show His love in our marriage. We are one with Christ and a part of His purpose because we are "of his flesh, and of his bones." We partake of the divine nature and life. Since we are all part of His body, we ought to love one another and care for each member of the body. The wife is part of the very life of her husband. Any disloyalty and unfaithfulness on her part will devastate his life as surely as his mistreatment of her would.

Verse 31. Paul quoted directly from Genesis 2:24, which Christ used as strong support for His teaching on the permanence of marriage and the wrongfulness of divorce (Matthew 19:3-9; Mark 10:2-12). God's original purpose for marriage was not for it to end in divorce but for God to be glorified. This statement provides a strong barrier to withstand Satan's attacks on marriage by polygamy, promiscuity, adultery, and divorce.

259

Christ used Genesis 2:24 to teach that God's intention was for man and woman, once married, to stay married until death separated them. Their life together in harmony and love would provide the best environment for godly living. Serving God together would make it easier for both to serve the Lord and provide a proper atmosphere to raise children in the fear of God. In order to establish a new family, a man must leave behind his former family.

Parental interference has ended many a marriage. It is difficult for two people to establish their marriage if their parents constantly try to intervene. It is understandable that parents have a difficult time staying out of their children's marital difficulties, for they want what is best for their children. But it invariably makes matters worse. God's purpose is for the man to leave his parents to establish his own life with his wife.

Verse 32. In essence Paul said, "This truth is no longer hid; it is clearly seen, but consider how wonderful it really is." The use of the word "mystery" (Greek: *musterion*) in reference to Genesis 2:24 implies that it contains greater truth than is seen on the surface. Through the gospel of Jesus Christ the mystery is now being manifested. The comparison to Christ and the church shows the beauty of the marital relationship. The rich symbolism reveals that the marriage bond has a much greater significance than the Jews or Gentiles had realized. The relationship between Christ and the church serves as a perfect pattern for the ideal marriage, with husbands and wives walking together in love and working together for the cause of Jesus Christ. Moreover, a successful marriage serves to point people to Christ and His church.

Paul used "mystery" to describe eternal secrets that had been hid from view until Christ came to reveal them. One of these mysteries is the role of marriage in disclosing God's eternal purpose for the church.

This verse shows that marriage is not just an earthly contract between two people, but a divine joining together of two people into one new unit. Marriage is a God-ordained institution. Because of the church's special revelation of the importance of marriage, she should hold this truth in her sacred trust, never violating the principle by condoning any immoral conduct.

Verse 33. Paul summed up his discourse on marriage with some practical admonitions. Each husband is to love his wife as himself. A husband is to give love (Greek: *agape*) sacrificially, because as the head of the house he holds the responsibility of nourishing his family. The husband must remember that he represents Jesus Christ to his family, and his concern for them, though imperfect, is a picture of Christ's concern for His church. A failure to live according to this ideal will not only injure his family and himself, but also the cause of Christ in general.

On the other hand, each wife should be loyal to her husband, showing respect for his position. She should do so with the knowledge that her dependence upon her husband's protection and her submission to his leadership represent the church's obedience to Christ. This reverence, or respect, is based on the knowledge that without her freely given loyalty, the marriage bond would be broken and the very life and mission of her husband severely affected. The wife should continually be aware that her submission serves as a pattern of how to live and act toward the Lord.

2. Parents and Children (6:1-4)

(1) Children, obey your parents in the Lord: for this is right. (2) Honour thy father and mother; (which is the first commandment with promise;) (3) that it may be well with thee, and thou mayest live long on the earth. (4) And, ye fathers, provoke not your children to wrath: but bring them up in the nurture and admonition of the Lord.

Verse 1. Paul provided instruction for the discipline of children. Pastors have scriptural authority to teach about the home, both about marriage and about rearing children.

Paul desired the walk of the believer to extend beyond the border of the church community into the home. He discussed the necessity of properly ordered marriages and then began a discussion of the proper relationship between children and their parents.

In this verse, Paul addressed Christian homes in which both parents serve the Lord. By no means did the apostle teach that children should obey parental commands contrary to the laws of God. The law of Christ would never allow for sinful or unrighteous demands upon a child. This is the significance of the words "in the Lord." What is done "in the Lord" will be done for the nurture and benefit of the child.

Children's willing obedience to their parents should come from their love for God, "for this is right." The parallel passage in Colossians 3:20 states, "This is well pleasing unto the Lord." When family discipline falters, society in general suffers. Christ set the example for the home by submitting to His parents (Luke 2:51).

Even in the animal kingdom the young ones are taught obedience. How much more should the Christian home be a showcase of Christian graces and virtues. The family structure is a God-ordained shelter in which people find safety and peace, to allow them to grow and flourish. Any nation that allows the destruction of the home is creating its own doomsday (Romans 1:30; II Timothy 3:2).

Verse 2. Paul appealed to the fifth commandment to support his teaching (Exodus 20:12; Deuteronomy 5:16). Children should honor their parents as well as obey them. When honor is given the child takes upon himself a personal concern for his parents' welfare. He will show both respect and concern for those who gave him life.

Paul noted that the fifth commandment is the "first commandment with promise." Some question this observation because the second commandment describes God's mercy to ensuing generations (Exodus 20:6). But that is a statement concerning God's character rather than a promise.

Nations fall apart when their family structure falls apart. A nation's survival depends on the home being a safe, orderly, and sacred place. Unfortunately in our day many homes are no longer safe because immorality prevails. It is the church's responsibility to raise up a standard against the decline of society by implementing the Word of God and displaying to the world a more perfect way of life in the home.

Verse 3. In Deuteronomy 4:40; 5:33 God promised peace, prosperity, and long life to those who kept the law. Here Paul cited the specific promise in Deuteronomy 5:16 of well-being and long life for children who obey their parents. The greater one's obedience to God's law, the less exposure to the hostile elements that threaten one's well-being. Sin will strip any person of dignity, demeaning that person and ruining the qualities that make life truly enjoyable.

This statement does not imply that if a person dies young he was disobedient to his parents. Rather it expresses a general principle. It shows the importance of family life and its effect on individuals and society. When the family is in disarray society's moral fiber is torn; the people who suffer the most are the children.

Verse 4. Again, the duties of one party are balanced by the duties of the other. Not only do children have a responsibility to their parents, but parents have a responsibility to their children. There is a mutual obligation. This principle holds true for all relationships (Ephesians 5:21). Mutual submission should characterize the entire life of Christians.

Parents cannot demand honor and obedience of their children; they must earn it by providing a loving atmosphere conducive for children to show their loyalty. Unreasonable demands and harshness only serve to cause discouragement, as the parallel passage in Colossians 3:21 points out. Dictatorial control in the home will cause its destruction. When children feel the pressure of having to perform beyond their ability, they can be severely damaged. Children have less patience and strength of character than adults, and parents, especially fathers, should take this into consideration.

Why did Paul address the fathers? The father is the head of the home. In Roman society he had total control over his family. He could sell them, kill them, or put them up for adoption. To counteract the abusiveness that this type of authority can create, Paul commanded the father to accept his children and raise them up in the nurture and admonition of the Lord. Moreover, fathers need to moderate their demands because their masculine nature can lend itself to harshness, which can be hurtful to children rather than helpful.

Parents, especially fathers, have a threefold obligation to their children:

1. "Provoke not your children to wrath." Instead of cultivating anger by harsh, unreasonable, and arbitrary actions, parents are to encourage their children. Children need the acceptance of their parents. In an atmosphere of encouragement children are able to achieve greater things. Without it they very seldom live up to their true potential.

2. "Bring them up in the nurture . . . of the Lord." The word "nurture" comes from the Greek word *paideia,* which means "discipline." Parents must couple encouragement with discipline. Children who are not taught proper discipline, even though they feel accepted, will not prosper. Discipline is too often left to the mother. A mother needs to uphold the discipline of the father, but he has the primary responsibility for the training and discipline of the children.

3. "Bring them up in the . . . admonition of the Lord." The word "admonition" comes from the Greek word *nouthesia,* which means "instruction." Parents need to teach their children to love, respect, and obey God. Many times they leave this task to the Sunday school teacher and the pastor, but God desires for the home to provide this teaching as well. But verbal instruction is not enough. The parents' lives should provide a path for the children to follow. Example is always the best teacher.

3. Masters and Slaves (6:5-9)

(5) Servants, be obedient to them that are your masters according to the flesh, with fear and trembling, in single-ness of your heart, as unto Christ; (6) not with eyeservice, as menpleasers; but as the servants of Christ, doing the will of God from the heart; (7) with good will doing service, as to the Lord, and not to men: (8) knowing that whatsoever good thing any man doeth, the same shall he receive of the Lord, whether he be bond or free. (9) And, ye masters, do the same things unto them, forbearing threatening: knowing that your Master also is in heaven; neither is there respect of persons with him.

Verse 5. Paul next addressed the relationship between masters and slaves. While slavery has been abolished, the principles taught here have relevance today for employers and employees.

Slavery was prevalent in Paul's day, and the issue had to be addressed. Since Paul discussed the duties of slaves more than masters, we can assume that the early church contained more slaves than masters. In the case of Philemon, both master and slave were converts.

It was possible, and history testifies, that a slave could become a church leader and minister in the church. This would present a problem for society, especially since slaves were not considered to be people, but possessions, tools to be used as the master wished. Therefore, Paul carefully outlined the proper behavior for slaves, to avoid appearing as though he were trying to create a slave revolution. This would have been disastrous for the fledgling church, which was already experiencing persecution.

The New Testament did not openly condemn slavery, yet the principles taught by Jesus and the apostles definitely opposed such a social order. The gospel was not designed to overthrow governments, but to overthrow sin in the hearts of people. Once delivered from sin, they would begin to view the world, including servants, with a new heart. Change from within is a more effective method of correcting the social disorders that plague society.

In the midst of this chaotic society Paul urged the servants to be obedient to their masters, "as unto Christ." They are not really serving their earthly masters, who only have authority "according to the flesh," but their Master in heaven. Becoming a Christian does not erase one's obligation to do a good job. Employees of today can take this good advice and become better witnesses for Jesus by giving their employers an honest day's work.

They are to do their job with "fear and trembling, in singleness of heart." The parallel passage of Colossians 3:22 explains that servants are to fear God, being careful to please Him. When Christians are on the job, they should devote all their attention to doing their very best because they are a witness for the church and represent Jesus Christ to the world.

Verse 6. Servants are to give their work the utmost attention, whether their master is watching them or not. Some people work hard only when they are being watched and can expect special favors from the boss. A true Christian knows that his work exemplifies his walk with God. He does not do a good job simply to be rewarded by his earthly boss, but because he is a servant of God. As a servant of the Lord he performs his duties, knowing that this is God's will for his life, and he does it from the heart.

Verse 7. Servants should be ready and willing to do their job, not grudgingly, but "with good will." Again,

Paul stressed that they should perform their tasks for the Lord and not merely for men. Upon their shoulders they carry the responsibility of representing Jesus Christ to their master and his household, which carries with it the greater purpose of being a witness of God's grace. A willingness to serve, which brings glory to God, ultimately serves as a witness that Jesus is Lord.

Verse 8. The principle discussed in this verse applies to all people, whether they are servants or masters, in slavery or freedom. If in obedience to God's Word someone performs a good deed, God in heaven, who is the Master of all, will reward him. Jesus taught this principle when He said, "And whosoever shall give to drink unto one of these little ones a cup of cold water only in the name of a disciple, verily I say unto you, he shall in no wise lose his reward" (Matthew 10:42).

All service is to be rendered with this truth in mind—that God is the true rewarder of those who diligently perform their Christian duties with the right attitude. The performance of duty does not affect people nearly as much as the spirit in which it is done.

This truth is given to encourage the believer. Even though the work is difficult and the master incorrigible, the servant is to work cheerfully, for God will reward him. The reverse is also true: "But he that doeth wrong shall receive for the wrong which he hath done: and there is no respect of persons" (Colossians 3:25).

The judgment seat of Christ is in view here. Every believer should realize that he will not receive some rewards on earth; they must wait until the final day. As long as they lay up treasure in heaven where the thief cannot steal and rust cannot corrupt, they will receive their reward at the appointed time (Matthew 6:1-6, 19-20).

Verse 9. Masters are to treat their servants in the same manner as servants are to treat their masters—with fairness, diligence, respect, and obedience to God. They must forego threats of abuse or, even worse, carrying out those threats. Under Roman law the master had complete control over the lives of his slaves, but this verse establishes restraints and duties for the master, transforming the relationship. The master must treat his servants in a way that would be pleasing to the Lord, knowing that God will judge him by the same standard that He will use for everyone else.

The master has a responsibility to reveal Christ to his household, which includes his servants. This should be done with the knowledge that God is no respecter of persons. He treats all people the same. He is the Heavenly Master of both masters and servants, and He will judge both according to their works.

The best observance of this principle is seen in Paul's letter to Philemon, which Paul sent by Onesimus, Philemon's runaway slave. Paul did not ask Philemon for the emancipation of Onesimus. He hinted that Philemon should grant Onesimus's freedom, but only as an act of Philemon's free will. If Paul had made a stronger appeal, using his apostolic authority to try to wrest freedom for the slaves, the legal wrath of the government could have fallen upon the church. Paul's purpose was to set down the principles of the gospel, which would provide a seedbed of truth where the emancipation of slaves could grow.

IV.

The Bride's Standing in Christ

(6:10-20)

A. Standing against the Wiles of the Devil (6:10-13)
B. Standing Clothed in the Armor (6:14-17)
C. Standing with All Prayer (6:18-20)

A.

Standing against the Wiles of the Devil

(6:10-13)

(10) Finally, my brethren, be strong in the Lord, and in the power of his might. (11) Put on the whole armour of God, that ye may be able to stand against the wiles of the devil. (12) For we wrestle not against flesh and blood, but against principalities, against powers, against the rulers of the darkness of this world, against spiritual wickedness in high places. (13) Wherefore take unto you the whole armour of God, that ye may be able to withstand in the evil day, and having done all, to stand.

Verse 10. The use of the word "finally" denotes Paul's effort to draw this epistle to a close. In conclusion, he turned the attention of the readers to the conflict that lies ahead of every believer. The use of "finally" also provides a connection with the previous revelations of the epistle.

Ephesians began with Paul opening the treasure chest of truth to make available the riches of Christ's mercy and grace. Then he revealed the eternal purpose for which these possessions are to be used. Thus he issued a challenge for believers to conduct themselves in a manner that promotes unity in the body—the church and the family. Now that he had outlined the riches and relationships with

Christ, the church, and the home, Paul discussed the final facet of a Christian's warfare.

From the home, he turned to the battlefield. He gave a call to arms because Satan is on the prowl, ready to pounce upon the untrained and unsuspecting soldier of the Cross. His purpose is to steal away the wealth and disrupt the unity of both church and home with the intention of ultimately destroying God's purpose. It is clearly a time for war.

The need for proper training in warfare becomes clear when we see the connection with the earlier revelations. Once believers have achieved unity through submission and love for one another, they must accept their place in the great controversy. Without spiritual warfare, this evil world would swallow up the church and make us unable to defeat the enemy. But before Paul gave instructions to train the believer for this battle, he proclaimed the need for strength in the inner man.

The concluding portion of the epistle gives help in the time of inevitable conflicts. These conflicts come to all the members of the body—not just ministers, but to the "brethren." No one is left out. Satan is not satisfied to destroy just the ministry, but he wants the saints as well. So what comes after "finally" is wise counsel for all who seek to live a victorious life in Christ.

When the believer is tried by Satan at some point in the future, in order to win the victory he must first recognize the source of strength. The revelations of the Bible will do no good if we do not recognize our need for strength that will defeat the foe in battle. The believer needs to know that God can make him strong enough to win, strong enough to defeat Satan.

The word "strength" (Greek: *endunamoo*) means "enabling." The same word is also used in Acts 9:22; Philippians 4:13; I Timothy 1:12; II Timothy 4:17. We are enabled for war! We are to be "made effective for the end contemplated . . . the work that must be done."[1] Now that we know who we are, what we have, and how we are to act, we can use that knowledge to wage an effective military campaign against the forces of darkness.

We must not quit or give up. Instead of looking at ourselves or at the enemy, we must look to the Lord. Christ has already won the victory. Strength is already available. We should call upon these inexhaustible resources to conquer the foe.

Where does this strength come from? It comes from the Lord. We are to be strong "in the Lord." We have steadfast assurance that strength is available through a vital union with Jesus Christ in the Spirit. This phrase "in the Lord" appears in one form or another about thirty-five times in this epistle alone, which shows the tremendous emphasis Paul placed on the development of a personal relationship with Jesus Christ.

Paul spoke of Jesus as a person, and not just as Messiah, or Savior, but as Lord. Jesus became the rightful ruler through His triumph at Calvary. The possessions, purpose, and power that are rightfully His now belong to the church, who are joint heirs with Him (Romans 8:17).

Being "in the Lord" is being hid in Christ (Colossians 3:3). This abiding enables us not only to walk uprightly but also to engage the enemy in spiritual combat.

In addition to strength, we also need "the power of his might." The person of Christ also possesses the power. This phrase is already familiar to us because of the same

Greek wording in Ephesians 1:19. That verse refers to the resurrection and ascension of Jesus Christ—in short, His exaltation. It is not a mere figure of speech. It is real! The enemy is real and the battle is real, but the power is also just as real. The power available to us is the same power that raised Christ from the dead and accomplished His exaltation. What makes Him Lord also makes the church triumphant.

The battle will be difficult and fraught with danger. Some may faint and become casualties. But if the believer can be properly trained and equipped by the fivefold ministry with the proper weapons, then the victory is assured.

We must understand that this battle is more than a moral conflict of the passions versus conscience. It is not a conflict between people. There is an ancient enemy who hates God and all He stands for. Likewise, he hates the people of God. Therefore we must receive strength for this inevitable conflict, seeking strength from the true source—the Lord Jesus Christ. God gives power to overcome, as the parallel passage in Colossians 1:11 confirms. We are commissioned to be strong, strong enough to be patient and longsuffering, with joyfulness. There is no better way to begin the good fight of faith.

Verse 11. The believer experiences the strength of God in his life by obeying the command to "put on the whole armour of God." Again, the Christian is urged to take on something other than himself. In essence Paul said to the church, "Not in your own energy will you conquer the devil but by what God supplies." This command is not unusual in Paul's writings. In Romans 13:12 he said, "Let us put on the armour of light," and in I Thessalonians 5:8 he wrote, "But let us, who are of the day, be sober, putting on the breastplate of faith and love; and for an helmet, the hope of salvation."

The believer is supposed to put on the "whole armour of God." Verse 13 repeats this command. In the Greek the word for "whole armour" is *panoplia,* which refers to the sum total of all the pieces described in greater detail in verses 14-17. Putting on the armor of God is much like what the Amplified Bible says happened to Gideon in Judges 6:34: "But the Spirit of the LORD clothed Gideon with Himself and took possession of him." When this happens victory is inevitable.

Paul found a precise analogy of Christian life in the armor of the Roman soldier to which he was chained. From it he drew the parallels that give striking insight into what is necessary for a believer to wage a successful spiritual campaign against the forces of darkness.

The purpose for diligence in Christian life is "that ye may be able to stand against the wiles of the devil." "Stand" is the key word in this entire passage. We must seek for power from the Lord because the devil will try to destroy every person who pledges faith in Jesus Christ. "Be sober, be vigilant; because your adversary the devil, as a roaring lion, walketh about, seeking whom he may devour" (I Peter 5:8). If we are going to endure the onslaught of the enemy we must be properly trained and equipped.

Who is this enemy? In this passage Paul calls him the "devil" (Greek: *diabolos*), which means "accuser." Throughout his writings Paul acquainted his readers with the devil, using various names and descriptive terminology. Compared to the New Testament, the Old Testament says little about Satan. When Jesus, the light of the world came, He exposed and defeated this fiend.

Paul described Satan in Ephesians 2:2 as the "prince of the power of the air" and in II Corinthians 4:4 as "the god of this world." Satan's sphere of influence is twofold: the air (spiritual realm) and this world (earthly realm). Right now he rules over the demons and the sinners of this world. Only through the new birth can a person be delivered from the power of Satan and translated into the kingdom of Jesus Christ (Acts 26:18; Colossians 1:13).

The devil has certain "wiles" that we must avoid and withstand. "Wiles" means "cunning craftiness" or "strategies." The devil has a plan of action to defeat God's plan. His purpose is to snare men (II Timothy 2:26) by tempting them with lies and deceitful lusts (Matthew 4:3; John 8:44).

He is a deceitful angel who transforms himself into an angel of light (II Corinthians 11:14). He is known as a serpent for his subtlety (Genesis 3:1; Revelation 12:9). The devil has his own religious followers with his own ministers that proclaim a false gospel and false doctrines (II Corinthians 11:13-15; Galatians 1:9; I Timothy 4:1; Revelation 2:9). Through their deception he seduces people into sacrificing to him in worship and fellowship at his table, drinking from his cup (I Corinthians 10:20-21). This drags people to his depths (Revelation 2:24). His power is destructive and supernatural.

Even though the devil possesses great power, he is not God. He does not have the attributes of God. He is not omnipotent, omnipresent, or omniscient. Therefore, he can be defeated. Not only has Jesus Christ defeated him both on earth and in the heavenlies, He desires to share that victory with His church. The church can now carry on the work of Jesus Christ in the earth.

We should not underestimate the destructive power of Satan, especially considering Job's experience. Therefore, it behooves every believer to prepare himself for his attacks. Satan is a real, supernatural being with a deep hatred for God and the church. If he were just a figure of speech, a moral evil, or a man, perhaps we could use earthly means to defeat him. But he is not! Therefore, we need God's strength. "Submit yourselves therefore to God. Resist the devil, and he will flee from you" (James 4:7). Our victory is assured when we understand the devil's tactics. "Lest Satan should get an advantage of us: for we are not ignorant of his devices" (II Corinthians 2:11).

Verse 12. Today, many deny the existence of a literal devil with an organized horde of evil spirits. However, Jesus and the New Testament writers used plain language to confirm the existence of the devil and demons (Matthew 4:1-11; Mark 5:9, 15; Luke 8:30; James 4:7; I Peter 5:8; I John 5:18).

Every division of the New Testament depicts the devil as a spirit being who is in control of other spirits that challenge Christ and His kingdom. This conflict is not imaginary or abstract. It is very real. "It is a conflict maintained, in Christ, with divine power and from a dominating position."[2]

We must understand that our enemy is more than just a man. "For we wrestle not against flesh and blood." The battle is not against humanity. "Flesh and blood" refers to other humans, not to moral weaknesses. The enemy is Satan and his well-organized group of demons. These spirits make up a kingdom that has established itself on this earth to tempt and provoke humans to sin. The more people succumb to Satan's temptations the more they come under Satan's control.

Paul moved from describing a soldier armed for battle to describing a wrestler grappling in hand-to-hand combat with an individual foe. Paul commonly used military terms and terms related to the Olympic games in his epistles. (See II Timothy 2:3-5.) But in this verse the word "wrestle" (Greek: *pale*) does not refer to the wrestling matches of the games, but to combat in which the soldier must grapple with the enemy one on one.

Every Christian is involved in such a struggle, whether he realizes it or not. The enemy's purpose is to establish strongholds in the minds of people with thought patterns that dominate their actions. If Satan can, by suggestions, cause the desired response, he can manipulate the individual for his own purposes. (See II Corinthians 10:3-5.)

Satan's kingdom is well organized. This verse implies, as does Daniel 10:13-20, that certain demons are assigned to certain geographical locations. In Daniel, the "prince of Grecia" and the "prince of the kingdom of Persia" momentarily hindered the progress of God's angelic messenger, Gabriel, but they could not stop the ultimate victory Daniel gained by persevering in prayer and fasting, for God sent the angel Michael to help Gabriel overcome.

The organization of Satan's kingdom is also indicated by the demons who called themselves "Legion" (Mark 5:9, 15; Luke 8:30). The use of this word reveals a large number of demons involved and also implies a military regimen maintained by Satan and his helpers. (See also Matthew 25:41; John 12:31; 14:30; II Corinthians 4:4; 12:7; Revelation 12:7-9.)

The leaders and members of Satan's organized kingdom of evil spirits are called "principalities and powers" and "rulers of the darkness of this world." The Greek word for "rulers" is *kosmokratoras* or "world rulers." Satan dominates sinful humanity through his kingdom. Consequently, the world lies in darkness, or wickedness (I John 5:19; Colossians 1:13). The darkness perpetuates its existence by dominating individual lives, governments, and worldly institutions. Against these evil spirits and their influences, the believers must declare war. These dark forces control the thoughts of sinners, and they can only be truly liberated through the light of the gospel (II Corinthians 4:4). The purpose of spiritual combat is not to destroy Satan, for Christ has already defeated him, but to liberate people from the bondage of darkness (II Corinthians 4:1-6).

The last description of our enemy is "spiritual wickedness in high places." Many commentators have a problem with this part of the verse because of its reference to the heavenlies as a dwelling place for these wicked spirits. (See commentary on Ephesians 2:2.) Their habitation is not physical, but spiritual. In the spirit realm they conduct all their malevolent activities against the people and purposes of God. This spiritual plane is the place where we wage the battle in prayer and where these powers are defeated.

"Spiritual wickedness" can mean "spirits of wickedness." This phrase describes evil spirits under the control of Satan and his demonic hierarchy. These evil spirits are directed to their attack on every believer.

Ephesians 1:21 and the parallel passage in Colossians 2:15 similarly list the enemies that confront the believer.

Both verses show conclusively that Jesus Christ, by His exaltation, has thoroughly defeated these *kosmokratoras*. This victory is already won and is available to every believer.

Verse 13 restates the command of verse 11. As the believer becomes aware of the spiritual enemy facing him, he should employ all the armor of the Lord to realize in his own personal life the triumph already available. No piece of this armor can be left out. Every piece is necessary if victory is to be assured. Each piece works together to provide the maximum protection in defense against the attacks of Satan.

Verses 14-17 list six items. Five items are for protection (defensive) and one is for attack (offensive). The equipment is available, but its availability does not guarantee the results. The believer must personally appropriate Christ's victory by: (1) believing that Christ desires him to put on this spiritual armor, (2) understanding the tremendous powers that war against him, and (3) realizing that only through faith, in union with Christ, can he find victory.

The purpose for taking this armor is "to withstand in the evil day." The "evil day" is the present evil of this world with its trials and difficulties, including moral and supernatural dimensions. It is a day of trial and testing but also a day to prove the power of our God. The armor provides the ability to "withstand" (Greek: *antistenai*) the enemy—to stand against all opposition, no matter how great. "Withstand" means to defend territory that has already been taken and to take new territory. In both cases, the armor helps bring down the opposing forces. This battle will intensify as Christ's second coming draws near (Matthew 24:22; Mark 13:20; Revelation 12:12).

The final command of this verse is, "Having done all, to stand." We have done all when we equip ourselves with every available item for both defense and offense, when we have applied every truth we know and prayed every prayer we can pray. After this, we must take our stand on what God has promised.

After every victory Satan will attempt to take back what we have gained in battle. We have to stand up to him and not let him have it back. God desires for every believer to maintain the ground taken and to remain victorious. We should resist Satan and give him no place to gain back what he has lost (Ephesians 4:27; James 4:7; I Peter 5:9).

Let us have confidence in what Jesus said: "In the world ye shall have tribulation: but be of good cheer; I have overcome the world" (John 16:33). Our God will not deliver us to the will of the enemy to be taken captive (Psalm 41:2), but we will overcome. "For whatsoever is born of God overcometh the world: and this is the victory that overcometh the world, even our faith" (I John 5:4).

Notes

[1]Westcott, 92.
[2]Moule, 151.

B.

Standing Clothed in the Armor
(6:14-17)

(14) Stand therefore, having your loins girt about with truth, and having on the breastplate of righteousness; (15) and your feet shod with the preparation of the gospel of peace; (16) above all, taking the shield of faith, wherewith ye shall be able to quench all the fiery darts of the wicked. (17) And take the helmet of salvation, and the sword of the Spirit, which is the word of God.

Verse 14. Taking a stand on the promises of God is an act of faith that requires the entire armor of God. In view of His provision for us, we must stand. By standing we receive power to accomplish what faith demands. We must take action by daily suiting ourselves in the armor God has provided. The pieces are listed in the order that a soldier would don them.

First, Christians are to have their "loins girt about with truth." In reality, the girdle is not a part of the armor itself but provides the means to attach the other pieces and hold them together. The flowing garments typical of the Middle East hampered the freedom of movement required for a race or battle. The only way for people to prepare themselves for such activity was to hitch their garments up with a girdle or belt. "Let your loins be girded about, and your lights burning" (Luke 12:35).

The Bible speaks of the "loins of your mind" (I Peter 1:13), suggesting that "truth" in this verse is not primarily the truth of the gospel, but more generally a sense of knowing what is right in the eyes of the Lord. The ability to ascertain the truth about sin and how it hinders forward progress will give the believer the power over that sin. To have truth as the girdle that binds all other armor provides freedom of movement—freedom to do the will of God. The importance of truth here shows why Paul earlier prayed for the church to receive enlightenment (Ephesians 1:18).

To know the truth is not enough. We need to know it, understand it, and apply it. "Behold, thou desirest truth in the inward parts: and in the hidden part thou shalt make me to know wisdom" (Psalm 51:6). Someone who does not have an understanding of what God wants will not be able to overcome the devil. The girdle of truth provides freedom of motion to fight the enemy, unhindered by personal doubt and guilt.

Truth includes sincerity of heart, which gives a person the liberty to do what God has called him to do. It empties the mind of lies and deceptions, so that the Christian soldier has clear direction for action. The Messianic prophecy in Isaiah 11:5 describes Jesus as having the girdle of righteousness and faithfulness. Truth also refers to one's ability to remain loyal to the cause and purpose of Christ's mission. If a Christian does not know what this mission is, or its purpose, then he cannot act with the decisiveness needed to defeat the wiles of Satan. Nothing gives one freedom and liberty any more than the knowledge of what to do and the rightness of one's cause.

Armed with this truth the believer is ready to don the rest of the armor and win complete victory.

The second piece of armor donned by the Christian soldier is the "breastplate of righteousness." Isaiah 59:17 mentions this piece of armor worn by Christ. He wears this breastplate to impute righteousness to the sinner (Romans 3:22). But this verse refers to more than the positional righteousness we gain by faith in Jesus Christ. It encompasses a practical righteousness that enables the believer to make the right choices, even when beset by severe temptations (II Corinthians 6:7).

The breastplate covers the vital organs of the body from wounds that could be immediately fatal. Every believer can find strength to defeat Satan in the truth of his right standing before God. But to protect himself from a fatal blow, he must have within him the ability to make right decisions every day and to take the right action in the face of temptations and disappointment.

Without the breastplate of righteousness, the believer would be snared. A believer cannot withstand the accusations of the devil unless he is living a life of victory over sin. Unrepented sin will give occasion for Satan to find fault and accuse him. Therefore, every believer needs righteousness in the Holy Ghost (Romans 14:17).

Ephesians 5:9 speaks of righteousness as an aspect of the fruit of the Spirit. As such, righteousness is more than one's right standing before God. It is strong character that gives power to the believer to remain loyal to God's purpose and law (Ephesians 4:24). Possessing this righteousness, or right character, will allow the believer to become useful for God's purpose (Romans 6:13).

A church that is unable to translate the righteousness

of Jesus Christ into right actions in the face of tempta-
tion will be vulnerable to satanic attack. For example, a
saint exposes himself to a mortal wound from Satan if
he allows hidden lust to remain in his heart. However,
when the church takes the righteousness of Christ and
transforms it into holy actions, it creates a testimony that
not only defeats the devil's purpose but also brings glory
to God.

Verse 15. The third piece of armor is likened to the
hobnailed sandals of the Roman soldier, which gave him
protection for his feet and a better footing, especially in
close-range combat. They enabled him to "stand" and
"withstand" the enemy's attacks. The shoes of the Christian's warfare are the "preparation of the gospel of
peace." In this context the word "preparation" (Greek:
hetoimasia) can refer to two things:

1. It can mean to be prepared for anything. Peace
prepares the believer for evangelism. It prepares him to
be ready to share the gospel of peace with anyone at any
time as the occasion arises. Isaiah 52:7 supports this meaning, as does Paul's quote of this Old Testament passage
in Romans 10:15. In short, the church fights for the salvation of others. Without the peace of God to give the
believer a firm footing, by ruling over his mind and spirit
(Colossians 3:15), he would not be protected. Nor would
he be able to bring the good news of the gospel to his
friends and family.

2. "Preparation" can also mean to be prepared in
one's spirit and heart by the peace that the gospel brings.
The gospel makes peace with God and humanity (Romans
5:1), bringing to the Christian an inner peace in the midst
of life's storms. This peace gives the believer a personal

victory in his own life over the discouragement caused by adverse circumstances (John 16:33; Philippians 4:7). Since we, as Christians, have peace through the gospel we can become ambassadors of peace and take the gospel and its blessing of peace to the whole world (II Corinthians 5:18-21).

Verse 16. The fourth piece of armor is "the shield of faith," which we are to take "above all." The shield of the Roman soldier covered most of the body and was flexible enough to be turned in any direction to block the blows of the enemy. The sides of the shield were designed to interlock with the other shields of fellow warriors. The soldiers could lock their shields together and march toward the enemy as one body.

Our shield is a shield of faith, not merely saving faith, but fighting faith. It means a trust and reliance upon the promises of God and His power to make those promises a reality.

Faith must cover all the other parts of the armor. Due to its flexibility, this shield can be turned to block the false accusations of the enemy, the temptations of the flesh, or tragedies that discourage. Faith can defeat whatever the enemy can throw against us. Whether an attack comes as a thought, a suggestion, or a word from someone Satan is using for his purpose, faith can defeat its influence.

The church becomes unbeatable when individual faith joins in unity with the faith of the other members of the church. Individual faith may be defeated, but the unified faith of the whole body creates an impregnable wall of invincibility. "Fight the good fight of faith, lay hold on eternal life, whereunto thou art also called, and hast professed a good profession before many witnesses" (I Timothy 6:12).

Paul proceeded to give another description of the enemy. This time he called him "the wicked," or, "the evil one," the one who loves to create troubles and trials without regard to the damage or pain inflicted upon the victims.

His weapons are "fiery darts." Fiery darts were common weapons in the arsenal of the armies of Paul's day. The dart, or arrow, was generally dipped in tar and ignited, giving the arrow maximum destructive power. Since most shields were made of wood, precautions were necessary to keep them safe from the fire. They were often covered with leather specially treated to quench the fire of an arrow. As an example, Isaiah 21:5 says, "Prepare the table, watch in the watchtower, eat, drink: arise, ye princes, and anoint the shield."

Faith is the shield that can quench all satanic temptations. Faith must be anointed with love. "For in Jesus Christ neither circumcision availeth any thing, nor uncircumcision; but faith which worketh by love" (Galatians 5:6). Only a true love that has complete trust in Jesus Christ and His purpose will be able to stand against the fears, disappointments, doubts, and lusts that Satan will launch against the believer.

Verse 17. The fifth piece of the soldier's protection is the final defensive part of the armor. The apostle urged the Ephesians to "take the helmet of salvation." Salvation is a gift to be taken by those who believe, and it provides deliverance in the midst of battle. It does more than deliver from the penalty of sin; it also protects from the power of sin. Ultimately it provides the hope of the final work of redemption as suggested in the parallel passage of I Thessalonians 5:8. Jesus Christ wears this helmet in

Isaiah 59:17, as both Creator and giver of salvation.

The helmet protects the head. Satan's first level of attack is on the mind. Through evil thoughts he can build strongholds that he uses to incite the imaginations, and from there he is able to control the actions. (See Proverbs 16:3; Isaiah 55:7; II Corinthians 10:4-5; Philippians 4:8.) The first attack the serpent made against Eve in the garden was to subtly corrupt her mind (Genesis 3; II Corinthians 11:3).

A mind controlled by the proper thoughts, especially armed with the truth of salvation's deliverance from the guilt of the past and the assurance of present and future help from the Lord, will ensure victory. That is the reason believers need a daily diet of the Word of God. They need to learn the Word in order to grow in the Lord and in the knowledge of His grace (II Peter 3:18).

The sixth piece of armor is the only offensive weapon mentioned in this list. It is the "sword of the Spirit, which is the word of God." The "word" is *rhema* in Greek, which refers to a specific truth that the Spirit applies to a specific situation. Jesus displayed this use of God's Word by quoting the written Word to defeat the devil's temptations (Luke 4:1-12).

Before the Day of Pentecost Peter attempted to use the wrong sword to protect Jesus (Luke 22:47-51), but he found a more effective sword in Acts 2:37 that cut to the heart and brought repentance. "For the word of God is quick, and powerful, and sharper than any twoedged sword, piercing even to the dividing asunder of soul and spirit, and of the joints and marrow, and is a discerner of the thoughts and intents of the heart" (Hebrews 4:12).

God gives the Christian soldier a word that is appropriate

to meet the present danger. By the use of the Word, the enemy can be overcome and the believer will triumph. "Therefore have I hewed them by the prophets; I have slain them by the words of my mouth: and thy judgments are as the light that goeth forth" (Hosea 6:5). The Word is a weapon that can bring conviction of sin into the lives of others, and it has been given to the Christian soldier by the Spirit (II Timothy 3:16; I Peter 1:11; II Peter 1:21). As the Spirit possesses the believer He provides a sword to use against the devil (John 14:17, 26; 16:13).

C.

Standing with All Prayer
(6:18-20)

(18) Praying always with all prayer and supplication in the Spirit, and watching thereunto with all perseverance and supplication for all saints; (19) and for me, that utterance may be given unto me, that I may open my mouth boldly, to make known the mystery of the gospel, (20) for which I am an ambassador in bonds: that therein I may speak boldly, as I ought to speak.

Verse 18. Prayer is not listed as part of the Christian soldier's armor, but it is necessary to the armor's function. Many people suit up but do not report for duty. The stand that a saint must take against the enemy must include prayer. For instance, there is no better way to use the Word of God than to use it in prayer. It is safe to say that without prayer the enemy would prevail. The manner in which Paul used the word "praying" can mean that each part of the armor should be put on with prayer and that prayer should continue as a result of putting on the armor.

In this verse Paul moved from the description of a believer's armor to the purpose for it, from the metaphor to the essence of the conflict. Four times in this verse he used the Greek word for "all," showing that prayer has the power to be effective regardless of occasion or circumstance. The duty of every Christian is to continually offer up strong supplications and crying to the Lord. Our Lord Jesus Christ set the example: "Who in the days of his flesh, when he had offered up prayers and supplications with strong crying and tears unto him that was able to save him from death, and was heard in that he feared" (Hebrews 5:7). This kind of prayer is to be done on behalf of others as well as for one's personal need.

Prayer requires discipline. It must become a habit to be effectual. A daily commitment to bring every need to God in prayer opens a new dimension of possibility for the believer. Satan's wiles may strike with a vengeance, but diligence in prayer is sure to defeat his every bombardment.

This verse sets before the church the need to take everything to God in prayer. Not only are we to "watch," but we are to do so "with all perseverance." Prayer is a discipline of endurance. The word "watch" simply means "to stay awake," to keep alert. The enemy is on the prowl, but a praying believer is aware of him and ready to meet the conflict head on, armed with the Word of God's promise. We must pray even when we do not feel like it, and even when it is not convenient, for only through prayer can we win the battle.

Prayer includes requests, or "supplications," but it is much more than that. Too many Christians consider prayer to be merely a time of placing their orders with God for what they want to receive personally. But prayer is communion with God. It is relationship. Thanksgiving is prayer. Intercession for others is prayer. Supplication is prayer. All of it is vital, not just for oneself, but for others also.

This verse reveals three very important truths about prayer:

1. There is more than one kind of prayer. The believer is armed with "all prayer." He is to continue in these prayers until they are answered. Even though the answer may not be immediate, it will come if one continues with perseverance. The power of prayer is unlimited. It is a resource that can never be exhausted, so we should use it to the glory of God.

2. All supplication must be "in the Spirit." Only the Holy Ghost knows exactly what we need and can lead us in God's will (Romans 8:26-27). Human effort is necessary if prayer is going to be a part of the daily walk of the believer, but without the Spirit's help that effort will ultimately fail. The Spirit provides wings to the earnest prayers of the church and lifts them above the earthly realm into the heavenly realm. Prayer can do anything God can do, because it is done "in the Spirit."

3. Prayer is to be given for "all saints." Prayer is not something that should be centered upon selfish desires. True spiritual warfare involves the entire body of Christ, not just one individual's need. No Christian who is truly at war with the enemy can neglect the camaraderie that develops between soldiers. This unity must be maintained if victory is to be assured.

Verse 19. Paul now offered his prayer request to the Ephesian church. It was a common practice for Paul to beseech others to pray for him after he had prayed for them (Colossians 4:3; I Thessalonians 5:25; II Thessalonians 3:1). Paul realized the tremendous battle he was in. He knew by experience the formidable foe he was up against. He also knew that he could not defeat the enemy within the limitations of his human efforts. So he requested the church to make strong intercession for his ministry. Satan may not stop a sermon, but he will fight to kill a ministry.

Paul asked for two things:

1. He asked that "utterance may be given unto me." It is very important for someone to have a word from God if he is going to speak for God. A ministry without a word from God will be ineffective, to say the least. Ability cannot make preaching powerful—only a word from God can. Jesus promised that the Spirit would give words to the disciples when they needed them the most (Matthew 10:19-20; Mark 13:11; John 14:26). Paul requested that the church pray this promise into reality. His desire was for God to give him the right opportunities as well as the right words at the right time. If he was to effectively declare the wonderful gospel to the Gentile world, he needed to possess the correct utterance that, under the anointing of the Holy Ghost, would have the maximum effect to bring glory to God.

2. Paul's second request, repeated in verse 20, was that he might have the boldness to declare words that God gave him to speak, thereby communicating the mystery of the gospel. In many cases, when God gives a minister the right words their profundity can make tremendous demands upon his courage. Just because one perceives the words to be from God does not mean those who hear will think so. Through boldness, Paul could make known the glorious mystery of the gospel, not for the praise of people but for the glory of Jesus Christ.

Paul set a wonderful example for the church with the nature of his request. His desire was not to be great or to receive earth's riches but that he might, with great wisdom and boldness, declare the truth of the gospel to the whole world. His burden was for the effective spreading of the gospel.

Verse 20. Throughout this epistle Paul made few references to himself, the only exceptions being his references to his imprisonment for preaching the gospel (Ephesians 3:1; 4:1; 6:20). Paul's request for prayer is made even more poignant when the reader's attention is drawn to his bonds. The chain that held him to a Roman soldier was there because he considered himself to be a personal representative of Christ's kingdom and message. His declaration of the gospel to the Gentiles had caused an uproar that led to his imprisonment.

Paul's situation was far from ideal, but he knew that regardless of his circumstances, he would be able to preach effectively because of the prayers of the church. Therefore, Paul called himself an "ambassador in bonds." In Rome, the ambassdors of various countries came and went to make their appeals to Caesar. As representatives of their respective nations, they came with their hopes and dreams to be reconciled to the mighty Roman Empire. Paul's primary desire was to represent the greatest kingdom on earth and heaven, to properly declare the truth that God had revealed to him.

Paul was not trying to evoke his readers' sympathy. Rather, he used himself as an example to them of God's grace, which was sufficient to carry him through this awful time of imprisonment and to further the preaching of the gospel. Through his circumstances they could see that their own lives could and would receive grace to overcome any hardship.

The devil could have used Paul's imprisonment to cause fear and to intimidate him to the point of keeping silent. Yet Paul was not too proud to request prayer for himself that he might be able to boldly declare the gospel in a manner that was fitting. His ambassadorial status demanded a bold declaration that had to be clear and correct. He already knew what he ought to speak, but as in verse 19, he stated his need to boldly declare the truth without fear for his own safety.

Was Paul's prayer answered? Yes! Acts 28:30-31 says, "And Paul dwelt two whole years in his own hired house, and received all that came in unto him, preaching the kingdom of God, and teaching those things which concern the Lord Jesus Christ, with all confidence, no man forbidding him."

V.

CONCLUSION

(6:21-24)

A. Tychicus, a Beloved Brother (6:21-22)
B. Prayer for Peace and Grace (6:23-24)

A.

Tychicus, a Beloved Brother
(6:21-22)

(21) But that ye also may know my affairs, and how I do, Tychicus, a beloved brother and faithful minister in the Lord, shall make known to you all things: (22) whom I have sent unto you for the same purpose, that ye might know our affairs, and that he might comfort your hearts.

Verse 21. Colossians 4:7 is almost identical to this verse. Tychicus was the bearer of the letters to the Colossians and the Ephesians, and possibly a letter to Laodicea (Colossians 4:16). This letter does not mention Onesimus, as Colossians does, because Colossae was the church where Onesimus belonged. Onesimus served Tychicus as his travel companion in the delivery of these epistles to the churches, as well as the personal letter he bore to Philemon.

Acts 20:4 mentions Tychicus as a member of Paul's party. He accompanied him on his journey with relief funds from the Gentiles to the saints in Jerusalem. Tychicus became a special messenger to the province of Asia because it was his home (II Timothy 4:12; Titus 3:12).

The churches in Asia were established as a result of Paul's ministry in Ephesus. It was Tychicus's responsibility to bear this letter to Ephesus and perhaps copies of it for the other churches in the province. Paul did not make many personal references to himself and no references to specific individuals in Ephesus, probably because he directed this letter, with its unique style, to a wider audience than a single church. Yet he knew that saints in every church would be concerned about his welfare and condition. Therefore, he sent Tychicus to convey this information because he considered him to be a "beloved brother" and a "faithful minister." They would trust the word he brought concerning the condition of Paul.

Being beloved and faithful are two enduring qualities of a Christian minister. If one is not loved by those to whom he ministers, regardless of how true or powerful his message, it will have little effect. Moreover, no ministry lasts long unless the minister remains faithful in times of storm and trial.

Undoubtedly, Paul and Tychicus were personal friends. This friendship extended beyond the mutual respect for one another's ministry. There was camaraderie that only develops when one has been faithful in extremely difficult circumstances. Such a trusted messenger would bring sure tidings about the affairs of the apostle.

This verse contains the epistle's final use of the phrase "in the Lord." The message of Ephesians resounds over and over again with the truth that brotherhood and faithful ministry can only develop in the context of a vibrant relationship in the Lord Jesus Christ.

Verse 22. Paul knew that the tidings of his condition and of the continued effectiveness of his ministry would bring comfort and cheer to the hearts of those who heard it. Whereas he wrote the epistle to minister to the saints spiritually, he sent Tychicus as a friend to let them know that, though Paul was in chains, all was well.

B.

Prayer for Peace and Grace

(6:23-24)

(23) *Peace be to the brethren, and love with faith, from God the Father and the Lord Jesus Christ. (24) Grace be with all them that love our Lord Jesus Christ in sincerity. Amen.*

Verse 23. To close the epistle Paul offered a greeting much like the one that opened the epistle in Ephesians 1:2. This greeting is more like a prayer. It accentuates three attributes that characterize a Christian life.

The first attribute is peace. Peace controls every aspect of a believer's life. It encompasses the inner peace of knowing that everything is all right between the believer and God, and peace among the brethren.

The second attribute is love, and it is coupled with the third, faith, because faith works by love (Galatians 5:6). Without love and compassion, faith cannot operate. Many times the New Testament says that Jesus was moved with compassion before He performed miracles.

Peace, love, and faith come from the only true source of all spiritual blessings: God Almighty Himself. God is the author of a wonderful life for us, but this life would not be possible without the mediatorial work of Jesus Christ. His work at Calvary secures all of God's blessings for the believer.

Verse 24. The final words of this epistle are, fittingly, a prayer for grace to remain with all who truly love Jesus. No matter how great the bounty of God's love toward us, there must be a reciprocation of love on our part in order to receive the fullness that God truly intends for us to have.

The word "sincerity" (Greek: *aphtharsia*) is translated as "immortality" in Romans 2:7 and II Timothy 1:10. God loves His people with an "everlasting love" (Jeremiah 31:3). Such an eternal love should be kept from every form of impurity, both spiritual and physical. The nature of God's love engenders a genuine response of love from the believer. This responsive love does not simply desire gifts and blessings to be consumed upon one's own desires and gratification, but it is a love that sincerely desires to have a personal relationship with the Lord Jesus Christ, to be a part of His family, and to fulfill His purpose. It is a love that seeks to know Him personally. God's love for us can only be answered by an unfailing love in return.

Where this kind of love exists in our hearts, we will always find grace to provide strength and encouragement, to discover the riches of relationship, to walk with Christ in peace, and to war against the enemy until ultimate victory is won. We can only summarize such sincere devotion and love for the Master by saying, "Amen."

Bibliography

Barclay, William. *The Letters to the Galatians and Ephesians*. Revised Edition. *Daily Bible Study Series*. Philadelphia: Westminster Press, 1976.

Bernard, David. *The Message of Colossians and Philemon*. Hazelwood, Mo.: Word Aflame Press, 1990.

Bernard, David. *The Message of Romans*. Hazelwood, Mo.: Word Aflame Press, 1987.

Bruce, F. F. *The Epistle to the Ephesians*. Old Tappan, N.J.: Fleming H. Revell, 1961.

Collier's Encyclopedia. Volume 18. New York: Macmillan, 1984.

Dale, R. W. *The Epistle of Paul to the Ephesians. Its Doctrine and Ethics*. London: Hodder and Stoughton, 1897.

Foulkes, Francis. *The Epistle of Paul to the Ephesians*. Volume 10 of *The Tyndale New Testament Commentaries*. Grand Rapids: Eerdmans, 1956.

Goodspeed, Edgar. *The Meaning of Ephesians*. Chicago: University of Chicago Press, 1933.

Hodge, Charles. *An Exposition of Ephesians*. Wilmington, Del.: Associated Publishers and Authors, 1972.

Mitton, C. L. *Ephesians*. Volume 19 of *The New Century Bible Commentary*. Grand Rapids: Eerdmans, 1973.

Moule, H. C. G. *Studies in Ephesians*. Grand Rapids: Kregel Publications, 1977.

Paxson, Ruth. *The Wealth, Walk and Warfare of the Christian*. Old Tappan, N.J.: Fleming H. Revell, 1939.

Tucker, W. Leon. *Studies in Ephesians*. Grand Rapids: Kregel Publications, 1983.

Westcott, Brooke. *St. Paul's Epistle to the Ephesians*. 1906. Reprint. Minneapolis: Klock and Klock, 1978.

Wiersbe, Warren W. *Be Rich*. Wheaton, Ill.: Victor Books, 1976.

Wood, Skevington A. *Ephesians*. Volume 11 of *The Expositor's Bible Commentary*. Frank E. Gaebelein Edition. Grand Rapids: Zondervan, 1978.